BEN JONSON

HIS VISION AND HIS ART

BEN JONSON

HIS VISION AND HIS ART

ALEXANDER LEGGATT

METHUEN

LONDON & NEW YORK

First published in 1981 by
Methuen & Co. Ltd
11 New Fetter Lane, London EC4P 4EE

Published in the USA by
Methuen & Co.
in association with Methuen, Inc.
733 Third Avenue, New York, NY 10017

Photoset by
Rowland Phototypesetting Ltd
Bury St Edmunds, Suffolk
and printed in Great Britain
at the University Press
Cambridge

British Library Cataloguing in Publication Data

Leggatt, Alexander
Ben Jonson.
1. Jonson, Ben – Criticism and interpretation
I. Title
822'.3   PR2638   80-49771
ISBN 0-416-74660-8

CONTENTS

for
WILLIAM BLISSETT

ACKNOWLEDGEMENTS

I have had the opportunity to read papers arising from my work on Jonson at the Ben Jonson Conference at the University of Toronto, at the annual conference of the Association of Canadian University Teachers of English, and at the Shakespeare Institute. I am grateful to those who made these occasions possible, and to the audiences who helped me formulate my ideas. I am grateful also to the University of Toronto for the sabbatical during which most of this book was written, to the Canada Council for the Leave Fellowship that made the sabbatical possible, and to the Director and Fellows of the Shakespeare Institute for their hospitality to me during that time.

Over the years Brian Parker has been unfailingly generous in sharing his work on Jonson. George Hibbard and Edward Partridge provided help and encouragement when they were particularly needed. William Blissett and Hugh MacCullum read my final manuscript and made many helpful comments. My thanks to them, and to Methuen's anonymous reader, for their advice. The follies and errors that remain are, of course, my own.

There is a more general debt to acknowledge. If to work on Shakespeare sometimes makes one feel like part of a multinational corporation, to work on Jonson is to join a fellowship of enthusiasts who have discovered something special. I have tried to acknowledge my debts to previous scholarship and criticism throughout the footnotes; but it is harder to acknowledge the debts that pile up, year by year, to fellow teachers and fellow students who have shared their knowledge of, and their delight in, Ben Jonson. To do so properly would require

Jonson's gift for writing about friendship. But I suspect that others who have worked on Jonson will know what I mean.

University College   ALEXANDER LEGGATT
University of Toronto
May 1980

A NOTE ON THE TEXT

All references to Jonson's work are to the text in *Ben Jonson*, ed. C. H. Herford and Percy and Evelyn Simpson (Oxford: Oxford University Press, 1925–52), abbreviated in the notes as Herford and Simpson. The spelling and punctuation of this text have been retained, except where the text is based on a manuscript; in such cases manuscript abbreviations have been expanded, and special manuscript forms have been regularized. Changes in typeface, except for roman and italic, have not been reproduced. Words marked by Herford and Simpson in square brackets have been omitted; words enclosed in pointed brackets have been included, and the brackets omitted. Titles of works have been modernized. References to *Every Man in his Humour* are to the Folio text unless otherwise specified.

PREFACE

In his pioneering essay on Jonson, T. S. Eliot declared that what Jonson's readers needed was 'intelligent saturation in his work as a whole'.[1] As the best Jonson criticism shows, many of his readers have achieved just that. Yet the criticism itself has tended to be highly selective. It is almost as though we have divided Jonson into three different writers – the dramatist, the masque-maker, and the poet – who can be examined in isolation. There are reasons for this. One is that Jonson's individual works – the plays especially – reward close study so richly that to report adequately on one's findings about a single work will leave no space for a larger view. Another is that Jonson's achievement is so varied it is not always easy to see the relations between the plays, poems and masques: he submits so thoroughly to the demands of each form that we seem to be left with little continuity overall. And yet the continuity is there; Jonson was one writer, not three, and Eliot's call for an examination of his work as a whole remains valid. That at least is the premise from which this study begins.

I want to see what happens when we put Jonson's writings together, tracing threads that run through the various forms he worked in. I have accordingly grouped the works not by chronology or genre but according to the ideas they consider and the experiences they explore; and it may be as well to indicate here the general pattern that has emerged. Chapter 1, 'False creations', considers Jonson's interest in the secondary worlds created by artist figures, mostly in the plays and masques, and examines the tension between his misgivings about the falseness of such worlds and his delight in the creative power that produces them. A similar tension emerges in Chapter 2, 'That Dead Sea of life', where Jonson's satiric depiction of humanity reduced to the subhuman is balanced against the pleasure he sees our lower natures giving when their energies are properly controlled and directed. Both these chapters show Jonson's imaginative side, his tendency to fantasy and stylization, and the curious mixture of alarm and delight his fantasies produce.

Chapter 3, 'Images of society', shifts the focus to Jonson the social artist, examining his views of the good society and of how societies become corrupted. Manners, culture and language are all involved, and the social role of the poet is of vital importance. But Jonson's images of the good social life are set against his awareness of the world's imperfection; and this leads to a broader discussion of the problems of virtue in Chapter 4, 'Virtue's labyrinth', where we see Jonson's depiction of the good struggling against not only the opposition of the world but the weakness of their own natures. Chapter 5, 'Judgement and transformation', explores two connected kinds of scene in Jonson: the moment of judgement when the true nature of a character is revealed; and the moment of transformation when a false vision is replaced by an ideal one. But, bearing in mind the difficulties of reality examined in Chapter 4, we see that judgement does not always work out smoothly and simply in practice. Once again there is a tension, this time between an ideal vision and a realistic one.

This tension is further explored in the last two chapters, 'The poet as character' and 'Art and its context'. Chapter 6 examines the variety of roles, both comic and serious, that Jonson plays as a character in his own work; more briefly, it considers how these correspond to the variety of ways in which he sees the function of his art. The final chapter conducts a similar analysis of his view of the audience, who (like the poet himself) become characters in his work; and this leads to a broader discussion of the relations between the controlled vision of the work of art and the larger, intractable reality that lies around it.

I have tried in the course of the argument to pause over most of the major works in each genre and to treat them in some

perhaps Jonson (through Timber) could be seen as a character in his own play.

detail; and I have tried to give some of the interesting minor ones
their due. While each chapter includes samples from the three
major genres, inevitably the emphasis shifts from one chapter to
another. For example, plays and masques dominate Chapter 1
because they are where secondary worlds are most obviously
created, while in Chapter 6 the study of Jonson's images of
himself leads to a concentration on the non-dramatic poetry,
where the major evidence is to be found. Simply in terms of
bulk, Jonson's drama has tended to dominate the discussion as it
dominates Jonson's work. But I do not see the other works as
simply adjuncts to the plays, and I have tried not to treat them
that way. The masques allowed Jonson to depict some of his
ideals in their purest form; and in the non-dramatic poems, free
of the constraints and hazards of theatrical performance, he
explored, with considerable depth and frankness, some of the
ideas and experiences that meant most to him. Indeed it may be
that in certain of these poems we are as close as we ever get to
the essential Jonson.

One point should be emphasized at the outset: my stress on
what I have loosely called Jonson's ideas does not mean that I see
him as a didactic artist, the essence of whose work can be
summarized in a series of 'messages'. For one thing, there is an
obvious tension between the moralist and the artist: in works
like *Volpone* and *Bartholomew Fair* the devil gets his due, and
sometimes (we may think) rather more than his due. More
important, while Jonson's art seems to move at times towards a
morality-play abstraction, he is never finally content with such
abstraction; there is an awareness of the solidity and complexity
of life, a respect for particular realities, that prevents him from
being as schematic or reductive as some recent criticism has
made him out to be. It is comforting to reflect that on the whole
Jonson was against sin and in favour of virtue; but he was more
concerned to attain an honest vision of life as it is, and to
embody that vision in the clearest form he could achieve. The
more widely one reads in Jonson, the more one admires his
refusal to take the easy way out, to settle for comfortable
orthodoxy on the one hand or glib cynicism on the other; or to
cover doubts and ambiguities with rhetoric. There is always a

keen critical intelligence at work, stopping such lines of retreat. I
hope that this study, besides suggesting some of the inner
connections of his work, will convey some sense (however
imperfect) of the honesty of Jonson's vision and the clarity of his
art.

I

FALSE CREATIONS

I

In the fourth act of Jonson's Roman tragedy *Sejanus*, the emperor Tiberius has retreated to the island of Capri, where like a demented Prospero he creates a little universe in which he can play the role of fate. Arruntius describes him:

> Retir'd
> (From all regard of his owne fame, or *Rome's*)
> Into an obscure Iland; where he liues
> (Acting his *tragedies* with a *comick* face)
> Amid'st his rout of *Chaldee's*: spending houres,
> Dayes, weekes, and months in the vnkind abuse
> Of graue *astrologie*, to the bane of men,
> Casting the scope of mens natiuities,
> And hauing found ought worthy in their fortune,
> Kill, or precipitate them in the sea,
> And boast, he can mocke fate.   (IV. 376–86)

[handwritten margin note: an image that describes the play as a whole.]

In a play with a wide-ranging vision of evil, this may look like just one more detail. It may even look like a minor embellishment, for it is not essential to the story. But as we examine it in the light of the entire play, it begins to emerge as a central image, one that through being withdrawn from the particular circumstances of the action can exemplify the world of the play as a whole. The Rome of *Sejanus* is dominated by power games, as characters work for control over each other's lives, or for the protection of their own. Tiberius is the most cunning, and therefore the most fascinating, of the players; and it may be objected that in withdrawing him from Rome at the end of the third act Jonson has prematurely removed his most interesting character.[1] But Tiberius withdraws only to brood over the play *a false creation.*

more ominously from a distance. And he withdraws in order to
play the game of power in its purest form, the creation of a little
universe in which he has absolute command. In so doing, he
reveals the game of power as ultimately empty. Nothing,
finally, is created or achieved; power is exercised for its own
sake, felt and tested for its own sake, in a vacuum. We may
admire Tiberius' skill in Rome, but when we see it in its essence
on Capri we see that it is pointless. The 'obscure Iland' is not just
(as in science fiction) a convenient place for a human laboratory;
it is an image of isolation from human reality, an isolation that
renders action meaningless. So with the larger world of the play:
characters like Sejanus and Macro work, plot, and kill for a
power that has in the end no purpose but itself.

it is not really creation, like poetry. 'To what end?'

this image is central to Jonson

Tiberius on his island presents a picture whose significance
reverberates not only through this play but through Jonson's
work as a whole. His characters are frequently seen, like
Tiberius, creating secondary worlds.[2] Volpone with his universe
of gold, Subtle and Face with their alchemy, and Morose with
his attempt to make a noiseless world – these are among Jonson's
best-known creations, and they exemplify one of his favourite
themes. The secondary world is usually an enclosed, isolated
place – an island in *Sejanus*, a house in *The Alchemist* and
Epicoene, a bedroom in *Volpone*. This withdrawal from ordinary
reality allows a certain imaginative freedom, but there can also
be something unhealthy about it. In the secondary world, true
nature is perverted: Volpone begets a small menagerie of freaks –
dwarf, eunuch, hermpahrodite – and Tiberius and his cohorts
practise 'strange' and new-commented lusts, / For which wise
nature hath not left a name' (IV. 400–1). The false creation is also
a kind of art: Volpone and Mosca constantly see themselves as
actors. But isolation from reality produces distortion in this
sphere as well: Tiberius, 'Acting his *tragedies* with a *comick* face'
(IV. 379), violates art as he violates nature. *a violation of art!*

Of course the effect varies from one work to another: few of
Jonson's secondary worlds are as horrible as that of Tiberius;
some are harmless, some are even delightful. The sheer enjoyment of creation is also part of Jonson's vision, and the man who
by his own account 'heth consumed a whole night in lying

looking to his great toe, about which he hath seen tartars & turks
Romans and Carthaginions feight in his imagination'[3] is not
always going to be censorious about private imaginings (though
even here we may remark that a man at peace with himself and
the world would surely sleep better than this). Moreover,
Jonson as a maker of plays is *ipso facto* a maker of secondary
worlds himself. Volpone and Mosca, Subtle and Face, manipu-
late their dupes and in so doing act as Jonson's own instruments
for creating the action of the plays. They are simultaneously *fatalistic?*
puppets and puppet-masters; and there is a natural analogy
between their activities and Jonson's business as a dramatist.[4]

The secondary world in its most depraved form is seen in the
SEJANUS LIVES IN HIS OWN FANTASY, WHICH HE CAN'T BE THE MASTER OF.
two Roman tragedies, *Sejanus* and *Catiline*, where rebellious
upstarts creating new power for themselves speak as though
they are actually creating new worlds. Sejanus in Rome tries to
achieve something like the new creation his master achieves on
Capri. He fails, not just because he is outwitted by the superior
cunning of Tiberius and his new henchman Macro, but because
there is something ultimately false and unstable in his own
vision. Tiberius' little world may be empty, but it is unassail-
able. Sejanus tries to be master of the universe not on an island
but in Rome – a city Jonson depicts as solid, bustling, full of
mixed but active humanity. Against this background, Sejanus
cannot be the centre of the world; he is merely one more player
in the power game, ultimately to be swept aside. Theatrically,
he does not dominate his play in the way (for example)
Tamburlaine and Bussy d'Ambois dominate theirs. He no
sooner declares: 'Tell proud IOVE, / Betweene his power, and
thine, there is no oddes' (II. 160–1), than Tiberius enters and we
are reminded that even in Rome there is a higher power.

Resisting the idea of Tiberius' dominance, Sejanus plunges
into fantasy. Tempting Livia, he uses the traditional imagery of
the flame of love; but as his imagination plays with it it quickly *this is cool.*
becomes sun-imagery (a recurring feature of Jonson's secondary
worlds) and *he* becomes the sun, giving light to lesser bodies.

> Then LIVIA triumphs in her proper spheare,
> When shee, and her SEIANVS shall diuide

The name of CAESAR; and AVGVSTA's starre
Be dimm'd with glorie of a brighter beame:
When AGRIPPINA's fires are quite extinct,
And the scarce-seene TIBERIVS borrowes all
His little light from vs, whose folded armes
Shall make one perfect orbe.   (II. 38–45)

Even the arms of embracing lovers suggest a world; but the little
world of love, self-sufficient in the poetry of Donne, is here
made part of an obsession with power. Once again, at the end of
this speech, the fantasy is interrupted, reminding us of the larger
world. Someone is outside the room. Sejanus thinks it is Livia's
husband Drusus; in fact it is one of Sejanus' servants, with a
message: the emperor wants to see him.

The connection in Sejanus' mind between political power and
the power to create a new universe is made ironically by one of
Sejanus' enemies, Silius:

> 'Tis he
> Makes vs our day, or night; Hell, and *Elysium*
> Are in his looke.   (I. 206–8)

This speech comes early in the play, and its heavy sarcasm alerts
us to the fundamental absurdity of Sejanus' view of himself as
the sun of a new universe. It is followed by a bit of gossip:
Sejanus' first step up in the world was from serving boy to male
prostitute (I. 212–16). Sejanus' own absurdity becomes flagrant
in the fifth act, when his pride swells to monstrous dimensions:

> My roofe receiues me not; 'tis aire I tread:
> And, at each step, I feele my'aduanced head
> Knocke out a starre in heau'n! Rear'd to this height,
> All my desires seeme modest, poore, and sleight,
> That did before sound impudent: 'Tis place,
> Not bloud, discernes the noble, and the base.
> Is there not something more, then to be CAESAR?
> Must we rest there? It yrkes, t'haue come so far,
> To be so neere a stay.   (V. 7–15)

also emphasises of power —>

Beneath the bravado is a desperate instability. The excitement of
feeling his power is threatened by a fear that there is nothing,
really, for that power to do. It is the same final emptiness we

Sejanus is mocked by the playwright. (Sej) as ridiculous character.

discern in Tiberius' human laboratory on Capri, but here it is
more explicit: a few lines later Sejanus describes himself as a
wind with nothing to blow against and a fire with nothing to
burn (v. 17–19). Though Sejanus does not see the implications
of his words, we may take the point that the private universe,
divorced from the real world, is ultimately pointless. And we
may also conclude, going back to an earlier line, that it is an
absurdly small universe in which a man can knock his head on
the stars. As the act proceeds, Sejanus appears increasingly
moody and unstable; there is even a crazy disproportion in the
omens of disaster that surround him – a fiery meteor appears, a
serpent leaps from his statue, a bed collapses, and a cat runs
between his legs. In the end 'He, that this morne rose proudly,
as the sunne' (v. 709) becomes a rag doll for the mob to tear to
pieces. He vanishes as though he had never been real at all; and in
a sense he never was. who was he, really ?

   A similar absurdity afflicts the hero of Catiline, but his
imagination is both steadier and more grotesque. Here we have a
rebellion decked out in images of false creation. The spirit of the
dictator Sulla, introducing the play, sees himself 'As a dire
vapor, that hath cleft the ground, / T'ingender with the night,
and blast the day' (i. 12–13). Sejanus imagined new worlds; he
actually did, or planned to do, comparatively little. Catiline sees
himself as a man of action: he plans a bloody uprising, and a
massive slaughter in Rome. His images of new creation are
accordingly more practical, and darker. Instead of a new sun
lighting the universe, we have a grotesque elaboration of Sulla's
image of false engendering. Life and death run backwards as
Catiline says of Rome:

> If shee can loose her nature, I can loose
> My pietie; and in her stony entrailes
> Dig me a seate; where, I will liue, againe,
> The labour of her wombe, and be a burden,
> Weightier then all the prodigies, and monsters,
> That shee hath teem'd with, since shee first knew MARS.
>
>   (i. 92–7)

Sulla invokes not so much a false dawn as a new and deeper
night that usurps the place of day:

> Let night grow blacker with thy plots; and day,
> At shewing but thy head forth, start away
> From this halfe-spheare. . . .   (1.61–3)

Mindful perhaps of the unity of time, of the single day in which the action would take place, Jonson began *Every Man in his Humour* with 'A Goodly day toward! and a fresh morning!' (1.i.1). The effect is parodied here. When the sun finally rises in *Catiline* it is a sick, dark sun, swollen and heavy:

> It is, me thinkes, a morning, full of fate!
> It riseth slowly, as her sollen carre
> Had all the weights of sleepe, and death hung at it!
> Shee is not rosy-finger'd, but swolne black!
> Her face is like a water, turn'd to bloud,
> And her sick head is bound about with clouds,
> As if she threatned night, ere noone of day!   (1.191–7)

Even conventional social greetings associated with morning seem out of place: 'It does not looke, as it would haue a haile, / Or health, wish'd in it, as on other mornes' (1.198–9). Catiline still uses sun imagery in addressing his associates. He says to Aurelia, 'Appeare, / And breake, like, day, my beautie, to this circle' (1.98–9) and to the dupe Lentulus, who fancies he will be king in Catiline's new Rome:

> CINNA, and SYLLA
> Are set, and gone: and we must turne our eyes
> On him that is, and shines.   (1.272–4)

But this is the small change of Catiline's conspiracy-talk; at the centre of his imagination is the idea of monstrous, dark engendering, of birth run backwards as the child digs its way back to the womb to create a new, reluctant life out of stony entrails.

Beneath the Jacobean blood and thunder of *Catiline*'s first two acts is a terrible sense of effort: it takes a slow, painful labour to get this conspiracy born. We sense the effort from Sulla's opening speech, with its long catalogue of Catiline's sins and its impatience for more horror to come (1.38–45). But the straining for effect is clearest, and most comic, in Cethegus' vow to kill Cicero:

> He shall die.
> Shall, was too slowly said. He's dying. That
> Is, yet, too slow. He is dead.   (III. 663–5)

Cicero sees the conspiracy in theatrical terms: 'It so farre
exceedes / All insolent fictions of the tragick *scene!*' (III. 258–9).
He may mean, in part, that the conspiracy is worse than a play
because it is real; but all the huffing and puffing of the
conspirators suggests that it is excessive in another way – it is a
bad, overdone play.[5]

And the hyperbolic manner of the conspiracy continually falls
into banality. Catiline, as a creator, has to work in a trivial
medium – his fellow conspirators. He sounds at times like
Subtle and Face manipulating their dupes (*The Alchemist* was
acted the previous year):

> I haue to doe
> With many men, and many natures. Some,
> That must be blowne, and sooth'd.   (I. 131–3)

There is Lentulus, with his dream of kingship; Cethegus, with
his vision of blood running in the streets; and the smaller fry:
'Some more there be, slight ayrelings, will be wonne, / With
dogs, and horses; or, perhaps, a whore' (I. 167–8) Catiline and
Aurelia lay in supplies like tradesmen: 'Get thee store, and
change of women, / As I haue boyes' (I. 171–2). For all his talk
of ruining the world, the rewards Catiline offers are prosaic:
houses, lands, and offices, debts paid and legal penalties lifted
(I. 453–60). And in the plotting of the conspiracy there is a
similar descent in tone:

> CVR I would there were more *Romes* then one, to ruine.
> CET More *Romes?* More worlds.
> CVR   Nay, then, more gods, and natures,
>   If they tooke part.
> LEN   When shall the time be, first?
> CAT I think the *Saturnalls*.   (III. 594–7)

The descent from apocalyptic imagining is twofold: to the
practical details, the clockwork of the conspiracy; and to an
image of disorder as a harmless game played once a year for fun.
The really effective conspirator in this play is Caesar, who will

prove more dangerous in the long run than Catiline, and the
notable thing about *his* language is its control. Even when
(urging Catiline to destroy Cicero) he uses a grotesque image,
there is a clinical precision in his words: 'A serpent, ere he comes
to be a dragon, / Do's eate a bat: and so must you a *Consul*'
(III. 523-4). Caesar is in control of his imagination; the imaginations of Catiline and his fellow conspirators are over-
inflated balloons, easily punctured.

And yet Jonson seems to have found something compelling
in Catiline's original vision. The idea of perverted creation, a
new world with a dark sun, returns in the description of Catiline
going to his final battle:

> And as he riss', the day grew black with him;
> And *Fate* descended nearer to the earth,
> As if shee meant, to hide the name of things,
> Vnder her wings, and make the world her quarrie.

$$(\text{v. }634-7)$$

Meanwhile the ordinary sun stands still, unable to rise (v. 660-2).
Jonson allows Catiline's last moments an apocalyptic grandeur
denied to Sejanus. As in the ending of *The Dunciad*, the world is
uncreated, and meaning itself – 'the name of things' – blotted
out. Not quite, of course: Catiline dies, and Rome goes on. But
Catiline, freed from his shabby followers and reduced to the
essential destructiveness with which he began, is allowed to be
surprisingly impressive. Jonson shows that, for all its absurdity,
the idea of false creation can – if only for a moment – capture the
imagination.

The fascination this idea held for Jonson is shown in a lighter
form in the masques, where it is one of his favourite images of
disorder. While the decorum of the masque keeps the tone light,
we know that Jonson is dealing with ideas that for him are
serious; and in the comic antimasques, in which the false creators
usually appear, we catch echoes from more sombre works. The
prefatory notes to *The Masque of Queens* define the function of
the antimasque as to 'haue the place of a foyle, or false-*Masque*'
(l. 13). In this case the hags of the antimasque dance backward,

in a parody of the essential action of the masque proper. But the reversal goes deeper, and becomes an attempt to reverse creation itself:

> Mixe Hell, with Heauen; and make *Nature* fight
> Within her selfe; loose the whole henge of Things;
> And cause the Endes runne back into theyr Springs.
>
> (ll. 147–9)

As the original Creation began with light, the Dame, leader of the hags, demands: 'Darken all this roofe, / With present fogges' (ll. 241–2) and tries to create an antiworld in which her magic can flourish:

> I'le speake a *charme*
> Small cleaue the ground, as low as lies
> Old shrunke-vp *Chaös*; and let rise,
> Once more, his darke, and reeking head,
> To strike the World, and *Nature* dead
> Vntill my Magick birth be bred.   (ll. 310–15)

Catiline is still a couple of years away; but we recognize the idea. The relative lightness of the verse, however, softens the horror and makes it playful; the backwards dance is still a dance.

In *Mercury Vindicated from the Alchemists at Court*, Mercury tells us that the alchemists 'professe to outworke the *Sunne* in vertue, and contend to the great act of generation, nay, almost creation . . . For, in yonder vessels, which you see in their laboratorie, they haue inclos'd *Materials*, to produce men, beyond the deedes of *Deucalion*, or *Prometheus* (ll. 132–7). They create, not real people, but satiric reductions of humanity – the recipe for a duellist includes ale, sugar, nutmeg, 'oyle of othes, sulphure of quarrell, strong waters' (ll. 151–2); for an Intelligencer, 'salt of confederacy, a pound of aduenture, a graine of skill, and a drop of trueth' (ll. 163–4). There is a point here that I want to return to in the next chapter: these satirically-conceived social types are not people at all, but unreal creatures, men reduced to their obsessions. When we are actually shown a sample of the alchemists' art, it is the fantastic collection of '*imperfect creatures, with helmes of lymbecks on their heads*' (ll. 183–4) who dance the second antimasque. This is what happens when man tries to usurp the function of nature. The effect is light and fantastic, but the idea is potentially horrible; and Jonson gets a bit closer to the horror in the 'imperfect creatures' of *Volpone*.

The most fully developed parody-creator in the masques is Vangoose in *The Masque of Augurs*. He scorns artists who are content to copy nature:

> dey have no ting, no ting van deir owne, but vat dey take vrom de eard, or de zea, or de heaven, or de hell, or de rest van de veir Elementen, de place a, dat be so common as de vench in de *Burdello*. Now, me vould bring in some dainty new ting, dat never vas, nor never sall be, in de *rebus natura;* dat has neder van de *materia,* nor de *forma,* nor de hoffen, nor de voote, but is a *mera devisa* of de braine –   (ll. 101–8)

Even his dialect is significant: as he has lost touch with nature, so he has lost touch with his own language: 'He is no *Dutchman*, sir, he is a *Britaine* borne, but hath learn'd to misuse his owne tongue in travell, and now speakes all languages in ill *English*' (ll. 111–13). He offers to create, with mirrors, a spectacular show of the Great Turk and the Great Mogul, with their armies, elephants, and camp-followers, and make them fight a spectacular battle 'and be all killen, and aliven! and no sush ting' (ll. 234–5). Finally, Vangoose's substitution of fantasy for nature is implicitly rebuked by the serious figures of Apollo and the augurers, who read the signs of nature and discover deep truths (i.e. compliments to King James) in what they see.

In some of Jonson's late plays, where the influence of the masques is strong, the idea of false creation is handled in a similar manner: playful fantasy with an edge of satire. In *The Devil is an Ass*, the projector Meercraft claims he can make money out of anything:

> Coyne her out of cobwebs,
> Dust, but I'll haue her! Raise wooll vpon egge-shelles,
> Sir, and make grasse grow out o' marro-bones,
> To make her come.   (II. i. 7–10)

Heated by the thought of money, his imagination cheerfully creates a new nature, violating the old one. The mines in *The Staple of News* show a similar, playful re-creation of the world:

> there, the molten siluer
> Runns out like creame, on cakes of gold. . . . And Rubies
> Doe grow like Strawberries.   (I. iii. 59–61)

The creation of the news-office itself is described as a parody of
birth (I. v. 73–9). Jonson implies throughout the play that money
(embodied in the Lady Pecunia) generates not only greed but a
mad ambition to remake the world. And there is indeed a
suggestion of a secondary creation in the social types who cluster
around Pecunia: Cymbal, Almanack, Shunfield, Broker,
Lickfinger, Fashion – compared with the rich comic creations of
Jonson's earlier plays these are small, puppet-like figures. None
has a full individual life, and together they make a tinny, tinkling
music. The court of Pecunia is like a miniature solar system:

> We know our places here, wee mingle not
> One in anothers sphere, but all moue orderly,
> In our owne orbes; yet wee are all *Concentricks*.   (II. ii. 54–6)

The ultimate irony is that Pecunia herself, the sun of this little
cosmos, longs to escape from it. She would like freedom,
action, and fresh air, but her attendants keep her locked up
(II. i. 45–9). As Sejanus' imaginings create, inadvertently, a
secondary world so small a man can bump his head in it, so the
new universe that gathers around Pecunia can be, like money
itself, shut up in a box (IV. iii. 41–6).

The fantasy of these parody-creations in the masques and late
plays is light and jocular, and it would be wrong to get too
solemn about it. But it acquires an extra, and distinctively
Jonsonian, piquancy through being recognizably a variation on a
serious theme. We can enjoy Vangoose by himself; but our
enjoyment is a little richer if we can also see him as one end of a
spectrum at the other end of which are Tiberius, Sejanus, and
Catiline. To play at making new worlds is a game that is both
engagingly silly and potentially dangerous; and the sense of
danger gives the fantasy a deeper hold on the imagination.

The idea of false creation is linked with other significant motifs.
In the incarceration of Pecunia we recognize one feature of the
secondary world that is particularly important for Jonson – its

enclosure from the real world. In Jonson's scheme of things, folly and vice cannot bear the open.[6] In the *Panegyre* Jonson wrote for King James at his first visit to Parliament, Jonson imagines the king looking 'Into those darke and deepe concealed vaults, / Where men commit blacke incest with their faults' (ll. 9–10). In *Timber* he writes of those who 'set the signe of the Crosse over their outer doores, and sacrifice to their gut, and their groyne in their inner Closets' (ll. 53–5). The idea of false creation is not explicit here, but we recognize the basic condition that is necessary for it – seclusion from the real world, the seclusion Tiberius achieves. We see in some of the early comedies that this involves not just seclusion from morality, but seclusion from common sense as well. The fools are safer in their follies if they can be left alone to spin their private fantasies. Bobadill, in *Every Man in his Humour*, emphasizes that he does not want his lodging generally known: 'I confesse, I loue a cleanely and quiet priuacy, aboue all the tumult, and roare of fortune' (I. v. 45–6). He is of course reluctant to be seen in such a mean house as Cob's; but I suspect the fundamental reason is that seclusion from the real world is congenial to his flights of fancy. His plan, for example, for a picked body of twenty men that would wipe out an army of forty thousand by the simple device of challenging and killing twenty a day shows that Bobadill, like Vangoose, likes to spin ideas from his own brain, unconstrained by the world as it is. As Littlewit in *Bartholomew Fair* remarks, 'I ha' such luck to spinne out these fine things still, and like a Silke-worme, out of my selfe' (I. i. 1–3).

Several characters in *Every Man out of his Humour* show the same tendency to self-enclosure. Sordido, the grasping farmer, sounds like a scaled-down version of Sejanus:

> I at home
> Can be contented to applaud my selfe,
> To sit and clap my hands, and laugh, and leape,
> Knocking my head against my roofe, with ioy
> To see how plumpe my bags are, and my barnes.
>
> (I. iii. 118–22)

There is something eerie about a man sitting alone, laughing and clapping his hands. Puntarvolo and his wife keep their romance

alive by going through a routine in which he is a knight errant lost
in an enchanted forest, and she is a lady who allows him shelter
in her castle; as soon as other characters appear, they break off
their act – 'Gods me, here's company: turne in againe' (II. iii. 88).
Like Bobadill, they require privacy. So does Fallace, for her
infatuation with Fastidius Briske: 'well, I will into my priuate
chamber, locke the dore to mee, and thinke ouer all his good
parts, one after another' (II. vi. 138–40). But the most striking
instance is Carlo Buffone, who stages a party in the last act. He
likes to see himself as a spirit of revelry, and this is a traditional
way to end a festive comedy – except that Buffone stages the
party all by himself, in a tavern room, using different voices,
drinking healths, and finally quarrelling and overturning everything on the table (v. iv.). What could have been a normal social
occasion becomes a grotesque, self-enclosed fantasy, as though a
comedy of courtship were to end not with a bedding but with an
act of masturbation.

If Jonson mistrusts this kind of seclusion from the world, he
also fears the loss of identity that goes with false creation. One of
the signs of a perverted nature in Jonson is constant shape-
shifting.[7] The vice-figures of the Epigrams are not given
individual names, because they have '*visards*', not faces ('Epistle
to the Earl of Pembroke', l. 39). And they live in an unreal,
shifting world in which the vizards are constantly changing.
Court-Worme completes an entire life-cycle without once becoming human:

> All men are wormes: But this no man. In silke
> 'Twas brought to court first wrapt, and white as milke;
> Where, afterwards, it grew a butter-flye:
> Which was a cater-piller. So't will dye.
> <div align="right">(<i>Epigrams</i>, xv: 'On Court-Worme', ll. 1–4)</div>

Sir Voluptuous Beast forces his chaste wife through various
disguises to satisfy his own lustful fantasy: 'And now, he
(hourely) her owne cucqueane makes, / In varied shapes, which
for his lust shee takes' (*Epigrams*, xxv: 'On Sir Voluptuous
Beast', ll. 5–6). Jonson attacks Inigo Jones, not just for being too
concerned with the material trappings of his art, but for being in
himself a man of too many parts:

By all your Titles, & whole style at ones
Of Tyre-man, Mounte-banck, & Iustice Iones,
I doe salute you! Are you fitted yet?
Will any of these express your place? or witt?

(Ungathered Verse, XXXIV: 'An Expostulation with
Inigo Jones', ll. 15–18)

Lighter, more comic images of shape-shifting are found in the plays. In *Every Man Out*, Fastidius Briske's constant changes of wardrobe, with Fungoso desperately following him one suit behind, suggest the evanescence of the fashionable world. Phantaste in *Cynthia's Revels* imagines herself in a variety of roles – citizen's wife, dairy-maid, empress – all of them conceived in cliché terms (IV. i. 171–214). She shows not a free imagination but an empty, derivative one. In *Poetaster*, Tucca piles up so many attributes for Chloe that she ends by having no fixed identity at all: 'Shee is a VENVS, a VESTA, a MELPOMENE: Come hither, PENELOPE; what's thy name, IRIS?' (IV. iii. 35–6). What's thy name, indeed?

In the more fantastic works, we encounter professional shape-shifters, who change their forms in the exercise of traditional magic, without losing their own identities. The witch Maudlin in *The Sad Shepherd* is one such character: for all the disguises she adopts 'Shee may deceive the Sense, but really / Shee cannot change her selfe' (II. vi. 124–5). Robin Goodfellow tries to gate-crash the masque *Love Restored* by adopting various disguises – a feather-maker, a citizen's wife, and so on – but succeeds only by resuming his own shape, and pretending to be – what he really is – one of the masquers. This kind of disguising is innocent and acceptable, well within the decorum of a festive occasion. Similarly, one enjoys the showmanship of Brainworm's disguises in *Every Man in his Humour* without thinking dark thoughts about possible threats to his identity. One of the epigrams to Lady Mary Wroth actually celebrates her ability to transform herself:

He, that but saw you weare the wheaten hat,
    Would call you more then CERES, if not that:
And, drest in shepheards tyre, who would not say:

You were the bright OENONE, FLORA, or *May*?
(*Epigrams*, CV: 'To Mary Lady Wroth', ll. 7–18)

The poem is anchored by the recurring 'you'. Through all the
disguises (she goes on to be Venus, Diana, Pallas and Juno) is the
one secure identity of Lady Mary herself; her name, characteristically, gives the poem its title. The disguises thus become
like the disguises of a Jonson masque: partly a pleasant game,
and partly a way of expressing through various forms the
different virtues of the central figure.[8] The same is true of the
next epigram in the collection, to Sir Edward Herbert:

If men get name, for some one vertue: Then,
  What man art thou, that art so many men,
All-vertuous HERBERT!
(*Epigrams*, CVI: 'To Sir Edward Herbert', ll. 1–3)

To be 'so many men' is normally, in Jonson, to be in grave
moral danger. But Sir Edward's central identity is secure and
can, again, be summed up in his name: 'All-vertuous HERBERT!'
In contrast, Jonson pretends to search through all Inigo Jones's
titles without once finding the real man.
  What Jonson fears is the disguising that leads to a loss of self.

  I have considered, our whole life is like a *Play*: wherein every
  man, forgetfull of himselfe, is in travaile with expression of
  another. Nay, wee so insist on imitating others, as wee cannot
  (when it is necessary) returne to our selves: like Children, that
  imitate the vices of *Stammerers* so long, till at last they become
  such; and make the habit to another nature, as it is never
  forgotten.   (*Timber*, ll. 1093–9)

(We may think of Volpone, forced by the Scrutineo to re-enact
for the rest of his life the role of a sick, broken man.) The
virtuous figures in the *Epigrams* all have their own names; the
vices have type-names, masks instead of faces; the vice has
replaced the man. The figures in question do not usually create
imitation universes to live in – or at least, not explicitly. But
they create imitation identities for themselves, and in the process
they become unreal.

An important variation on the theme of false creation is found in one of Jonson's favourite recurring jokes – the reproduction of classical mythology in comic, miniature forms. Here we have, not imagination cut free of reality, but rather the reverse: figures that belong properly to the realm of the imagination are reduced to the concrete and material. The ultimate effect is the same: a mock creation. The Master Cook in *Neptune's Triumph* is, like Vangoose, a parody-artist, though there is more enjoyment and less satire in Jonson's depiction of him. He 'Makes *Citadels* of curious foule, and fish' (l. 91), and 'raiseth ramparts of immortall crust' (l. 95); he has '*Nature* in a pot' (l. 102). He also has classical mythology in a pot:

> Some twentie *Syrens*, singing in the kettel,
> With an *Arion*, mounted on the backe
> Of a growne Conger, but in such a posture,
> As, all the world should take him for a Dolphin.
>
> (ll. 188–91)

Elsewhere the effect is to bring classical mythology down to reality – a small, local reality. *Christmas his Masque* is a show brought to the court '*from little little little little* London' (l. 76) in which Cupid becomes an apprentice in a flat cap and Venus a deaf tire-woman who lives in Pudding Lane. In *Chloridia* even the torments of Hell are comically reduced to the local and familiar:

> Sisyphus *ha's left rowling the stone, and is growne a Mr. bowler;*
> *challenges all the prime gamesters, Parsons in hell, and giues them*
> *odds: vpon Tityus his brest, that (for sixe of the nine acres) is*
> *counted the subtlest bowling-ground in all* Tartary.   (ll. 140–4)

In passages like these, one could hardly say that any serious point is being made; Jonson is having a classicist's holiday, sharing a few professional jokes over the College port.

But this light joking is mixed with a more pointed satire in the most notable miniaturized creation in Jonson's work: the puppet show in *Bartholomew Fair*. Here the story of Hero and Leander is reduced to 'little little little little London', with the Thames for the Hellespont and Cupid as a drawer. There are reductions of a more basic kind as well: love to lechery, language to a senseless babble of noise. Indeed the puppets seem to present a tiny,

concentrated image of the coarse energy that informs the whole
Fair.[9] Specific details of the main play are parodied in miniature:
the quarrelling friends Damon and Pythias may recall Quarlous
and Winwife;[10] their bickering reminds us of the game of
vapours. Hero is smitten with love through a pint of sherry, as
Madam Overdo has been made a daughter of the game and filled
with Ursula's ale. Guy Hamel has detected echoes from the
Induction, in the costuming of Dionysus as a scrivener and in the
varying prices the audience pays.[11] Yet the parallels are never
too obvious. Jonson concludes *A Tale of a Tub* with a series of
'motions' summing up the action of the whole play; the device is
too glib to be interesting. In *Bartholomew Fair*, he is subtler.
Instead of giving us a neat overall structure to admire, he
unsettles us with half-buried suggestions. There are just enough
hints and echoes that at times we feel the whole play being
pulled down to the level of the puppets, and we may wonder if
we are being pulled down with it. What we are being pulled
down to is a loss of identity, even of humanity itself: man and
puppet, Thames and Hellespont, merge and lose their distinctive
natures; in the carved features of the puppets we glimpse faces
we think we know; and in the end the puppet Dionysus hoists
up its garment to reveal blank wood where its genitals ought to
be.

Whit calls Leatherhead 'Mashter o' de *Monshtersh*' (v. iv. 28)
and in the Induction Jonson mischievously suggests that the
puppets are his answer to Shakespeare's violations of nature:

> If there bee neuer a *Seruant-monster* i' the *Fayre;* who can helpe
> it? he sayes; nor a nest of *Antiques?* Hee is loth to make Nature
> afraid in his *Playes,* like those that beget *Tales, Tempests,* and
> such like *Drolleries,* to mixe his head with other mens heeles,
> let the concupiscence of *Iigges* and *Dances,* raigne as strong as it
> will amongst you: yet if the *Puppets* will please any body, they
> shall be entreated to come in.   (Induction, ll. 127–34)

Jonson has his own way of making nature afraid: not stretching
the laws of space, time and logic but reducing the world to a
series of mad little images, at once laughable and disconcerting –
laughable because we know the puppets are comic imitations of
humanity, not the real thing; disconcerting because they seem at

times perilously close to the real thing. In the end their whole
world can be shut up in a box, and carried off to Justice
Overdo's. And in the dialogue between Cokes and Leatherhead
there is a strange little joke that may be worth pausing over:

> LAN   . . . indeed, I am the mouth of 'hem all!
> COK   Thy mouth will hold 'hem all.   (v. iii. 78–80)

With Ursula's pig-tent fresh in our minds, is it too much to
think of bodies disappearing into a Hellmouth?[12] A vein of
cannibalistic humour runs through Jonson (most notably in the
Cock-Lorell song in *The Gypsies Metamorphosed*), but in the odd
notion of Leatherhead popping the puppets into his mouth there
may be another suggestion as well – of the little world ending as,
according to some theories, the big one will.

In Jonson's secondary worlds, then, there is much to be
uneasy about: self-enclosure, shape-shifting, loss of identity, the
reduction and trivializing of reality itself. But that is very far
from being the whole picture. Eliot saw Jonson as more a
creator than a satirist,[13] and in most of the works under discussion the violation of reality triggers not just moral condemnation but a mischievous delight in the nonsense that is produced. The puppets in *Bartholomew Fair* are a good example: in
the study, we may shake our heads wisely over the degradation
of humanity they represent; in the theatre, they· are the high
point of the evening. On two occasions when I have seen the
play, their bawdy antics brought hoots of startled laughter from
the audience. They are Jonson's answer to Shakespearean fantasy
in two ways – they violate nature and in doing so they produce
delight.

There are many instances in Jonson where the secondary creation
is presented in a spirit of pleasure, free from critical misgivings.
In *Poetaster*, the poetry of Virgil is seen as a new creation,
brimming with life; but unlike the bogus life created by the
alchemists of *Mercury Vindicated* it is a valid creation that men can
admire, and in which they can see an image of truth (v. ii. 17–20).
Similarly, Clement Edmonds is praised for his work on Caesar's
Commentaries, which has restored the ancient writer by 'Thy

learned hand, and true *Promethean* art / (As by a new creation)'
(*Epigrams*, CX: 'To Clement Edmonds . . .', ll. 17–18). The
pleasure in making a secondary world is strongest in the
masques. In *The Masque of Beauty* the masquers are seen as
imitating the movement of the heavens by their dance; far from
being a blasphemous parody, it is an imitation that reflects the
integrity of the masquers themselves; the security of their own
natures gives them the right to imitate the order of the heavens:

> Still turne, and imitate the heauen
>   In motion swift and euen;
>   And as his Planets goe,
>   Your brighter lights doe so:
> May *youth* and *pleasure* euer flow.
>   But let your state, the while,
>   Be fixed as the Isle.   (ll. 399–405)

As in the conventional love poetry of the time (including some
of Jonson's),[14] love creates its own artificial world, reversing
day and night: 'This same night / Is CVPID's day. Aduance your
light' (*The Haddington Masque*, ll. 167–8). For the young men of
the court, the ladies are a sufficient cosmos in themselves: 'Those
softer circles are the young mans heauen, / And there more
orbes and Planets are then seuen' (*Mercury Vindicated*, ll. 216–17).
We have seen how such ideas can be perverted by figures like
Sejanus and Catiline; here we see them in their innocent form,
with the sting removed.

   But Jonson's main interest is in the ruler as creator and in his
realm as a little world. In *Love Freed from Ignorance and Folly*,
Love answers the Sphinx's riddle:

> 'Tis done, 'tis done. I haue found it out,
> Britayne's the world, the world without.
> The King's the eye, as we do call
> The sunne the eye of this great all.   (ll. 284–7)

The idea of James as the sun is most elaborately developed in
The Masque of Blackness, in which the daughters of Niger,
wanting a cure for their blackness, are told to seek a land where
they will be free from the sun that heats the normal world:

> *where bright* Sol, *that heat*
> *Their blouds, doth neuer rise, or set,*
> *But in his Iourney passeth by,*
> *And leaues that* Clymat *of the sky,*
> *To comfort of a greater* Light,
> *Who formes all beauty, with his sight.*   (ll. 190–5)

This new sun is, of course, King James. Unlike the sun of the great world, which burns and blackens and then hides for the night, he is a sun 'Whose beames shine day, and night, and are of force / To blanch an AETHIOPE, and reuiue a *Cor's*' (ll. 254–5); 'This *sunne* is temperate, and refines / All things, on which his radiance shines' (ll. 264–5). Taken literally, the identification of James as the sun of a new, benevolent cosmos is gross flattery; from the author of *Sejanus* and *Catiline* it looks like blasphemy as well. To say that the conventions of the masque allow, even require, such flattery is part of the answer. But Jonson is not simply following the decorum of the genre; he gives the idea its own integrity by the way he develops it. The new suns of *Sejanus* and *Catiline* were expressions of an egocentric obsession with power; therein lay the root of the blasphemy. The identification of James with the sun, on the other hand, is a way of stressing his benevolence. To see Britain as a little world is not so much national *hubris* as a way of celebrating the kingdom's good fortune; it is unique in the world, in having such a kindly ruler. The idea of the secondary world, then, is not a serious violation of nature but a graceful way of turning a perfectly legitimate compliment.

Jonson returns to this idea in *Oberon*, but the tribute to James is more comprehensive and a different kind of safety device is required to keep it under control. The first suggestion of a secondary world is in the revelation of the palace of Oberon, the fairy prince:

> Looke! Do's not his *Palace* show
> Like another *Skie* of lights?
> Yonder, with him, liue the knights,
> Once, the noblest of the earth,
> Quick'ned by a second birth. . . .   (ll. 143–7)

The source of all life in this secondary creation is James; and the main function of Oberon (Prince Henry) and his attendants is not to show their own virtue but to pay tribute to the King:

> 'Tis he, that stayes the time from turning old,
> And keepes the age vp in a head of gold.
> That in his owne true circle, still doth runne;
> And holds his course, as certayne as the sunne.
> He makes it euer day, and euer spring,
> Where he doth shine, and quickens euery thing
> Like a new nature: so, that true to call
> Him, by his title, is to say, Hee's all.   (ll. 350–7)

We could say that, as in *The Masque of Blackness*, this is a graceful compliment to the King's virtues, well within the convention and not to be taken literally. But there is a new daring in the language here, a new comprehensiveness in the claims for the King – especially that startling, climactic 'Hee's all' – that suggests we need to look for another answer. Jonson, this time, is not working easily within the convention but seeing how far the convention can be pushed. The image of James as a new nature is not just a vehicle for other ideas (his power, his benevolence); it seems to be the idea itself. As in *Catiline*, Jonson, against what we might have thought was his better judgement, has become fascinated by the idea of new creation for its own sake.

But the idea never finally takes over, any more than it does in *Catiline*. James does not engulf the world; Jonson's sense of the evanescence of the masque itself sees to that. It is a transitory spectacle, for one night only; and elsewhere Jonson can write quite sharply of 'the short brauerie of the night' (*The Forest*, III: 'To Sir Robert Wroth', l. 10), the ridiculous expenditure of wealth on spectacles that vanish in a day (*Timber*, ll. 1404–13). Nor was this thought confined to moments when Jonson was feeling sour about the masque; the masques themselves often end with graceful admissions of their own impermanence. *Oberon* ends this way. James may be the sun of a more beautiful universe; but he is not the sun we have to live with every day:

> O Yet, how early, and before her time,
> The enuious *Morning* vp doth clime,
>   Though shee not loue her bed!

What haste the iealous *Sunne* doth make,
His fiery horses vp to take,
   And once more shew his head!
Lest, taken with the brightness of this night,
The world should wish it last, and neuer misse his light.

                                (ll. 448–55)

We see here a half-jocular resentment at the ending of an
evening's pleasure; a wistful feeling that the false world is finer
than the true one; and beneath it all, a frank admission that the
show is over. This puts the view of James as the centre of a new
creation in its proper context; it is not an idea that requires final
commitment, but an idea that can safely be played with for an
hour or two. We are safe with it because Jonson remembers, and
expects us to remember, that in the last analysis we live under
the ordinary sun.

The acknowledgement that the new world is a temporary
invention leads in some of the later masques to a fantasy that is
simply playful, allowing us to enjoy the secondary world
without taking it too seriously. *News from the New World
Discovered in the Moon* offers fabulous, grotesque creatures in the
antimasque, and a new race formed by James himself in the
masque proper; the notion of James as a creator is presented
lightly, as part of the evening's pleasure (ll. 300–8). In *Chloridia*,
Charles as creator brings forth not a new cosmos but a painted
garden 'By warmth of yonder Sunne' (l. 59). The modest scale,
which makes us think more prosaically than we usually do about
a masque, suggests a perfectly natural interpretation of the
compliment – the masque has been created by royal command,
and comes out of the King's budget.

One of the pleasantest of these later masques is *The Vision of
Delight*, in which we move naturally from one kind of fantasy to
another, each being accepted and enjoyed for its own sake.
'Phant'sie' offers the audience dreams, given comically solid
form, 'Some that are tall, and some that are Dwarffes, / Some
that are halter'd, and some that weare scarffes' (ll. 65–6), as part
of a long speech of jingling nonsense. But she is not a false
creator to be dispelled: she also presents the main vision, of the
Bower of Zephyrus where the masquers are discovered as the

glories of the Spring. Even the final yielding to time so that the masque can end is quick and simple:

> They yeild to Time, and so must all.
> As Night to sport, Day doth to action call,
>   Which they the rather doe obey,
> Because the Morne, with Roses strew's the way.   (ll. 244–7)

The nonsensical creatures of the antimasque, and the graceful figures of Spring, are all parts of a secondary world that can be cheerfully accepted, and – when the time comes – lightly surrendered.

II

Jonson, then, was both repelled and attracted by the idea of false creation. This puts us in touch with a central paradox of his work: he constantly expresses allegiance to nature, 'deedes, and language, such as men doe vse' (*Every Man in his Humour*, Prologue, l. 21); yet he is one of the great masters of fantasy in English literature. Even in his most 'realistic' plays we feel we are watching a distinctive world that only Ben Jonson could have created. This paradox, and the other ideas that cluster around it, ideas I have tried to explore in this chapter, can be seen most fully in two masterpieces of Jonson's maturity, *Volpone* and *The Alchemist*, and in that unstable but fascinating late play *The New Inn*.

That Volpone presides over one of Jonson's secondary worlds is clear from his opening speech:

> Good morning to the day; and, next, my gold:
> Open the shrine, that I may see my *saint*.
> Haile the worlds soule, and mine. More glad then is
> The teeming earth, to see the long'd-for sunne
> Peepe through the hornes of the celestiall *ram*,
> Am I, to view thy splendor, darkening his:
> That, lying here, amongst my other hoords,
> Shew'st like a flame, by night; or like the day
> Strooke out of *chaos*, when all darkenesse fled
> Vnto the center.   (1.i.1–10)

Volpone acknowledges, briefly, the sun of the normal world; but that brief acknowledgement is enough to create a critical perspective on what follows. Volpone creates a new universe with his gold as the sun – a sun, we might note, that can be shut up in a box.[15] He goes from false creation to blasphemy as he compares the first sight of his gold to the light that began the first Creation. The blasphemy becomes flagrant a few lines later:

> Deare *saint*,
> Riches, the dumbe god, that giu'st all men tongues:
> That canst doe nought, and yet mak'st men doe all things;
> The price of soules; euen hell, with thee to boot,
> Is made worth heaven!   (ll. 21–5)

The expansion in one line from 'saint' to 'god' suggests Volpone's imaginative excitement, an excitement that to some degree carries us with it. But there is something dead about this god. The words that follow – 'That canst doe nought, and yet mak'st men doe all things' – parody the idea of the unmoved mover, the still point of the turning world;[16] but we may infer that if the source of action in this universe is itself dead, then the action it creates must be empty and meaningless. This also expresses the relationship between Volpone and his dupes: they are whipped into feverish but nonsensical activity by a motionless figure on a bed. Like Pecunia's attendants they are '*Concentricks*' but the point they revolve around is not so much still as dead.

The shape-shifting that goes with false creation is expressed theatrically in the many disguises Volpone adopts, and poetically in his wooing of Celia. When left alone with her (like the fools of *Every Man Out* he requires privacy) he transforms himself, instantly, from a sick old man to a lusty young lover; and urges her to see herself as a power that can raise the dead to life (though not to *true* life, for she has raised Volpone in many different shapes):

> Why art thou maz'd, to see me thus reuiu'd?
> Rather applaud thy beauties miracle;
> 'Tis thy great worke: that hath, not now alone,
> But sundry times, rays'd me, in seuerall shapes,
> And, but this morning, like a mountebanke,
> To see thee at thy windore. I, before

I would haue left my practice, for thy loue,
In varying figures, I would haue contended
With the blue PROTEVS, or the horned *Floud*.

(III. vii. 145–53)

If Volpone has the versatility of Proteus, he has also the desperate, novelty-seeking sensuality of Sir Voluptuous Beast. In their love-making, he and Celia will be everyone but themselves. The sheer length of Volpone's speech suggests an attempt not so much to seduce Celia as to dominate her; and the special form this domination takes is a breaking of her identity, so that an endless variety of roles can be imposed on her:

Whil'st, we, in changed shapes, act OVIDS tales,
Thou, like EVROPA now, and I like IOVE,
Then I like MARS, and thou like ERYCINE,
So, of the rest, till we haue quite run through
And weary'd all the fables of the gods.
Then will I haue thee in more moderne formes,
Attired like some sprightly dame of *France*,
Braue *Tuscan* lady, or proud *Spanish* beauty;
Sometimes, vnto the *Persian Sophies* wife;
Or the grand-*Signiors* mistresse; and, for change,
To one of our most art-full courtizans,
Or some quick *Negro,* or cold *Russian;*
And I will meet thee, in as many shapes:
Where we may, so, trans-fuse our wandring soules,
Out at our lippes, and score vp summes of pleasures.

(III. vii. 221–235)

Behind the fantasy is a certain desperation; Volpone is easily bored, easily wearied, and needs constant novelty to keep him excited. When he is tried of classical fancy dress, he will turn to modern fancy dress. The drawing forth of the soul in kissing is a traditional image of ecstasy; but it also suggests a loss of self, even a kind of damnation: the soul leaves the body and wanders.[17] And Volpone can think of nothing to do with his wealth but waste it: offering jewels to Celia, he invites her to 'Dissolue, and drinke 'hem . . . weare, and loose 'hem' (III. vii. 193, 198).

There is, finally, something sterile and self-enclosed about

Volpone. His love is not a 'mutual flame' but a fire that lashes about in a closed furnace:

> But angry CVPID, bolting from her eyes,
> Hath shot himselfe into me, like a flame,
> Where, now, he flings about his burning heat,
> As in a fornace, an ambitious fire,
> Whose vent is stopt. The fight is all within me.   (II. iv. 3–7)

Volpone is enclosed in other, more basic ways. The essence of his trickery is to stay at home in bed, shut up like his gold. When he leaves his room he runs into danger;[18] notably, when he goes to the Scrutineo:

> I ne're was in dislike with my disguise,
> Till this fled moment; here, 'twas good, in priuate,
> But, in your publike, *Caue,* whil'st I breathe.   (V. i. 2–4)

And when he ventures on to the Piazza, as Scoto of Mantua, he produces a parody of his own parody of creation: the life-giving properties he attributed to his gold he now attributes to a mountebank's oil.[19] It is a trivial, miniaturized form of an idea that in the first scene had a certain imaginative power. When he presides over his little world in the bedroom, Volpone can be allowed to have a certain grandeur; but when he ventures outside his enclosure, he becomes a lightweight, even vulnerable figure. We have seen the same pattern in *Sejanus* and *Catiline*.

He has no proper social relations, and no posterity of the normal kind: 'I haue no wife, no parent, child, allie, / To giue my substance to' (I. i. 73). Like Shylock, he breeds gold and silver; Mosca, laying a plate (Volpone's latest present) to one side, says, 'Stand there, and multiply' (I. iv. 2). Volpone has also a freakish progeny of 'imperfect creatures', the dwarf, the eunuch, and the hermaphrodite.[20] Nano in particular is, like the puppets of *Bartholomew Fair*, a small-scale parody of humanity: '*And, why a pretty ape? but for pleasing imitation / Of greater mens action, in ridiculous fashion*' (III. iii. 13–14). In particular, Volpone's own artistry, his role-playing and shape-shifting, are parodied by the freaks. Nano's speech on the transmigration of the soul of Pythagoras reduces the whole process to meaningless bustle:

> *and the next tosse of her*
> *Was, againe, of a whore, shee became a Philosopher,*
> CRATES *the* Cynick: *(as it selfe doth relate it)*
> *Since, Kings, Knights, and Beggers, Knaues, Lords and Fooles*
> *gat it,*
> *Besides, oxe, and asse, cammell, mule, goat, and brock,*
> *In all which it hath spoke, as in the Coblers cock.*
>
> (I. ii. 19–24)

King, philosopher, whore, mule, and goat are all jumbled together; the distinctions that give life meaning are reduced to a blur. If Volpone's speeches to Celia were played at double speed, the effect would be similar.

Self-enclosed, shape-shifting, the dead centre of a meaningless universe, generating only miniature perversions of humanity who are also parodies of himself – it is easy enough to build a case against Volpone. Thomas M. Greene sums it up: 'The subject of *Volpone* is Protean man, man without core and principle and substance.'[21] But this Protean man has also an energy that compels attention. Against our better judgement, he appeals to us, and his appeal is undeniable. No one who has ever felt like breakfast in bed can watch Volpone in the first act without a touch of envy. No one who enjoys the game of dressing up can feel that a purely moral reading of the speeches to Celia (like the one I offered earlier) tells the whole story. And the wit Volpone and Mosca display in manipulating their dupes puts us, in the gulling scenes, firmly on their side. It also establishes a link between them and their creator. Their disguises (which proliferate madly in the last act) make them seem like actors;[22] their power to make their dupes do whatever they want is like the power of the dramatist himself. They frequently use theatrical language for what they are doing: 'And, as I prosper, so applaud my art' (II. iv. 38). While this contributes to our sense of the falseness of their lives, it also creates an analogy between their activities and those of the dramatist. Jonson in his Prologue promises to make us laugh:

> Onely, a little salt remayneth;
> Wherewith, he'll rub your cheeks, til (red with laughter)
> They shall looke fresh, a weeke after. (ll. 34–6)

In this image of giving pleasure there is something a little aggressive, as there is certainly something brutal in the art of Volpone and Mosca. Jonson is giving us fair warning that we may find the fun a little rough, but he expects us to stand up to it. Volpone and Mosca are doing his work, not only in their wit and inventiveness, but in their occasional brutality as well.

The theatricality of Volpone in particular is, paradoxically, both his destruction and his salvation.[23] After their triumph in the first trial, Mosca urges his patron,

> We must, here, be fixt;
> Here, we must rest; this is our master-peece:
> We cannot thinke, to goe beyond this. (v. ii. 12–14)

But Volpone is not content. His artist's instinct urges him to finish his comedy and put it in its final form, and the best ending he can think of is to pretend to die and leave Mosca the heir. It is indeed a fine, decisive ending for the comedy he has played with his dupes and as he hides behind the curtain and watches the reading of the will he shows all the glee of an author on a successful first night. But we see also that he has surrendered his power over this little world, as an author must surrender his work when he finishes it and turns it over to the public (a surrender Jonson himself always found very difficult to make). Volpone has not really thought this through – his 'O, my recouery shall recouer all' (v. iii. 109) is far too casual; as Mosca strips off the mask and tells each dupe in turn what he thinks of him, it is hard to see how Volpone will be able to cheat these people again. Nor has he thought of the consequences of giving Mosca this much power. The parasite becomes a rival creator, devising a new play in which he is the hero and Volpone is his dupe. He even has a title for it: 'the FOXE-trap' (v. v. 18). (Has he been watching *Hamlet*?)

The rapid bargaining between Volpone and Mosca in the final scene is not just over Volpone's estate; it is a fight between two rival artists, each trying to end the play on his own terms. In the end, Volpone realizes that he can gain the mastery only by stripping off his disguise and revealing all:

I am VOLPONE, and this is my knaue;
This, his owne knaue; this, auarices foole;
This, a *Chimaera* of wittall, foole, and knaue;
And, reuerend fathers, since we all can hope
Nought, but a sentence, let's not now despaire it.

(v. xii. 89–93)

The gesture is at once self-destructive and self-fulfilling. 'I am VOLPONE' is not an admission of defeat but a flourish of defiance, ranking with 'I am Duchess of Malfi still'; and 'Richard's himself again'. He fixes each of his victims in turn, including Mosca, with a final insult that sums him up. Because he has ended the comedy – his comedy – on his own terms, he can accept almost gaily whatever punishment the court has for him in the larger play in which he is simply one of Ben Jonson's characters. When the terrible sentence is delivered he greets it with a wry shrug, 'This is call'd mortifying of a FOXE' (v. xii. 125). And in the end Jonson allows him to escape from the play and appeal to the audience as a court higher than the *Scrutineo*:[24]

> The seasoning of a play is the applause.
> Now, though the FOX be punish'd by the lawes,
> He, yet, doth hope there is no suffring due,
> For any fact, which he hath done 'gainst you;
> If there be, censure him: here he, doubtfull, stands.
> If not, fare iouially, and clap your hands.   (Epilogue, 1–6)

If the audience applauds – and it will – it is registering its approval of a character who has broken rule after rule in a serious moral scheme that lies beneath the entire Jonson canon. That Jonson allows this shows he is willing to identify Volpone with his own delight in artistic creation, a delight that supplements and at times overrides his critical judgement of the character.

After the rough boldness of *Volpone*, *The Alchemist* may seem a smoother, smaller work. But it is as finely constructed and delicately balanced as any comedy in the language, and the idea of false creation lies at its centre. Lovewit's house is a special, closed world in which false images proliferate. As E. B. Partridge has shown, the transforming power of alchemy

touches not just minerals but man himself; alchemy becomes a
parody religion with the alchemist as Creator.[25] The cheaters'
transformations begin with themselves. 'Dol, Subtle, and Face
speak as though they had set up a commonwealth . . ., with an
instrument and articles, a King and a Queen, and a whole world
of subjects.'[26] At the same time Face and Subtle in their opening
quarrel taunt each other with the essential dirt from which they
sprang, and to which they could so easily return. Subtle reminds
Face of what he was, and of what the house was, before they were
both transformed by the alchemist's art:

> Thou vermine, haue I tane thee, out of dung,
> So poore, so wretched, when no liuing thing
> Would keepe thee companie, but a spider, or worse?
> Rais'd thee from broomes, and dust, and watring pots?
>
> (I. i. 64–7)

Subtle, as creator, made Face out of the dust of the earth. But he
himself was once a thin, grovelling creature, as Face reminds
him:

> When you went pinn'd vp, in the seuerall rags,
> Yo'had rak'd, and pick'd from dung-hills, before day,
> Your feet in mouldie slippers, for your kibes,
> A felt of rugg, and a thin thredden cloake,
> That scarce would couer your no-buttocks.　　(I. i. 33–7)

Among Jonson's secondary worlds, this one is especially precarious. We do not usually get such a clear view of the mean
truth behind the grand illusion; normally we are left to infer it
from the hollow ring the illusion itself gives off. This little
world is also made precarious by the fact that it has not one
creator but two. There is so much energy in the quarrel of Subtle
and Face that we feel sure their reconciliation is unstable; sooner
or later they (like Volpone and Mosca) will have to square off.
The privacy that is a necessary condition of the illusion is also
threatened. As we sense the grubby reality beneath the common-
wealth of cheaters, we sense also the neighbourhood that lies
around their little state:

> 　　　Will you haue
> The neighbours heare you? Will you betray all?
> Harke, I heare some body.　　　　　　　(I. i. 7–9)

They inhabit, not a remote island where they can give free rein to their fantasies, but one house in a crowded London street. It is not even their house. The return of the owner, like the internal collapse of the commonwealth itself, is anticipated from the beginning.

But it is a grand game while it lasts. They take in a cross-section of English society, making their clientèle seem like England itself in miniature.[27] Dapper stands for law, Drugger for trade, Kastril for the landed (soon to be unlanded) gentry, and the Puritans, 'my brace of little IOHN LEYDENS' (III. iii. 24), for civil and religious dissent. The cheaters create in turn a hall of mirrors in which these parody images of society are themselves parodied. It is, like the universe of Sejanus, a small world where you can knock your head on the ceiling: Face and Subtle, gloating over the cheating of Mammon, feel as light 'as balls, and bound / And hit our heads against the roofe for ioy' (IV. v. 98–9). But within it there is something for everybody. Dapper is made to see himself as a comic image of a complete man – rich, cultivated and professionally accomplished (I. ii. 50–8). Drugger is offered a spirit world in which the unseen powers of the air conspire to help the tobacco trade (I. iii. 63–8); Kastril, a perspective glass in which he can see at a glance the borrowers and lenders of London (again, London miniaturized) and thus more conveniently dispose of his estate (III. iv. 87–93). Even Surly is, in a curious way, satisfied, for the alchemist gives plenty of scope for his cynicism:

> I'll beleeue,
> That *Alchemie* is a pretty kind of game,
> Somewhat like tricks o'the cards, to cheat a man,
> With charming.   (II. iii. 179–82)

Like the dupes he sees what he expects to see, and it is a mocking reflection of his own face; he himself is a gamester.[28] In creating this hall of mirrors, Subtle, Face and Dol show an endless versatility. Subtle, as John J. Enck has pointed out, changes his manner for each dupe;[29] he is awestruck before Dapper, testy with Ananias, gentle and holy for Mammon and Surly. Face is now a captain, now a laboratory assistant; Dol is the Fairy

Queen, and a gentlewoman who has addled her brains with
theology. What Face says of her in the latter role might apply to
all three of them:

> she'll mount you vp, like *quick-siluer,*
> *Ouer the helme;* and *circulate,* like *oyle,*
> A very *vegetall:* discourse of *state,*
> Of *mathematiques, bawdry,* any thing.   (II. iii. 254–7)

They transform themselves so easily that they seem to have the
properties of elements rather than those of human beings; in this
new creation of theirs the distinctions between one form of life
and another vanish. Or at least it suits the cheaters to claim that
they do; but in this play hard reality is never very far from our
minds. Dol, as the Fairy Queen, is still recognizably Dol: 'the
Queene of *Faerie* do's not rise / Till it be noone' (I. ii. 146–7).

What we see in most of the play is more a comic miniaturizing
of society than a blasphemous challenge to God's universe. The
tone is closer to *Bartholomew Fair* than to *Volpone.* But when Sir
Epicure Mammon enters in Act Two, he brings a new grand
manner with him. Subtle introduces him:

> He will make
> Nature asham'd, of her long sleepe: when art,
> Who's but a step-dame, shall doe more, then shee,
> In her best loue to man-kind, euer could.
> If his dreame last, hee'll turne the age, to gold.   (I. iv. 25–9)

Mammon aspires, in fact, to the powers attributed to James in
the masques. After this build-up, he enters with a grand flourish:

> Come on, sir. Now, you set your foot on shore
> In *nouo orbe*; Here's the rich *Peru*:
> And there within, sir, are the golden mines,
> Great SALOMON's *Ophir!*   (II. i. 1–4)

His new world is at first locatable on a map, one of the fabulous
places of the known world. But Subtle's view of the real depth
of his ambition is shortly justified, as he speaks a new creating
Word '*be rich*' (II. i. 7) that will allow him to redraw the maps –
'I'll purchase *Deuonshire*, and *Cornwaile*, / And make them
perfect *Indies*' (II. i. 35–6), to run time backwards – 'In eight, and

twentie dayes / I'll make an old man, of fourescore, a childe'
(II. i. 52–3), to transform anything he touches – chaste wives to
whores, grave divines to flatterers (II. ii. 53–61). He himself will
be transformed, not simply restored to youth and potency but
broken into multiple images:

> Then, my glasses,
> Cut in more subtill angles, to disperse,
> And multiply the figures, as I walke
> Naked betweene my *succubae*.   (II. ii. 45–8)

The suggestion is that he would like to people the world with
endless reproductions of himself. Later, he promises Dol the
same variety of wardrobe Volpone had promised Celia (IV. i.
166–9). It is in the scenes with Mammon that we get closest to
the heart of alchemy, in the debate between Subtle and Surly on
its basic assumptions about how nature operates. It is here that
nature seems most deeply challenged, as the inanimate becomes
humanized: 'Blushes the *bolts-head*? . . . Like a wench with child,
sir' (II. ii. 9); 'H. ha's his *white shirt* on?' (II. iii. 83).

In the end, Mammon's vision lies in ruins, and he waxes
apocalyptic: 'I will goe mount a turnep-cart, and preach / The
end o' the world, within these two months' (V. v. 81–2). Putting
his first scene and his last together, we have seen a whole cosmos
begin and end. But the turnip-cart, and the way the grand
flourish of 'preach / The end o'the world' is frittered away by the
anticlimax of 'within these two months', suggest that Mammon's
end has not quite the *panache* of Volpone's. As usual in this play,
grubby reality intrudes. And for all the similarity of their
orgiastic fantasies, Mammon has never had Volpone's authority.
Volpone (like Richard III) begins his play, and sets the stamp of
his mind upon it; when he claims to be able to create a new
world, we can almost believe him. Mammon enters *The Alchemist*
a whole act late; he is placed in the context of a fully established
con game in which he is just one more victim.

Finally, the play descends to the hard reality with which it
began. The whole world that Subtle and Face have created can
be packed up in two trunks (IV. vii. 121–3). It all comes down in
the end to a miscellaneous collection of things – money, rings,

cups, fire irons. The neighbours build a rich picture of the bustling life that has gone on around the house:

NEI 3		I, some as braue as lords.
NEI 4	Ladies, and gentlewomen.	
NEI 5		Citizens wiues.
NEI 1	And knights.	
NEI 6		In coches.
NEI 2		Yes, & oyster-women.
NEI 1	Besides other gallants.	
NEI 3		Sailors wiues.
NEI 4		*Tabacco*-men.

(v. i. 2–5)

On the appearance of Face (reduced now to Jeremy) it all collapses to 'I thinke I saw a coach' (v. ii. 35). And the house, on being opened, is empty and derelict:

> Here, I find
> The emptie walls, worse then I left 'hem, smok'd,
> A few crack'd pots, and glasses, and a fornace,
> The seeling fill'd with *poesies* of the candle:
> And MADAME, with a *Dildo*, writ o' the walls.

(v. v. 38–42)

There was some life here, but it has left only a few bits of dirty rubble behind.

Jeremy the butler seems a smaller, more pallid figure than Face; he will even *look* smaller, as he has been shaved. It is as though Face is the real character, Jeremy his shadow. But though he may be reduced he is not finished. He offers his master Lovewit the sort of prize he had offered his dupes – youth and wealth – but with a new practical frankness:

> I'll helpe you to a widdow,
> In recompence, that you shall gi' me thankes for,
> Will make you seuen yeeres yonger, and a rich one.
> 'Tis but your putting on a *Spanish* cloake,
> I haue her within. You need not feare the house,
> It was not visited.
> LOV   But by me, who came
> Sooner then you expected.
> FAC   It is true, sir.   (v. iii. 84–90)

In place of the mumbo-jumbo of the alchemist's routines there is a disarming frankness between master and man. And Lovewit benefits. In the contest for the hand of Dame Pliant, he succeeds where Subtle, Face, Surly and Drugger have failed, but he succeeds at the same game, played for the same motives – money and sex – and not because he is more honest and deserving than the others, but because he is dealt a winning hand, and knows how to play it.

The false visions of the alchemist's world vanish, the transformations are undone. But the wit and inventiveness that went into the creation of that world still have their value, and we are allowed to enjoy them to the end. Even the idea of transformation is seen as having some practical validity. Lovewit seems an old man with the potency of youth – Kastril calls him 'a fine old Boy, as ere I saw' (v. v. 133) – not because of some magic charm but because of something natural and recognizable: a vivid, salty personality. Face's epilogue, like Volpone's, is an appeal beyond morality to our sense of delight:

> I put my selfe
> On you, that are my countrey: and this pelfe,
> Which I haue got, if you doe quit me, rests
> To feast you often, and inuite new ghests.   (v. v. 162–5)

As in the prologues to *Epicoene* and *The New Inn*, the play is a feast and we are the guests. But there is a disconcerting suggestion that the play is also a con game and we are the victims.[30] We have seen how Face treats his guests. If we have been caught up in the play – and surely we have – then we have been taken in by an illusion. Once again Jonson has devised a false creation and expected us both to deplore it and delight in it, for it reflects both his satiric vision and his conjurer's skill. But the final approach to the audience is more sly and ironic than in *Volpone*, and suggests that the last laugh may be on us.

In *The New Inn*, Jonson attempts a wider range of feeling and experience than is customary in his drama. In particular, he gives us a tale of lost children and multiple disguises so bizarre in its complications that critics have been unable to decide whether this is a clever parody or simply a bad play.[31] The play's self-consciousness about theatre itself has frequently been seen as one clue to the puzzle,[32] and it is a clue I would like to follow up here. The imaginative scale of the play is smaller than those of some others discussed in this chapter: there are, this time, no false suns rising over new worlds. But the concern for false creation, and the balance of criticism and delight, are still there, notably in the games of dressing up and pretending that the characters play.

The identification of the inn with the play itself is made in the first line of the Prologue: '*You are welcome, welcome all, to the* new Inne.' Like Lovewit's house, or Volpone's, the inn is a special place, set apart, in which we can see a concentrated image of humanity. The Host likes to see himself not just as a tradesman dealing with all comers but as an artist creating an idealized holiday world: 'I must ha' iouall guests to driue my ploughs, / And whistling boyes to bring my haruest home' (I. i. 22–3). He resents the behaviour of his principal guest Lovel, who has shut himself up in his room to conduct mad little experiments with insects. Already we have an ironic view of the Host. Insisting that his house is a place of pleasure, he is testy and irritable with anyone who will not co-operate; he wants his guests to have a good time whether they like it or not. (A similar irony touches the figure Jonson himself presents in the prologue; he is a cook serving a banquet for his guests' pleasure, and sternly lecturing anyone who has the temerity to dislike it.) The Host also likes to see his inn as giving him a special perspective on the world:

> Where, I imagine all the world's a Play;
> The state, and mens affaires, all passages
> Of life, to spring new *scenes*, come in, goe out,
> And shift, and vanish; and if I haue got
> A seat, to sit at ease here, i' mine Inne,
> To see the *Comedy*.   (I. iii. 128–33)

This laughing detachment from the world may not be all that far from the morose detachment of Lovel shut up in his room; each man cuts himself off from life. And the Host's claim to be above the shifts and changes of the world denies the fact that he himself is disguised, that his true identity is that of Lord Frampul, a man who ran away from his family. His retreat was the result not of a philosophical temperament but of a giddy and unstable personality. Jonson, in the *Argument*, calls him 'cock-braind' (l. 9), and his name means 'peevish'. Nor can he preserve the detachment he claims here. His tendency to see the world in artistic terms leads him to view himself not just as an observer but as a playwright. (Earlier in his career he was a puppet-master.) In that he is like Volpone, but more self-conscious and less shrewd. Early in the last act, he laments the way his creation is going out of control:

> I had thought to ha' sacrific'd,
> To merriment to night, i' my light Heart, *Fly*.
> And like a noble Poet, to haue had
> My last act best: but all failes i' the plot.
> *Lovel* is gone to bed; the Lady *Frampull*
> And Soueraigne *Pru* falne out: *Tipto*, and his Regiment
> Of mine-men, al drunk dumbe, from his whoop *Barnaby*,
> To his hoope *Trundle*: they are his two Tropicks.
> No proiect to reare laughter on, but this,
> The marriage of Lord *Beaufort*, with *Laetitia*.
> Stay! what's here! The sattin gowne redeem'd!
> And *Pru* restor'd in't, to her *Ladyes* grace!   (v. i. 24–35)

What he misses, of course, is the simple fact that a state of total confusion is the ideal way for the last act of a comedy to begin. But Jonson knows better than he does, and is already at work setting the confusion right – beginning with the entrance of Pru, restored to favour and in her new gown.

The Host has none of the brutality of Tiberius, of course; but he has the same tendency to see the world as a little creation he can laugh at and occasionally meddle with. Jonson allows some of the Host's pleasure to communicate to us, but delicately suggests that the laughter is finally against him. He also suggests that his disguise, and the story of loss and wandering in which he participates, are signs of an unstable nature. The Host likes to see himself as Democritus; he is closer to Proteus. There are other Protean figures in the play. Fly (a poor relation of Mosca's), a former gypsy and now the Inn's resident parasite, has a variety of titles: 'Some call him Deacon *Fly*, some Doctor

Fly, / Some Captaine, some Lieutenant' (II.iv.33–4). Bat Burst
is 'One that hath beene a Citizen, since a Courtier / And now a
Gamester (III.i.171–2). The strangest identity shift is that of
Stuffe the tailor, who when he has made a fine gown that will fit
his wife dresses her as a Countess and himself as a footman, and
takes her off for a dirty weekend (IV.iii.66–74). As Beaufort
comments, 'A fine *species*, / Of fornicating with a mans owne
wife' (IV.iii.76–7). Even words at this point become unstable.

But with the figure of Lady Frampul's maid Pru, the idea of
shape-shifting acquires a new dimension. Lady Frampul, later
revealed to be the Host's daughter, has inherited her father's
giddy nature; she is '*a* Lady *of great fortunes, and beauty, but
phantasticall*' ('The Persons of the Play', ll. 32–3), and her
ambition to have many 'servants', coupled with her refusal to
love any, has driven her suitor Lovel to distraction. As part of
her toying with him, she sets up an elaborate parody of a Court
of Love, over which Pru presides as Sovereign. But Lady
Frampul gets more than she bargained for. As she sees it, the
game of dressing up is simply a reflection of the comic emptiness
of life itself; she has something like her father's detached view of
the world. She says of the gown in which she makes Pru dress
up:

> 'Twill fit the *Players* yet,
> When thou hast done with it, and yeeld thee somwhat.
> PRU   That were illiberall, madam, and mere sordid
> In me, to let a sute of yours come there.
> LAD   Tut, all are *Players*, and but serue the *Scene*.   (II.i.35–9).

Pru is much less casual than her mistress about the play-acting
she is expected to indulge in, and more practically concerned
with what the rest of the world will think:

> What will they say of you? or iudge of me?
> To be translated thus, 'boue all the bound
> Of fitnesse, or *decorum*?   (II.i.53–5)

In the business of the scene Jonson emphasizes that the dress
goes on with real difficulty, and this bears out Pru's misgivings
about the disguise. In the mental world of a character like
Volpone, costumes can be changed with the speed of thought.

But Pru takes us to a practical world, in which for a servant to wear a fine lady's gown is a tricky and embarrassing business.

She takes, then, a clear-eyed view of the false creation she is expected to preside over. But preside she does, and to some purpose. Whatever misgivings she has, she acts the role of Queen with decisiveness and authority. She strikes firmly the balance between engagement and detachment that the Host never quite manages, and in so doing represents the paradox of the artist – like Jonson himself – who can stand back from his own creation and yet be deeply committed to it. This paradox is reflected in Jonson's handling of the Court of Love sequences, which are among the most complicated set-pieces in all his plays. Lovel and Lady Frampul have not properly come to terms with each other: she has refused to love; he has vowed not to declare his feelings. Pru's solution is to make them, like a pair of wayward children, sit still for a couple of hours. During each hour Lady Frampul will extend to Lovel the rights and privileges of principal 'servant'; he in turn will spend the hour in a discourse on love and courtship, to which Lady Frampul must listen and at the end of which he may claim a kiss. One of Pru's first acts is to make the Lady give Lovel an initial kiss. (The Lady, who does not like even this degree of commitment, protests, but Pru insists on her authority.) The brief moment of the kiss seems to Lovel to sum up the beauty and the transience of love:

> How soone it pass'd away! how vnrecouered!
> The distillation of another soule
> Was not so sweet! (II. vi. 120–2)

So with the two hours Pru has given him. During this time he has undreamed-of access to the Lady, and at the end of each hour the privilege of a kiss. But, Pru warns him,

> those howres past, and the two kisses paid,
> The binding caution is, neuer to hope
> Renewing of the time, or of the suit,
> On any circumstance. (II. vi. 175–8)

To which Lovel protests, 'Who would be rich to be so soone vndone?' (v. vi. 200). The two hours are, like the 'two hours'

traffic' of a play, a special, privileged time, in which the
relationship of Lovel and his Lady will be brought into focus.
But Lovel must achieve what he can within those two hours, for
he can count on nothing more. This suggests both the discipline
of art, with its self-imposed limits, and the transience of the
special worlds that art creates – like the transience of a Jonson
masque.

The setting up of the Court is elaborately ceremonial, but the
ceremonies have the effect of parody – as when Lovel and the
Lady are made to swear on a copy of Ovid's *De Arte Amandi*.
Lovel's first discourse, on love, is a set-piece of dignified, high-
minded oratory, which Jonson constantly undercuts with irony.
Lovel sees love as spiritual and immutable; yet he has been
excited by a kiss, and the condition imposed on his love is that
he must cease to think of it in two hours. His high view of love
is comically juxtaposed with the behaviour of his friend
Beaufort, flirting with Laetetia on the sidelines:

> L O V   True loue hath no vnworthy thought, no light,
>   Loose, vn-becoming appetite, or straine,
>   But fixed, constant, pure, immutable.
> (B E A   I relish not these *philosophicall* feasts;
>   Giue me a banquet o' sense, like that of *Ovid*. . . .)
>   (III. ii. 122–6)

But there is more than simple undercutting here. Lovel is
resisting the conditions imposed on his love, not only by the
two-hour time limit, but by his own sensual nature. He uses his
privileged time not just to express his own desires, but to try to
rise above them, to express not so much what he feels for the
Lady as what an ideal lover ought to feel. That he is claiming
more than normal humanity is content with is clear from
Beaufort's mocking asides; but if at this point we side too easily
with Beaufort, we are then shamed by his cynical treatment of
Laetitia towards the end of the play. The low view of love is not
just amusing, and is certainly not the whole truth.

Towards the end of the first hour, Lovel builds to a climax,
and a series of complicated ironies develops:

> So knowledge first, begets beneuolence,
> Beneuolence breeds friendship, friendship loue.

And where it starts or steps aside from this,
It is a mere degenerous appetite,
A lost, oblique, deprau'd affection,
And beares no marke, or character of Loue.
LAD How am I chang'd! By what alchimy
Of loue, or language, am I thus translated!
His tongue is tip'd with the *Philosophers stone,*
And that hath touch'd me thorough euery vaine!
I feele that transmutation o' my blood,
As I were quite become another creature,
And all he speakes, it is proiection!
PRU Well fain'd, my Lady: now her parts begin!
LAT And she will act 'hem subtilly.
PRU She fails me else.   (III. ii. 165–79)

Lovel depicts the creation of love as a steady, logical process.
But it strikes Lady Frampul suddenly, with the transforming
power of alchemy, leaving Lovel's theoretical description far
behind. (Yet the theory is not to be despised, for Lovel sees
'knowledge' as the start of the process, and the Lady can be said
here to know Lovel for the first time.) But such is the Lady's
wayward, flirtatious nature that Pru, whose creation has at this
point passed beyond even her understanding, cannot believe the
profession of love is serious. Even Lovel assumes she is pretending, and betrays his own ideal of steady love by descending to
bitter, passionate resentment: 'Tut, she dissembles! All is
personated, / And counterfeit comes from her!' (III. ii. 259–63).
This is the price Lady Frampul has paid for her waywardness.
Later, defending her old ways, she admits:

I was somewhat froward,
I must confesse, but frowardnesse sometime
Becomes a beauty, being but a visor
Put on. You'l let a Lady weare her masque, *Pru.*
PRU But how do I know, when her Ladiship is pleas'd
To leaue it off, except she tell me so?   (IV. iv. 292–7)

The danger in the conventional games of courtship the Lady has
played is that they can make sensible relations between men and
women impossible; and the anger with which Lady Frampul
attacks Pru for her misunderstanding may be in part anger with

herself. Like other Jonson characters, Lady Frampul has by her
fascination with masks placed her true nature in jeopardy.

The special conditions that Pru has created allow Lady
Frampul to see Lovel at his best, and to feel a love she has never
allowed herself to feel before. They also allow Lovel to break
out of his melancholy, to the Host's delight (III. ii. 264–8), and to
show the heights his mind is capable of reaching. But his
behaviour falls below those heights. The gap between his theory
and his practice is more obvious in the second hour, when the
lecture topic (set by the Lady herself) is the nature of true valour.
It is exercised, he says, for the public good, and is above all free
from anger: 'I neuer thought an angry person valiant: / Vertue is
neuer ayded by a vice' (IV. iv. 64–5). This dignified view sits
rather oddly on a preceding incident in which Lovel had
expended *his* valour rescuing Pinnacia Stuffe from the below-
stairs ruffians of the inn – hardly a worthy object for his
chivalry. And it sits very oddly indeed on the end of the
sequence, when Lovel is given his last kiss:

> LOV   One more – I except.
>   This was but halfe a kisse, and I would change it.
> PRU   The Court's dissolu'd, remou'd, and the play ended.
>   No sound, or aire of *Loue* more, I decree it.
> LOV   From what a happinesse hath that one word
>   Throwne me, into the gulfe of misery?
>   To what a bottomlesse despaire? how like
>   A Court remoouing, or an ended Play
>   Shewes my abrupt precipitate estate,
>   By how much more my vaine hopes were encreas'd
>   By these false houres of conuersation?   (IV. iv. 245–55)

The two hours are over, vanished like a play or masque. And
with them go not only Lovel's privilege of speaking, his sight of
the Lady, and his three precious kisses, but the fine figure he has
cut and the fine ideals he has defended. He lapses into the passion
that he said had nothing to do with either love or valour;[33] he
wants to change the rules, like a spoiled child; and his idealized
celebration of love collapses into bitterness (IV. iv. 264–71).

It is as though everything he has achieved in the Court of Love
has been as much illusion as the secondary worlds of Subtle and

Volpone. But we cannot say that any of these secondary worlds, when they collapse, 'leave not a rack behind'. In this case Lovel, without knowing it, has kindled love in Lady Frampul; far from losing his chance, he has achieved his end. The Court of Love sequences are full of irony – Pru in her unaccustomed fancy dress, Beaumont heckling in the background, the Nurse's drunken indifference to the whole procedure,[34] and above all Lovel's betrayal of his own ideals. But those ideals are serious, he is genuinely eloquent in defence of them, and through the charade he and Lady Frampul make contact in a way that was never possible before.

It may be there is a similar balance in Jonson's attitude to the romantic ending. The tangle of lost children and multiple disguises is grotesquely complicated, and I will not try to summarize it here. A sour note is added by Beaufort's cynical attitude to Laetetia, whom he marries (thinking she is high-born), repudiates (thinking she is low-born), and just as quickly re-accepts when he finds she is Lord Frampul's second daughter. Jonson may be parodying the fantastic endings of romance; and there is certainly a scaling-down of the wanderings of a romance hero when Lord Frampul describes his own travels, which were not through mysterious corners of the world but through the more disreputable parts of England (v. v. 91–102). Yet the multiple weddings are touched with an atmosphere of peace and beauty:

> LOV   Stay, let my Mrs.
> But heare my vision sung, my dreame of beauty,
> Which I haue brought, prepar'd, to bid vs ioy,
> And light vs all to bed, 'twill be instead
> Of ayring of the sheets with a sweet odour.
> HOST   'Twill be an incense to our sacrifice
> Of *loue* to night, where I will woo afresh,
> And like *Mecaenas,* hauing but one wife,
> Ile marry her, euery houre of life, hereafter.
>   *They goe out, with a* Song.   (v. v. 149–57)

There is a real problem of tone in the last scene. When the old drunken nurse reveals herself to be Lady Frampul, by the simple expedient of opening the eye she has kept shut for the last seven years, we wonder if this is parody or just ineptness. And if it is parody, how far is it meant to affect passages like the one quoted above? Jonson's intentions are not as clear in this case as they usually are. But we may, I think, assume that he intends some sort of balance between a delight in the creative fantasy and a satire on its absurdity. The fact that romantic love is not in his usual range of dramatic subjects may account for his uncertain treatment of this material; but in the double attitude toward the creative act – both the false creations his characters devise, and his own creation of the play of which they are a part – we realize that though Jonson may be old and sick, and though his powers may be failing, he is still the same man who wrote *The Alchemist* and *Volpone*. He sees the creation of the false image as a betrayal of reality, a departure from nature; but it is also a way of concentrating reality in order to see one aspect of humanity more clearly.

2

THAT DEAD SEA OF LIFE

I

In Jonson, the secondary world can appear to be not merely a substitute for reality but an alternative to it, and there is something positive in the creative energy that goes into its making. But there is another kind of unreality that Jonson finds more alarming. We see it when a character descends below full humanity, not to some other specific form of life – as figures in mythology become animals or plants – but simply to inert matter, without form, purpose or identity. Epigram XI, 'On Something that Walks Somewhere', is a particularly clear instance. Like the description of Tiberius on his island, this is one of those points at which an important aspect of Jonson's imaginative world comes into sharp focus, and we see the essential form of an idea that runs with variations through all his work:

> At court I met it, in clothes braue enough,
>   To be a courtier; and lookes graue enough,
> To seeme a statesman: as I neere it came,
>   It made me a great face, I ask'd the name.
> A lord, it cryed, buried in flesh, and blood,
>   And such from whom let no man hope least good,
> For I will doe none: and as little ill,
>   For I will dare none. Good Lord, walke dead still.

Towards the end of the poem the vision is given a particular satiric point: Jonson is attacking a worthless lord he has just met at court, one who will never use his position to achieve any good. Many a satirist would have been content with that point, but Jonson's imagination pushes him further. The lord will 'dare' no evil, either; like Eliot's hollow men, he is in a moral

limbo. But while Eliot's images suggest desolation and emptiness, Jonson gives us heavy, inert matter. There is not enough
spirituality in the lord even to make us aware of the blank where
the soul should be. Instead we are shown a walking corpse – and
perhaps even to say that is to give the figure more identity than
Jonson does.

In his epigrams of praise Jonson names the parties addressed,
often making a special point of the name itself as a sign of
virtue.[1] Here the title of the poem calls attention to the fact that
the thing has no name; it is not even 'he' but 'it'. What is most
horrible is that while it is not alive, it is not really dead either. In
fact, the signs of life it gives are unnaturally exaggerated – the
'great' face, the startling 'cryed' for the answer to a simple
question. And it seems strangely articulate about its own nature.
The analysis of what is wrong with it – it will do neither good
nor evil – comes from its own voice. For a moment we may
think of one of Dante's encounters with the damned. But there is
no suggestion that the creature is at all perturbed by its own
nature, and at the end of the poem it walks on, impassive. The
heavy tread of the last three words, 'walke dead still', gives us an
imaginative horror to match the moral horror. So does the
dreadful paradox earlier in the poem, 'buried in flesh, and
blood', where life and death, as in *Catiline*, seem reversed. The
creature is dead, buried in its own body, knows it; and far from
being disturbed by this knowledge, proclaims it shrilly and
without shame. The poem goes beyond social satire to produce a
deep imaginative horror at the idea of a subhuman being that
talks and walks like a man.

In the ode 'To the Immortal Memory and Friendship of that
Noble Pair, Sir Lucius Cary and Sir H. Morison' (*The Underwood*,
LXX), Jonson gives us a view of a similar creature, seen from a
greater distance. The early death of Morison has prompted the
reflection that it is not the length but the perfection of life that
matters: 'And in short measures, life may perfect bee' (l. 74). To
illustrate the point, Jonson describes the career of a public man
whom he does not bother to name – not just as a sign of
contempt, but to indicate that like 'something that walks somewhere' he does not really have a human identity:

Here's one out-liv'd his Peeres,
And told forth fourescore yeares;
He vexed time, and busied the whole State;
Troubled both foes, and friends;
But ever to no ends:
What did this Stirrer, but die late?
How well at twentie had he falne, or stood!
For three of his foure-score, he did no good.

THE TURNE.

Hee entred well, by vertuous parts,
Got up and thriv'd with honest arts:
He purchas'd friends, and fame, and honours then,
And had his noble name advanc'd with men:
But weary of that flight
He stoop'd in all mens sight
To sordid flatteries, acts of strife
And sunke in that dead sea of life
So deep, as he did then death's waters sup;
But that the Corke of Title boy'd him up.   (ll. 26–42)

Out of context, there might be a suggestion of ordinary corruption in 'He purchas'd friends,' but the context implies that he got them – and fame and honour – honestly, by his virtues. The sheer length of his life is what undid him. He was corrupted not by a particular evil but by the impossibility of maintaining virtuous action that long. Jonson, as I will argue in Chapter 4, saw virtue as something dynamic, requiring constant effort. The struggle is not just against vice but against inertia – a threat that in Jonson is often more serious than traditional evil. The figure began as a virtuous man but was simply tired of keeping it up, 'weary of that flight'. From the particular 'sordid flatteries' through the more general 'acts of strife' Jonson goes to one of his most comprehensive and alarming images – 'that dead sea of life'. The fuller ramifications of the image will be seen later in this chapter; but we should note here the suggestion that not this evil or that but life itself can overwhelm and destroy, as implacably as the sea.

In both poems, Jonson looks beyond social observation and satire to an essential imaginative horror. Drummond of Haw-

thornden described him as 'oppressed with fantasie, which hath
ever mastered his reason, a generall disease in many poets'.[2]
Whether this is Drummond's own observation or his report of
Jonson's self-description, it urges us to look beyond Jonson as an
artist preoccupied with judging man and society, and to see a
darker, less rational side to his work. Behind the satire is a fear
that a human being can become a dead thing, that life itself can
be a meaningless, oppressive weight. There is a link here with
the images of uncreating examined in the last chapter. Sulla's
ghost, in the prologue to *Catiline*, threatens Rome not just with
darkness and death but with an inhuman weight that crushes the
city as though an inert mass were lying on it:

> Do'st thou not feele me, *Rome*? not yet? Is night
> So heauy on thee, and my weight so light?
> Can SYLLA's Ghost arise within thy walls,
> Lesse threatning, then an earth-quake, the quick falls
> Of thee, and thine? shake not the frighted heads
> Of thy steepe towers? or shrinke to their first beds?
> Or, as their ruine the large *Tyber* fills,
> Make that swell vp, and drowne thy seuen proud hills?
>
> (I. 1–8)

The image of drowning is particularly significant. The city
sinks, the river rises: social life is overwhelmed by a massive
elemental force.[3] And Sulla seems to be such a force himself. It is
traditional to describe a ghost as insubstantial, but Jonson's
imagination moves in the other direction: Sulla is a great lifeless
weight pressing down on Rome. In his own creation of perverted life, Catiline imagines himself returning to the 'stony
entrails' of his mother Rome, where he will

> be a burden,
> Weightier then all the prodigies, and monsters,
> That shee hath teem'd with, since shee first knew MARS.
>
> (I. 95–7)

This false creation is not (as some of Shakespeare's are) insubstantial, but unnaturally heavy.

With this in mind, we may see an extra dimension to the
grotesque comedy of Arruntius' description of the senators in
Sejanus, hurrying to take their places:

See, SANQVINIVS!
With his slow belly, and his dropsie! looke,
What toyling haste he makes! yet, here's another,
Retarded with the gout, will be afore him!
Get thee *liburnian* porters, thou grosse foole,
To beare thy' obsequious fatnesse, like thy peeres.

(v. 454–9)

The senators are lumps of heavy matter, forced into unwonted, desperate activity by fear, the only emotion of which they are capable. The savage irony of the passage lies in the suggestion that life is stirred in them not by higher feelings, but by baser ones; they are not normally corrupt, but normally inert.

Elsewhere in Jonson, reduction below the human takes more conventional forms. In particular, characters in the plays are frequently seen in animal terms. Sometimes this has the effect of emphasizing cruelty or sensuality – as in *Volpone*, where what the birds and beasts may lack in full humanity is made up in energy and concentration of purpose, or in *Sejanus*, where a brace of informers is described as 'Two of SEIANVS bloud-hounds, whom he breeds / With humane flesh, to bay at citizens' (III. 376–7). But more often than not, the animal world to which Jonson's characters descend is not energetic but stupid and passive. In *Epicoene*, Truewit advises John Daw to be as melancholy as 'a snaile, or a hog-louse: I would roule my selfe vp for this day, introth, they should not vnwinde me.' (II.iv. 141–2). The most haunting animal images in *Sejanus* are not hounds or wolves but lower, softer forms of life. Sabinus compares himself and his friends to the common run of courtiers:

We haue no shift of faces, no cleft tongues,
No soft, and glutinous bodies, that can sticke,
Like snailes, on painted walls.   (I. 7–9)

Later, we see those soft and glutinous bodies hurrying to the Senate, and the effect is grotesque. In the session itself, Arruntius observes, 'Gods! how the spunges open, and take in! / And shut againe!' (v. 506–7). They are reduced to one stupid, passive movement. When Jonson wants an animal image for

sexuality he turns not to goats and monkeys but to shellfish:
'Firke, like a flounder; kisse, like a scallop, close' (*The Alchemist*,
III. iii. 69); 'And wilt thou kisse me, then? . . . As close as shells /
Of cockles meet' (*Catiline*, II. 344–5). The emphasis is not on the
creature's fierce lust (shellfish lead a quiet life) but on 'the
mechanics of its shell'.[4] A slow stupidity is also characteristic of
Jonson's human animals. Preamble sums up the rustics of *A Tale
of a Tub* with 'Still let them graze; eat Sallads; chew the Cud'
(I. v. 23). Finally, the connection between the animal state and
the inert life that is really no life at all is made in the lines,
'Th'Ignoble never liv'd, they were a-while / Like Swine, or
other Cattell here on earth' (*The Underwood*, LXXV: 'Epithalamion . . .', ll. 153–4). Behind the conventional satiric point
about man descending to the animal is a more characteristic
Jonsonian fear of life descending to non-life.

The same is true of another conventional satiric motif, man's
idiotic fascination with clothes. For Jonson, this is not just
foppery but a descent to the subhuman. All too literally, clothes
make the man. In *The Staple of News* Pennyboy Junior is
transformed by Fashion, his tailor:

> I thinke this Suite
> Has made me wittier, then I was.
> FAS   Belieue it Sir,
> That clothes doe much vpon the wit, as weather
> Do's on the braine; and there comes your prouerbe;
> *The Taylor makes the man.*   (I. ii. 107–11)

This goes beyond conventional satire on foppery to the suggestion that Pennyboy Junior has lost his human integrity and
become a mechanical thing that reacts to external stimuli.

We see the reduction of man to mechanism in the epigrams.
The title of Epigram XCVII, 'On the New Motion', speaks for
itself. Another poem speculates wickedly on a Frenchified
Englishman:

> Or is it some *french* statue? No: 'Tdoth moue,
>   And stoupe, and cringe. O then, it needs must proue
> The new *french*-taylors motion, monthly made,
>   Daily to turne in PAVLS, and helpe the trade.
>   (*Epigrams*, LXXXVIII: 'On English Monsieur', ll. 13–16)

Like 'something that walks somewhere' the fop has become less than human, and is denied even the dignity of a personal pronoun. He acquires a new shape – in fact, a new life – every month, as fashions change. Even his stooping and cringing seem as much a matter of clockwork as his turning round and round to display himself to the customers. Jonson suggests that the creature was not begotten in the common way: 'Or hung some MOVNSIEVRS picture on the wall, / By which his damme conceiu'd him, clothes and all?' (11–12). Unlike the rest of us, he did not come naked from his mother's womb.

Frequently in Jonson, as man loses his humanity, lower forms of life become unnaturally animated as though all matter, high and low, were converging towards a strange half-life (So in *Epicoene*, Captain Otter, described as '*animal amphibium*' (I. iv. 26), gives his drinking cups animal names and treats them as if they were alive.) As man becomes a creature of clothes, the clothes start to become human. In *The Magnetic Lady*, clothes are 'wounded desperately' (III. iv. 11) in a skirmish, as though they were human flesh.[5] But what seems to fascinate Jonson particularly, perhaps because it indicates a confusion of the living and non-living in the most basic possible way, is the participation of clothes in the sexual act – not just as enticements (in *Volpone*, for instance), but as actual partners. There is even a certain snobbery about the kind of material used: 'To do't with Cloth, or Stuffes, lusts name might merit; / With Velvet, Plush, and Tissues, it is spirit' (*The Underwood*, xv: 'An Epistle to a Friend, to Persuade him to the Wars', ll. 57–8). In the elegy 'Let me be what I am . . .' we hear of a tailor who, like Stuffe in *The New Inn*, dresses his wife in gowns made for his customers; this time, however, his interest seems to be in copulating with the clothes rather than the woman: 'his Letcherie / Being, the best clothes still to praeoccupie' (*The Underwood*, XLII, 'An Elegy', ll. 41–2). In the same poem Jonson goes into more grotesque detail about a groom who

> did make most solemne love,
> To ev'ry Petticote he brush'd, and Glove
> He did lay up, and would adore the shooe,
> Or slipper was left off, and kisse it too,

Court every hanging Gowne, and after that,
　　Lift up some one, and doe, I tell not what.　　(ll. 53–8)

Modern psychology has its own explanations for this sort of
behaviour; for Jonson, a man is descending to the subhuman.

Man as animal, man as a creature of clothing – these are
conventional satiric motifs, but they acquire an extra dimension
by the time Jonson is through with them. The same is true, I
think, of the stock comic device of giving characters reductive
names. This begins as conventional Elizabethan fooling, like the
jokes on Onion's name in *The Case is Altered*:

> VALEN　Faith thou hast made me weepe with this newes.
> ONION　Why I have done but the parte of an *Onion*, you must
> 　　pardon me.　　(i. iii. 40–2)

Squire Tub's name gives *A Tale of a Tub* not only its title but a
number of its incidental jokes: ''Tis two to one but *Tub* may
loose his botome' (i. i. 101); '*the fortune of most empty Tubs /
Rowling in love*' (Epilogue, ll. 3–4). Even that last line is not just
a simple pun but a comment on the character's stupidity; there is
indeed something 'empty' about him. When Justice Preamble
(alias Bramble) speculates on why Toby Turfe wants to marry
his daughter to John Clay, the inevitable puns also suggest that
these characters are creatures of the earth not just in their names
but in their low, dull natures (to which Bramble, as a growing
thing, is slightly superior):

> Whereas the Father of her is a *Turfe*,
> A very superficies of the earth;
> Hee aimes no higher, then to match in *Clay*;
> And there hath pitch'd his rest.
> HUG　　　　　　　　　　　　　Right *Justice Bramble*:
> You ha' the winding wit, compassing all.　　(i. v. 5–9)

Jonson never tires of jokes like this. Elsewhere we have Butter
melting (*Christmas his Masque*, ll. 87–90) and spreading (*The
Staple of News*, Second Intermean, 51–2), Waxe soft (*Ibid.*,
ii. ii. 33–4) and hard (*Ibid.*, iv. iii. 47–9), Burst springing a leak
(*Ibid.*, i. ii. 72–3) and Ingine declaring:

> Breake me to pieces else, as you would doe
> A rotten Crane, or an old rusty *Iacke*,
> That has not one true wheele in him.
> *(The Devil is an Ass,* I. iv. 49–51)

Many of these jokes relate to Pecunia's attendants in *The Staple of News* – Mortgage, Statute, Band, Waxe – who make up the little subhuman world that surrounds her. The cumulative effect goes beyond punning to a picture of humanity dissolving and reducing itself to mechanism, or to pure matter.

The result is a subhuman creation – as in *Mercury Vindicated from the Alchemists at Court*, where men are created by alchemy from such ingredients as ale, sugar, nutmegs and tobacco (ll. 150–3). In the *Epigrams*, certain characters are reduced to mere physical processes. Gut is not a man, but a single organ, and his sins bring on not conventional damnation but reduction to the mechanical:

> He makes him selfe a thorough-fare of vice.
> Thus, in his belly, can he change a sin,
> Lust it comes out, that gluttony went in.
> *(Epigrams,* CXVIII, 'On Gut': ll. 4–6)

Defining the 'tribe of Ben', Jonson excludes those who 'make it their proficiencie, how much / They'have glutted in, and letcher'd out that weeke' (*The Underwood*, XLVII: 'An Epistle Answering to One that Asked to be Sealed of the Tribe of Ben', ll. 12–13). The vicious man is not so much a sinner as a mechanism for turning one kind of material into another. Mistress Otter, in *Epicoene*, is a collection of moving parts, whose one function when assembled is to make a loud noise:

> She takes her selfe asunder still when she goes to bed, into some twentie boxes; and about next day noone is put together againe, like a great *Germane* clocke: and so comes forth and rings a tedious larum to the whole house, and then is quiet againe for an houre, but for her quarters. (IV. ii. 97–101)

In *The Staple of News*, Pecunia's worshippers show a lifeless activity:

They are a kinde of dancing engines all!
And set, by nature, thus, to runne alone
To euery sound! All things within, without 'hem,
Moue, but their braine, and that stands still! mere monsters.

(IV. ii. 134–7)

What life they have is mechanically induced, as is the case with
the Beotians of *Pan's Anniversary*, who have fire struck into them
by a tinder-box, and who are wound up by a clock-keeper
(ll. 115–18, 123–7).

But Jonson's subhuman creatures do not always have even
this degree of animation. They can be mere lifeless things, to be
played upon, measured, or sliced to pieces. In the Quarto
version of *Every Man in his Humour*, Stephano is compared to 'a
Barbers virginals, for euery one may play vpon him' (II. iii.
184–5). In the Folio the comparison is with a drum and a child's
whistle (III. ii. 23–5). In *A Tale of a Tub*, rank is something that
can be measured physically, like cloth: 'A Gentleman and a halfe;
almost a Knight; / Within zixe inches: That's his true measure'
(IV, 'the scene interloping', ll. 39–40); in *Epicoene*, John Daw is
'two yards of knighthood, measur'd out by *Time*, to be sold to
laughter' (II. iv. 151–2). Anything that can be measured can be
cut. Truewit balks at the idea of amputating Daw's left arm:
'How! Maime a man for euer, for a iest? what a conscience has
thou?' But Dauphine insists that Daw will not miss a few spare
parts: ''Tis no losse to him: he has no employment for his armes,
but to eate spoone-meat' (IV. v. 135–8).

Some figures, like Gut in Epigram CXVIII, are reduced to one
organ only, since only one organ really matters. Morose thinks
of his servants this way: 'Where are all my eaters? my mouthes
now?' (III. v. 33–4). The most startling fragmentation, however,
occurs in the masque *Time Vindicated to Himself and to his Honours*,
in which the 'Curious' are broken down into specialized senses,
each concentrating on its own narrow function and incapable
of full human understanding:

FAME   *entreth, follow'd by the* Curious, *the* Ey'd,
          the Ear'd, *and the* Nos'd.
FAME   Give eare, the worthy, heare what *Time* proclaimes.
EARES What? what? Is't worth our eares?

EIES   Or eyes?
NOSE   Or noses?
　　For we are curious, *Fame*: indeed, the *Curious*.
EIES   We come to spie.
EARES   And hearken.
NOSE   And smell out.
FAME   More then you understand, my hot Inquisitors,
　　Is't not so?
NOSE   We cannot tell.   (ll. 3–15)

The quick, broken lines suggest the fragmentation the characters
themselves embody. Jonson's main purpose, of course, is to
attack impertinent gossips in general and hard-to-please audiences in particular; but the fable he constructs for doing so
becomes a striking image of inhumanity, of man reduced to the
physical and thereby rendered incapable of functioning. It is like
a parody of Menenius' fable of the belly and the members. The
different parties are incapable of co-operating because there is no
understanding to control them. Far from working together,
they squabble, agreeing only that they would like to see a mad
chaos:

NOSE   Something that is unlawfull.
EARES   I, or unreasonable.
EIES   Or impossible.
NOSE   Let't be uncivill enough, you hit us right.
EARES   And a great noyse.
EIES   To little, or no purpose.   (ll. 241–6)

Jonson attacks the complaining element in his audience, not so
much for failing to know its own mind as for not having a mind
to know. Understanding being absent, the senses have it all their
own way, and the result is like watching an integrated human
being going to pieces. Yet the fragmented organs remain alive,
talking shrilly and rapidly. They lose their proper functions:
instead of recording, they demand and judge, taking on the role
that the mind should be playing. There is an edge of anger here
that we do not often get in the comic section of a masque; and
behind the anger may be one of Jonson's basic fears – the fear of
a descent below normal humanity, resulting not in death but in a
terrible parody of life.
　　This passage also suggests Jonson's concern with what happens
to the mind when men become subhuman. Like the body it

continues to function, but in a limited, mechanical way. It records without understanding, and asserts without judging. The main action of *A Tale of a Tub* concerns the competition for the hand of Audrey, but there seems to be no particular reason why she should marry one suitor rather than another, or why she herself should be worth winning. As Sir Hugh remarks, 'I smile to thinke how like a Lottery / These Weddings are' (I.i. 97–8); and Audrey herself, the prize in the lottery, has (like Dame Pliant in *The Alchemist*) no mind of her own, but will fit her judgement to that of the person who has spoken to her most recently:

> TUB Why, did you ever love me, gentle *Awdrey*?
> AWD Love you? I cannot tell: I must hate no body,
>   My Father sayes.
> TUB   Yes, *Clay*, and *Kilburne*; Awdrey,
>   You must hate them.
> AWD   It shall be for your sake then. (II.iv.71–4)

In her habit of picking up ideas mechanically, Audrey is like more fully developed characters in other plays, who have recording devices where their brains ought to be. Crispinus, in *Poetaster*, shapes himself so thoroughly to his company and his surroundings that he has (like Audrey) no mind of his own. Finding himself in conversation with Horace, he declares he would like to be like Horace:

> Nay, we are new turn'd *Poet* too, which is more; and a
> *Satyrist* too, which is more then that: I write iust in thy veine,
> I. I am for your *odes* or your *sermons*, or anything indeed; wee
> are a gentleman besides: our name is RVFVS LABERIVS
> CRISPINVS, we are a prettie *stoick* too. (III.i.23–8)

We see here a man who has no identity and is casting about to find one, using whatever material comes nearest to hand. No judgement controls his search; he is at the mercy of external stimuli. Even this problem cannot occupy his mind for more than a few seconds; needing something else to talk about, he takes again the material nearest to hand:

> By PHOEBVS, here's a most neate fine street, is't not? I protest
> to thee, I am enamour'd of this street now, more then of halfe

the streets of *Rome*, againe; 'tis so polite, and terse! There's the
front of a building now. I studie architecture too: if euer I
should build, I'de haue a house iust of that *prospectiue*.

(III. i. 30–5)

Even when he has found his subject he can do nothing with it.

Sir Politic Would-be in *Volpone* is equally receptive to suggestion, as we see when Peregrine begins ironically to feed his
companion's fantasies of espionage:

PER   I haue heard, sir,
     That your *Bab'ouns* were spies; and that they were
     A kind of subtle nation, neere to *China*.
POL   I, I, your *Mamamuluchi*. Faith, they had
     Their hand in a *French* plot, or two; but they
     Were so extremely giuen to women, as
     They made discouery of all.   (II. i. 87–93)

In another character this would be bluff; but I suspect that to Sir
Politic the Mamamuluchi, once Peregrine has planted the idea in
his mind, are as real as Stone the fool and all his other
obsessions. He does not discriminate; he simply collects. The
same is true of John Daw's efforts at picking up culture:

CLE   What a sacke full of their names he has got!
DAVP   And how he poures 'hem out! POLITIAN, with VALERIVS
     FLACCVS!   (II. iv. 72–4)

Dauphine later says of Daw and La-Foole, 'They'll beleeue
themselues to be iust such men as we make 'hem, neither more
nor lesse. They haue nothing, not the vse of their senses, but by
tradition' (III. iii. 97–9). In depicting his fools, then, Jonson is not
content with stock signs of idiocy. He is scientifically precise in
the way he identifies certain characteristic mental processes that
distinguish the fool. In particular, he shows minds reduced to
mechanical recording, and this is of a piece with his general
vision of man reduced to the material, the sub-human. Yet these
things seem to be the products of nature, and a question is raised
here that seems as much metaphysical as satiric: 'O manners!
that this age should bring forth such creatures! that Nature

should bee at leisure to make 'hem!' (*Every Man In*, iv. vii.
146–7).[6] What was Nature thinking of? Why did she bother?
The answer may be implied in the word 'leisure': men of this
kind are not Nature's central work but an odd amusement for
her idle hours. Once again, not just their value but their reality
as human beings is called into question.

At times it seems that what Nature has created is not a collection
of individual fools or knaves but a vast amorphous mass of
undifferentiated material. Jonas A. Barish has noted that in
Sejanus 'The huge crises, when they come, have the jolting
impact of geological cataclysms, the product of centuries of
shifting of subterranean rock.'[7] This is because there is something amorphous in the characters themselves: a glance at the
huge cast list suggests a play that will show not individuals but a
mass of humanity, like the expressionist plays of the 1920s and
1930s with their toiling armies of extras. In fact individual voices
do rise from the general hubbub – Sejanus, Tiberius, Arruntius,
Macro – but the sense of an undifferentiated mass is always there
in the background. It is strongest in the Senate scenes, in which
characters seem to coalesce into a single voice expressing the
reactions of a single unthinking mind. This mind, like those of
individual fools in Jonson, simply responds to stimuli: as
Tiberius' view of Sejanus switches, the Senate mechanically
follows. The mob that tears Sejanus to pieces and then weeps at
what it has done is a frighteningly logical extension of what we
have already seen in the Senate. (Jonson repeats the effect in a
modified and more overtly comic form in *Volpone*, where the
Avocatori seem at times to be a single jabbering voice, not
showing an intelligent understanding of the case before them
but simply responding to the latest piece of information.)

The conspirators in *Catiline*, like the senators of the earlier
play, sink at times to a single amorphous mass, and the
irrationality that results is even more striking. The scene of the
omens goes far beyond the conventional dramatization of such
moments in its suggestion of a collective panic, a group instinct
like that at work in a flock of birds:

VAR How is't, AVTRONIVS!
AVT LONGINVS?
LON   CVRIVS?
CVR   LECCA?
VAR   Feele you nothing?
LON A strange, vn-wonted horror doth inuade me,
  I know not what it is!
LEC   The day goes back,
  Or else my senses!   *A darkenesse comes*
CVR   As at ATREVS feast!   *ouer the place.*
                              (I. 309–13)

The omens that follow, '*a grone of many people . . . vnder ground*', and a fiery light, seem projections of the collective, fevered imagination of the conspirators themselves. Similarly, the participants in the mock banquet of the gods in *Poetaster* are mysteriously struck with a 'sodaine and generall heauinesse' (IV. v. 184) in the midst of their revelry, shortly before they are raided by Caesar and his officers.

Frequently, even in lighter plays, the fools coalesce into groups – the courtiers of *Cynthia's Revels*, the pretenders to culture in *Poetaster*, the collegiate ladies of *Epicoene*. This is partly Jonson's desire 'to behold the *Scene* full' (*Every Man out of his Humour*, II. iii. 297–8); but behind that technical consideration is a desire to show the sheer alarming *mass* of folly. In *Epicoene*, Sir Amorous La-Foole speaks with pride of the multiplying spawn of his tribe: 'They all come out of our house, the LA-FOOLES o' the north, the LA-FOOLES of the west, the LA-FOOLES of the east, and south' (I. iv. 37–9). The effect is not unlike the fantasies of proliferation in the plays of Ionesco – chairs, eggs, rhinoceroses. One of Jonson's favourite images (related to the idea of life as a dead sea) is the image of flood[8] – in *Epicoene*, a flood of noisy folly that threatens to engulf Morose's house: 'O, the sea breakes in vpon me! another floud! an inundation! I shall be orewhelm'd with noise. It beates already at my shores' (III. vi. 2–4). Volpone similarly fears a 'floud of words! a very torrent!' (III. iv. 64) from Lady Would-be, who is an inundation in herself.

The image of flood relates to the idea of a shared, subhuman consciousness among the fools; and to the well-known theory of 'humours'. The definition of humour in the Induction to *Every Man Out* emphasizes its liquid properties:

> what soe're hath fluxure, and humiditie,
> As wanting power to containe it selfe,
> Is Humour. (Induction, ll. 96–8)

In *Epicoene* there seems to be a water-table of humours that rises when the fools become collectively excited: 'OTTERS wine has swell'd their humours aboue a spring-tide' (IV.iv. 168–9). The sea of humour, like the dead sea of life, can be overwhelming and destructive. In *Every Man in his Humour*, Cash comments on the dangerous power of Kitely's obsession:

> Where should this floud of passion (trow) take head? ha?
> Best, dreame no longer of this running humour,
> For feare I sinke! the violence of the streame
> Alreadie hath transported me so farre,
> That I can feele no ground at all! (III.iii. 140–4)

Death by humour is also a threat in *Cynthia's Revels*, as Crites says of the foolish courtiers:

> But how more cheape
> When, euen his best and vnderstanding part,
> (The crowne, and strength of all his faculties)
> Floates like a dead drown'd bodie, on the streame
> Of vulgar humour, mixt with commonst dregs? (I.v. 35–9)

Many implications of the 'dead sea of life' image come together in this passage. The understanding is drowned, and man becomes part of a collective irrational mind, suffering a kind of death in the process. The irony is that the fools of *Cynthia's Revels* welcome this state, and are like stranded fish without it (II.v. 16–24). The only life of which they are capable is to float drowned in the sea of humour.

The creative energies of Jonson's dramatic characters – energies that lead them, for example, to construct secondary worlds like those examined in Chapter 1 – are in constant tension with an underlying sluggishness and torpor. The sensual world in Jonson is a world asleep. In *Poetaster*, Horace's friend Trebantius

ironically advises him not to bother with writing, but to lapse
into idleness with the rest of the world:

> Rather, contend to sleepe, and liue like them,
> That holding golden sleepe in speciall price,
> Rub'd with sweet oiles, swim siluer *Tyber* thrice,
> And euery eu'en, with neat wine steeped be.   (III. v. 12–15)

The temptation to sleep is subtly blended with the temptation to
surrender to a flood – of water, or of wine. In *Part of the King's
Entertainment in Passing to his Coronation*, the Thames itself is
rebuked for sluggishness:

> Vp thou tame RIVER, wake;
> And from thy liquid limbes this slumber shake:
> Thou drown'st they selfe in inofficious sleepe;
> And these thy sluggish waters seeme to creepe,
> Rather than flow.   (ll. 302–6)

'An Epistle to a Friend, to Persuade him to the Wars' (*The
Underwood*, xv) opens with the exhortation, 'Wake, friend, from
forth thy Lethargie,' and claims that the wars 'would yet revive /
Mans buried honour, in his sleepie life' (ll. 6–7).

The exhortation to rise from lethargy into action is subjected
to a grisly parody in *Catiline*. The conspirators see themselves
whipping a sleepy world into life; Cethegus chides his colleagues:

> Come, we all sleepe, and are meere dormice; flies,
> A little lesse then dead: more dulnesse hangs
> On vs, then on the morne. W'are spirit-bound,
> In ribs of ice.   (I. 211–14)

The end of that passage suggests that the conspirators are a
frozen river, a subhuman force waiting to be released; and
Catiline picks up the image later:

> That, when the sodaine thaw comes, we may breake
> Vpon 'hem like a deluge, bearing downe
> Halfe *Rome* before vs.   (I. 523–5)

We have seen already what the flood image means for Jonson.
Even without the evidence from other works, what we see of

the conspirators of this play – noisy, pretentious and funda-
mentally stupid – would tell us that the action they create in
response to the torpor they fear is in its own way just as
subhuman, just as dead. The complacency of the Roman senate
is also described as sleep (I. 437–8) and Cicero wonders for a
while if the gods themselves are sleeping (III. 237–41). He
manages to rouse the senate, Catiline leaves Rome, and the
conspirators who remain are betrayed (according to Catiline) by
'the sloth, / And sleepinesse of LENTVLVS' (v. 380–1). But the
torpor in which the play began returns towards the end. Cicero
– for reasons that will be examined in Chapter 4 – wins his
victory over the Catiline conspiracy but in so doing leaves Rome
still open to the much graver threat posed by Caesar. Both the
conspiracy and the forces of virtue are stymied.[9] This may
account for the most curious feature of the play's structure: the
pace gets slower and slower in the last three acts. It is not that
Jonson does not know how to pace a play; he has by this time
written *Sejanus*, *Volpone*, and *The Alchemist*. Rather, he seems to
want, at whatever cost to the play's theatrical viability, the effect
of a whole world grinding slowly to a halt.

A subtler depiction of creative energy pulling against torpor is
found in *Volpone*. In Chapter 1 I suggested some of the ironies
that surround the central figure – he becomes the source of
action in his world by lying, inert, in bed, and the feverish
activity he himself indulges in suggests a man with no real
identity of his own. The tremendous creative energy released in
the play is a reaction against inertia, non-being, even death.[10]
Behind the bustle of Jonson's Venice we catch glimpses of a dead
world. There are small touches in the language: 'When you doe
come to swim, in golden lard' (I. iii. 70) – the most sluggish flood
imaginable; 'when I am lost in blended dust' (I. ii. 119) – the final
loss of individuality. Volpone mocks Corbaccio in particular:

> So many cares, so many maladies,
> So many feares attending on old age,
> Yea, death so often call'd on, as no wish
> Can be more frequent with 'hem, their limbs faint,
> Their senses dull, their seeing, hearing, going,
> All dead before them.   (I. iv. 144–9)

He and Mosca predict that their victims, when finally discomfited, will simply go dead and curl up:

MOS   Your Aduocate will turne stark dull, vpon it.
VOLP It will take off his oratories edge.
MOS   But your *Clarissimo*, old round-backe, he
      Will crumpe you, like a hog-louse, with the touch.

                                                (v. ii. 88–91)

In contrast, Volpone sees himself, especially in the scenes with
Celia, as a vital figure, and his gold as a life-giving force, much
like Scoto's oil with its power to sharpen the senses (II. ii. 192–
203). He parodies death in his own impersonation of it – thus,
perhaps, trying to win some power over it by bringing it under
the control of his imagination:

             he, now,
      Hath lost his feeling, and hath left to snort:
      You hardly can perceiue him, that he breathes.   (I. iv. 52–4)

Like the 'Curious' in *Time Vindicated* he is reduced to one
faculty:

      Put it into his hand; 'tis onely there
      He apprehends: he has his feeling, yet.
      See, how he grasps it!   (I. v. 18–20)

By impersonating so wittily a man half-dead, Volpone is
actually demonstrating his own vitality.

   Yet there is an uncomfortable truth in the impersonation. The
vitality has to be artificially stimulated, by entertainment –
'Bring forth your sports / And helpe, to make the wretched time
more sweet' (III. iii. 1–2); and by drink – 'Giue me a boule of
lustie wine, to fright / This humor from my heart' (v. i. 11–12).
In the encounter with Celia, Volpone tries to present himself as a
lusty young lover, but the argument of his song – that most
basic persuasion to love – betrays him:

      Time will not be ours, for euer,
      He, at length, our good will seuer;
      Spend not then his gifts, in vaine.
      Sunnes, that set, may rise againe:
      But if, once, we lose this light,
      'Tis with vs perpetuall night.   (III. vii. 168–73)

The tension persists to the end of the play. Clifford Leech has aptly described the sentences on Volpone and Mosca as 'living deaths'.[11] Mosca is to be a 'perpetuall prisoner' (v. xii. 114) and Volpone, 'crampt with irons, / Till thou bee'st sicke, and lame indeed' (v. xii. 123–4), is doomed to enact his impersonation of death till death itself frees him. He will be in reality as inert as he pretended to be. But when he steps forward to deliver the epilogue, it is as though Volpone's disguise has been imprisoned and the essential character – the showman, trickster and creator – has gone free. The tension between Jonson's moral criticism of the character and his delight in his creative power is matched by a parallel tension – between the death-like torpor that threatens even this liveliest of Jonson's plays and the stubborn vitality of the fox who may feign death but refuses to die. Volpone may have sunk beneath the fully human; but unlike 'something that walks somewhere' he has a function and – despite his Protean nature – a final identity that fixes him in our minds. The role of the fox by which Volpone identifies himself in the epilogue may be a substitute for a full human identity; but for all our misgivings we have to recognize and respect its vitality. Where other Jonson characters sink to living death, Volpone has created an alternative life.

II

Just as Jonson's criticism of the false secondary world is countered by his delight in creation, so his horror at the subhuman is countered – occasionally – by a fascination with the vitality our lower natures can display when the restraints imposed by our higher ones are removed. In theory, the first antimasque of *Pleasure Reconciled to Virtue* shows the sort of reduction to the subhuman that Jonson deplores; it is a dance of men disguised as bottles, 'figures who have ceased to be men and who have become mere containers for what will satisfy their appetites'.[12] Hercules, the figure of virtue in the masque, routs them as he later routs those other subhuman creatures, the pygmies: 'Burdens, & shames of nature, perish, dye, / For yet you neuer liv'd' (ll. 101–2). But if the dancing bottles never

really lived, that is not altogether true of the subhuman figure
who dominates the antimasque:

> Roome, roome, make roome for the bouncing belly,
> first father of Sauce, & deuiser of gelly,
> Prime master of arts, & the giuer of wit,
> that found out the excellent ingine, the spit,
> the plough, & the flaile, the mill, & the Hoppar,
> the hutch, & the bowlter, the furnace, & coppar.   (ll. 13–18)

And so on, through a long list of the belly's inventions. It is a
triumphant entrance. The belly may be only one organ, 'for
when did you ever read, or heare, that the Belly had any eares?'
(ll. 49–50), but the reduction of human possibilities he represents does not mean he is a dead thing, like 'Gut' of Epigram
CXVIII. He is, rather, the 'bouncing belly', and his vitality
extends beyond mere gluttony to a considerable, if single-
minded, inventiveness. A whole range of activities springs from
the one basic need the belly represents. Finally, the belly expands
and explodes – not to destruction but to apotheosis:

> All which haue now made thee, so wide i' the waste,
> as scarce with no pudding thou art to be lac'd:
> but eating & drincking, vntill thou dost nod
> thou break'st all thy girdles, & breakst forth a god.   (ll. 33–6)

The spirit in which the belly is presented is suggested by the
Bowl-bearer's rebuttal of one particular accusation: 'Some in
derision call him the father of farts: But I say, he was the first
inventor of great ordynance: and taught vs to discharge 'hem on
feastivall daies' (ll. 60–3). It is the liberty of a festive occasion –
in this case Twelfth Night, the date of the performance – that
allows the belly his triumph, and allows us to keep more
responsible feelings in check for a while:

> I know it is now such a time as the saturnalls for all the world,
> that every man stands vnder the eaves of his owne hat; & sings
> what please him, that's the ryte, & the libertie of it.
>   (ll. 41–4)

The belly's ancient retainer Hunger has been turned away 'for
being vnseasonable: not vnreasonable, but vnseasonable' (ll.
53–4). The belly would not object to anything unreasonable,

being essentially unreasonable himself; but Hunger has no place in a festive occasion. Of course there is much more to *Pleasure Reconciled to Virtue* than a celebration of cakes and ale. The sort of pleasure the belly represents is condemned by Hercules, and is replaced by the higher pleasures of the courtly revels, the serious and morally significant pleasures of music and dance. But to take a simply moral interpretation of the Bowl-bearer's speeches is to ignore their tone: for a while, we are allowed to relax and enjoy the belly's triumph. We may imagine that, for all the moral seriousness behind the image, the dance of bottles had a similar effect. And in *The Vision of Delight*, the reduction of man to belly is accepted as cheerful fantasy:

> As for example, a belly, and no face,
> With the bill of a Shoveler, may here come in place;
> The haunches of a Drum, with the feet of a pot,
> And the tayle of a Kentishman to it; why not?   (ll. 107–10)

If we expected Jonson to be morally earnest all the time, we could read a long lecture on that passage, based on disorder, reduction, and subhumanity; but the flippant 'why not?' warns us to read it instead in the spirit of the occasion.

The frequent references in *A Tale of a Tub* to the fact that the action takes place on Saint Valentine's day add a similar dimension to our response. The comedy of mindless courtship is perhaps more genial and less censorious for taking place on the day when the birds, naturally, choose their mates. Even the formidable dowager Lady Tub acknowledges the occasion:

> This frosty morning wee will take the aire,
> About the fields: for I doe meane to be
> Some-bodies *Valentine*, i'my Velvet Gowne,
> This morning, though it be but a beggar-man.   (I. vi. 2–5)

The characters' lack of judgement and discrimination, noted earlier, is mostly their own rustic stupidity, but the sense of occasion gives it at least a temporary warrant, and helps to lighten the tone of the play. But the most notable festive occasion in Jonson is Saint Bartholomew's Day. At the opening of *Bartholomew Fair* Littlewit calls attention to the date (I. i. 6–8), and while not much is made of this in the play as a whole, we take the point that the Fair is a special occasion, taking place at a time set aside for it.

This is not to say that Bartholomew Fair is simply one big party. In fact, it is Jonson's most detailed and comprehensive vision of man reduced below his proper level. At the centre of the early Fair scenes in particular is Ursula's pig tent, where human flesh and swine's flesh are sold in the same breath: 'heere you may ha' your Punque, and your Pigge in state, Sir, both piping hot' (II. v. 40–2). Ursula herelf is a great lump of matter, as fat and greasy as her pigs, and threatened by her own heat with even further reduction: 'I am all fire, and fat, *Nightingale*, I shall e'en melt away to the first woman, a ribbe againe, I am afraid' (II. ii. 50–1). She is also massive, overwhelming, a great bog: 'Yes, hee that would venture for't, I assure him, might sinke into her, and be drown'd a weeke, ere any friend hee had, could find where he were' (II. v. 95–7). There is a brisk trade in human beings, as well as goods, at the Fair, and no real difference is made between them. When Knock'em persuades Win Littlewit to become a punk, he itemizes her 'points' 'as he would those of a horse'.[13] Waspe suggests that Leatherhead could be sold like one of his own toys: 'Cry you mercy! you'ld be sold too, would you? what's the price on you? Ierkin and all, as you stand' (III. iv. 110–111). The sensuality of the Fair is not life-enhancing but life-diminishing; even its sexuality is sterile. The Fair's energy is ultimately concentrated in the puppets, who are not only noisy and quarrelsome but aggressively lecherous. They are, however, not flesh and blood but wood, and the ultimate revelation about them is that they are sexless.[14]

Those who come to the Fair are quickly dragged down to its level. Some, of course, do not need much dragging. Zeal-of-the-Land Busy has natural affinities with Ursula, having been 'a notable hot Baker' (III. ii. 50–1) in his Banbury days. Our first glimpse of him shows an impressive concentration of purpose: 'I found him, fast by the teeth, i'the cold Turkey-pye, i' the cupbord, with a great white loafe on his left hand, and a glasse of *Malmesey* on his right' (I. vi. 34–6). When he tries to locate the pig tent, he relies on one sense alone: 'Therefore be bold (huh, huh, huh) follow the sent' (III. ii. 84). The accompanying stage direction reads, 'Busy *sents after it like a Hound.*' He is reduced not only to an animal, but to an animal whose faculties are concentrated in one direction only. In the last scene, he can debate with a puppet on equal terms. Waspe (reduced already by his name) also shows a natural affinity with the Fair. His mental tic is an irritable contradiction of whoever is speaking to him; as Busy is reduced to one sense, Waspe is reduced to one mechanical reaction. This means that the 'Vapours' game, whose whole point is senseless contradiction, finds him in his element:

> WHI Yesh, I am i' de right, I confesh it, so ish de little man too.
> WAS I'le haue nothing confest, that concernes mee. I am not i'the right, nor neuer was i'the right, nor neuer will be i'the right, while I am in my right minde. (IV. iv. 70–4)

The idea of a mechanical response to stimuli is clearest in the case of Troubleall, who behaves like one of Pavlov's dogs:

> hee will doe nothing, but by Iustice *Ouerdoo's* warrant, he will not eate a crust, nor drinke a little, nor make him in his apparell, ready. His wife, Sirreuerence, cannot get him to make his water, or shift his shirt, without his warrant.
> (IV. i. 58–62)

The character who takes most enthusiastically to the Fair – even to the point of claiming it as *his* fair, because it bears his name (I. v. 65–7) – is Bartholomew Cokes. And Cokes is one of the fullest portrayals in Jonson of man reduced to a noise-making machine. He has many affinities with the puppets in which he takes such delight. Whatever his head is stuffed with, it is not a brain. Waspe speculates on the subject:

> he that had the meanes to trauell in your head, nów, should meet finer sights then any are i'the *Fayre;* and make a finer voyage on't; to see it all hung with cockle-shels, pebbles, fine wheat strawes, and here and there a chicken's feather, and a cob-web. (I. v. 93–7)

He has, like John Daw, detachable parts. Waspe despairs of bringing him home from the Fair undamaged: 'If a legge or an arme on him did not grow on, hee would lose it i' the presse. Pray heauen I bring him off with one stone!' (I. v. 114–16). The cutpurse Edgeworth remarks, 'a man might cut out his kidneys,

I thinke; and he neuer feele 'hem' (IV. ii. 42–3). His mind is simply a recording device, that picks things up indiscriminately. According to Waspe,

> I dare not let him walke alone, for feare of learning of vile tunes, which hee will sing at supper, and in the sermon-times! if hee meete but a Carman i' the streete, and I finde him not talke to keepe him off on him, hee will whistle him, and all his tunes ouer, at night in his sleepe! (I. iv. 76–81)

The fact that his mind does not discriminate is shown most clearly when he catalogues his losses in the Fair, putting everything on the same level of importance:

> I ha' lost my selfe, and my cloake and my hat; and my fine sword, and my sister, and *Numps*, and Mistris *Grace*, (a Gentle-woman that I should ha' marryed) and a cut-worke handkercher, shee ga' me, and two purses to day. And my bargaine o' Hobby-horses and Ginger-bread, which grieues me worst of all. (IV. ii. 81–6)

A mind that records and repeats without thinking, a body with detachable parts – Cokes is the perfect victim for the Fair, and sinks into it completely.

But the real test of the Fair's power is what it will do to the three most intelligent characters in the play: Quarlous, Winwife and Grace. Each maintains, even while attending the Fair, a certain ironic detachment from it. Yet they are all affected by the Fair, and all three emerge from it with marriage partners. Moreover, the marriage partners are not the ones anticipated in the first act of the play. Almost our first piece of plot information is that Grace is engaged to Cokes; she emerges from the Fair betrothed to Winwife. Winwife is paying court to Dame Purecraft; Quarlous scorns the idea, and delivers racy lectures on the folly of marrying a Puritan widow. Yet at the end of the play Quarlous and Purecraft are betrothed. The Fair is like a parody of the enchanted wood of *A Midsummer Night's Dream:* couples enter it, are spun into confusion, and emerge in different configurations. Grace, who seems sensible and discriminating about marriage – 'I must haue a husband I must loue, or I cannot liue with him' (IV. iii. 16–17) – speaks of the impossibility of choosing between Quarlous and Winwife, both of whom want her (IV. iii. 21–6). Her solution is not to delay her choice but to put it to a lottery; each man is to write a word in a table-book, and the first passer-by – who turns out, of course, to be the mad Troubleall – is to mark one of them. The whole idea of choice is rendered meaningless. While Cokes is incapable of discriminating, Grace refuses to.

There are many reasons why the two men regard Grace as a desirable prize; but one may be the basic, instinctive sex drive suggested by Winwife's bawdy pun at the start of the courting sequence: 'let's goe enter our selues in *Grace*, with her' (III. iv. 75). And the reason why Quarlous is prepared to settle for Dame Purecraft, despite his lectures on the folly of marrying widows, is equally basic: 'Why should not I marry this sixe thousand pound, now I think on't?' He adds, 'The tother wench, *Winwife* is sure of; there's no expectation for me there' (v. ii. 75–9), as though one wench is as good as another so long as she has money. Quarlous is at this point disguised as Troubleall, and Purecraft's sudden infatuation with him is a mechanical response to a prophecy that she must marry a madman: 'I loue him o' the sudden, (the cunning man sayd all true)' (IV. vi. 170–1); but when she proposes, some instinct – probably her own materialist nature – tells her to put her most compelling argument first: 'I am worth sixe thousand pound, my loue to you, is become my racke' (v. ii. 50–1). The marriages of *Bartholomew Fair* are almost as meaningless as the courtship intrigue of *A Tale of a Tub*. Identities are flattened, money, sex and superstition are the only impulses that count, and ultimately chance rules all, embodied in the figure of the mad Troubleall, who touches each of the engagements but has even less sense of what he is doing than Puck in *A Midsummer Night's Dream*.

All this having been said, why do we not simply turn away from Bartholomew Fair in disgust? One answer is that the play is at pains to show there is no turning away from it. Winwife and Grace both scorn it; yet they owe their betrothal to it. Justice Overdo seeks to judge and correct it, but finds himself over-whelmed by it when he discovers his own wife has been trans-formed into one of Ursula's punks. Even the Fair's enemies are drawn to it like iron filings to a magnet. The obvious clue to its significance is Quarlous' final admonition to Overdo:

> remember you are but *Adam*, Flesh, and blood! you haue your frailty, forget your other name of *Ouerdoo*, and inuite vs all to supper. There you and I will compare our *discoueries;* and drowne the memory of all enormity in your bigg'st bowle at home. (v. vi. 96–100)

The Fair is an overwhelming force; what it represents is as common to us as our flesh and blood. To resist a descent to our lower nature is, finally, impossible. It is worth noting that the last voice heard in the play is not that of some conventional figure of authority or judgement, but that of Bartholomew Cokes: 'Yes, and bring the *Actors* along, wee'll ha' the rest o' the *Play* at home' (v. vi. 114–15).[15] The Fair, like Volpone's false world, is also enjoyable for its sheer theatrical vividness, for the creative flair Jonson displays in figures like Ursula and Mooncalf; and for the skill and dedication with which the rogues ply their trade. Edgeworth illustrates the latter point when Quarlous hires him to steal Cokes's license:

> Would you ha' the boxe and all, Sir? or onely that, that is in't? I'le get you that, and leaue him the boxe, to play with still: (which will be the harder o'the two) because I would gaine your worships good opinion of me. (III. v. 251–4)

It is impossible not to admire professionalism at that level.

But if there is one consideration that is finally decisive in making the Fair enjoyable while many other images of the sub-human in Jonson produce only scorn or alarm, it is the sense that the Fair is a special occasion. It is not a flood to overwhelm us or a dead sea in which we could sink and be lost forever. Its energies are contained. It is emphasized that the Fair is held at a special time, and a special place – Smithfield – that we can leave as well as enter.[16] The play itself, that embodies the Fair, is likewise a special, deliberately limited occasion. The Induction sets up an agreement

> between the *Spectators* or *Hearers*, at the *Hope* on the Bankeside, in the County of *Surrey* on the one party; And the *Author of Bartholomew Fayre* in the said place, and County on the other

party: the one and thirtieth day of *Octob.* 1614 and in the
twelfth yeere of the Raigne of our Soueraigne Lord, IAMES by
the grace of God *King of England, France, & Ireland;* Defender
of the faith. And of *Scotland* the seauen and fortieth.

(Induction, ll. 64–72)

There is no other play of Jonson's in which the theatrical
occasion is so elaborately prepared, its special conditions so
clearly spelled out. Even in his choice of the disreputable Hope
theatre, 'the *Author* hath obseru'd a speciall *Decorum*, the place
being as durty as *Smithfield*, and as stinking euery whit'
(Induction, ll. 158–60). At the end of the play, the festive
energies of the Fair are reduced to a manageable domestic
compass as Overdo takes up Quarlous' suggestion and invites
the company home to supper.

There are times when it is safe for man to surrender his cooler
reason, even his individual identity, and become part of a mass.
Such a surrender need not involve a loss of humanity, provided
it takes place within the institutions of society and under the
shaping order of art. 'Something that walks somewhere' and the
dead lord of the Cary–Morison ode have surrendered not just
their individual identities but their social natures; the public
positions they both occupy serve to emphasize that point. In
Pleasure Reconciled to Virtue and *Bartholomew Fair*, social occasions
and artistic form protect us from the worst possibilities of the
descent to the subhuman, putting that descent within limits that
make it acceptable. This is not to say that it is a matter of pure
rejoicing; Jonson does not finally sentimentalize either the
belly-god or the Bartholomew-birds. If something is gained in
energy and concentration, much is lost in dignity, intelligence
and simple human decency. But it is worth noting that on a
couple of occasions Jonson adapted the image of the flood – so
frequently used to express his fear of man drowning in a life that
is no life at all – and made it a matter of celebration. In *Part of the
King's Entertainment in Passing to his Coronation*, Tamesis, roused
from his sleep, speaks of a flood of rejoicing at the King's
progress:

> To what vaine end should I contend to show
> My weaker powers, when seas of pompe o'reflow

The cities face: and couer all the shore
With sands more rich than TAGVS wealthy ore?
When in the flood of ioy, that comes with him,
He drownes the world; yet makes it liue and swimme,
And spring with gladnesse: not my fishes heere,
Though they be dumbe, but doe expresse the cheere
Of these bright streames.   (ll. 309–17)

To be 'drowned' in joy at the arrival of King James is not just to
lose oneself, but to participate in a fuller, richer life. In *Poetaster*,
the power of poetry is celebrated in similar terms:

In her sweet streames shall our braue *Roman* spirits
Chace, and swim after death, with their choise deeds
Shining on their white shoulders; and therein
Shall *Tyber*, and our famous riuers fall
With such attraction, that th'ambitious line
Of the round world shall too her center shrinke,
To heare their musicke.   (v. i. 25–31)

Individuality is surrendered – to a social occasion, or a form of
art. The flood that overwhelms the individual mind is not a
lifeless force but one that exalts and clarifies. Its strength is not
that of inert matter, but of humanity intensified by social and
artistic form; and that makes all the difference.

3
IMAGES OF SOCIETY

I

While Spenser and Shakespeare generally find their great images of order in celebrations of love, marriage and the family, Jonson turns more to the public institutions of society. In his 'Epithal-amion' for Jerome Weston and Frances Stuart (*The Underwood*, LXXV) he pauses in his account of the marriage to write two stanzas of tribute to the groom's father, Lord Weston, in his public role as Lord High Treasurer of England. Jonson also emphasizes the good judgement of King Charles in showing favour to Weston and his son. At times, indeed, the King and Queen seem to take the focus away from the bridal pair, and to become themselves the centre of the occasion:

> It is their Grace, and favour, that makes seene,
>   And wonder'd at, the bounties of this day:
> All is a story of the King and Queene!   (ll. 89–91)

While Spenser in his *Epithalamion* speaks of raising posterity for Heaven, Jonson is more political in his wishes for the future: 'And never may there want one of the Stem, / To be a watchfull Servant for this State' (ll. 177–8). Throughout the poem, the wedding is placed in a firmly social context: service to the state, and the favour of the Crown, seem at least as important as the religious and romantic values we would expect in such a poem.

Even Jonson's one pastoral is a very civil one. Renaissance pastoral is of course a highly cultivated genre; in *The Sad Shepherd* we find this not so much in the characters' elegance of style as in the attention Jonson pays to social form. Though there is a love-plot of the traditional kind, the main preoccupation of

Jonson's pastoral world is the attempt to hold a sheep-shearing feast. The emphasis is not on bringing lovers together so much as on bringing a community together. Robin Hood and his band are defined by their social roles: he is 'The chiefe Wood-man, Master of the Feast'; Friar Tuck is 'The Chaplaine and Steward', George a Green 'Huisher of the Bower', and Much 'Robin-Hoods Bailiffe'. The shepherds are grouped under the general title 'The Guests invited' ('The Persons of the Play', ll. 1–10). While the play is incomplete and any judgements of it must be tentative, it would appear that Jonson intended to found his pastoral drama less on a story of love, and more on a social occasion, than was usual in the genre.

But the most striking instance of Jonson's preoccupation with society is The Speeches at Prince Henry's Barriers. The ostensible subject of this entertainment is Prince Henry's revival of the spirit of chivalry. It is Jonson's only extended treatment of the Arthurian material that has fascinated so many English poets; it is also our only substantial evidence of what Jonson might have been like as a writer of English history.[1] The material could have called for a romantic celebration of English legends. Jonson gives us some of that, with Merlin rising from his tomb and Arthur (now changed into a star) speaking from above and exhorting Prince Henry to high deeds; but his real interest is in civil order:

> These were bold stories of our ARTHVRS age;
> But here are other acts; another *stage*
> And *scene* appeares; it is not since as then:
> No gyants, dwarfes, or monsters here, but men.
> His arts must be to gouerne, and giue lawes
> To peace no lesse than armes. (ll. 171–6)

Jonson's treatment of the Arthurian material anticipates Tennyson's and has its roots in Virgil's vision of Rome's responsibility in the *Aeneid*. The true adventure is the advance of civilization, the ordering of society.

In his panorama of English history, Jonson constantly reminds us of the civil arts. He pays tribute to Edward III's encouragement of the cloth trade, Henry VII's gift for making money, Henry VIII's build-up of the militia, and Elizabeth's

development of shipping. His view of the Tudors, though
idealized for the sake of the lesson he wants to draw, is as
practical and unmystical as that of a modern historian. The
lesson for Prince Henry is

> That ciuill arts the martiall must precede.
> That lawes and trade bring honors in and gayne,
> And armes defensiue a safe peace maintayne.   (ll. 212–14)

Jonson's parade of English kings is in fact an anatomy of kingship, stressing not only the king's power but the principles that
restrain that power. It must be underpropped by civil arts, and
governed by moral virtue. As a crusader, Richard Coeur de Lion
did 'Deedes past an angell, arm'd with wroth and fire' (l. 227).
But in his treatment of Austria, he was following his own pride,
and he came to grief for it – in Jonson's view, quite rightly
(ll. 231–6). That other popular hero of chivalry, the Black Prince,
is seen as a more civilized figure because he acts under the law
(ll. 253–5). The same civilized restraint is urged on Prince Henry's
imperial ambitions. Jonson seems to be writing with one eye on
King James, with his pacific foreign policy. The memory of
British conquests abroad

> may make to'inuite
> Your valure vpon need, but not to'incite
> Your neighbour Princes, giue them all their due,
> And be prepar'd if they will trouble you.
> He doth but scourge him selfe, his sword that drawes
> Without a purse, a counsaile and a cause.   (ll. 329–34)

The terse concluding line reminds us of the practical as well as
the moral restraints on kingly action.

But the entertainment ends with a vision of British im-
perialism as boundless:

> behold your *Britaine* fly
> Beyond the line, when what the seas before
> Did bound, shall to the sky then stretch his shore.
>   (ll. 436–8)

Here, and at other points in the work, Jonson seems to throw
caution to the winds. Every court entertainment had to pass

muster before James; but this one was written for Prince Henry in particular, and in trying to satisfy both the pacific policy of the father and the warlike ambition of the son, Jonson has created an unresolved tension. He is also writing on a panoramic scale less congenial to him than the smaller occasions he deals with in works we will examine later in this chapter. But *The Speeches at Prince Henry's Barriers* commands our interest as Jonson's most comprehensive attempt to deal with the idea of the state. Jonson could always rise to the special demands of an occasion, and this particular one – Prince Henry's attempt to revive the spirit of chivalry – took him outside his usual range of subjects. The result is a handling of the theme of England as eclectic within its smaller compass as is Spenser's in *The Faerie Queene*. It combines history and legend, chivalry and imperial splendour, law and economics. The imaginative energies of the imperial vision are played off against the restraints of civil and moral order: Jonson cannot write of chivalry without bringing in the cloth trade as well. This suggests a concern for civil life that many another poet handling the same theme would have thought irrelevant. It also suggests a fundamental Jonson idea that we can trace through more familiar works: namely, that society is an organic whole and no one part of it can be examined in isolation. In the remainder of this chapter I would like to consider Jonson's view of the inner connections of social life, and in particular his concern – more characteristic than the concerns of *Prince Henry's Barriers* – for the role of manners, culture and language in determining the health of a state.

From small occasions Jonson can draw broad significance; even apparently casual pleasures have their importance. Visiting Sir Henry Goodyere, and watching him at the sport of hawking, Jonson draws from the flight of the hawk a message for the behaviour of men, 'That they to knowledge so should toure vpright, / And neuer stoupe, but to strike ignorance'; he concludes, 'Now, in whose pleasures I haue this discerned, / What would his serious actions me haue learned?' (*Epigrams*, LXXXV: 'To Sir Henry Goodyere', ll. 6–7, 11–12). The last couplet might be taken as a rebuke to Sir Henry for not being wholly serious; but the effect of the entire poem is to cancel that possibility and suggest rather that Sir Henry is serious enough even in his sports. At the end of *Time Vindicated to Himself and to his Honours*, hunting is seen to have a similar moral value, training the hunter in a skill that exemplifies man's control over his lower nature (ll. 516–36).

Jonson could even harness one of the chief vices of the Jacobean court, and make it serve virtue. According to G. P. V. Akrigg, 'the senseless display with which too many of the courtiers bankrupted themselves passed all measure of taste or sanity';[2] Jonson himself attacked it many times. But through the masque, he was able to turn the courtiers' fondness for revelry and fancy dress into serious forms, using their opulence to express the beauty, dignity and harmony that ought to be the fundamental principles of court life.[3] For all the value Jonson placed on the text, the heart of the masque in performance was the dancing; and Jonson saw to it that the courtly performers and the audience did not see this as simply an occasion to show off:

> For Dauncing is an exercise
>   not only shews the mouers wit,
> but maketh the beholder wise,
>   as he hath powre to rise to it.
>
>   (*Pleasure Reconciled to Virtue*, ll. 269–72)

Jonson prefaced one of his last court masques, *Love's Triumph through Callipolis*, with a statement significantly titled 'To make the Spectators vnderstanders,' and insisting that

> all Repraesentations, especially those of this nature in court, publique Spectacles, eyther haue bene, or ought to be the mirrors of mans life, whose ends, for the excellence of their exhibiters (as being the donatiues, of great Princes, to their people) ought alwayes to carry a mixture of profit, with them, no lesse then delight. (ll. 2–7)

In social life, if properly conducted, there are no idle pleasures; a linked system of analogies holds the whole structure together, so that dancing, hunting, and even fancy dress are virtuous acts, training the participants and educating the beholders in the art of living well. According to E. B. Partridge, 'the arts of living and creating usually meant to Jonson all that later ages separated out into morality, manners, poetics, philosophy and piety.'[4] This means that there is, ideally, no distinction between pleasures and serious actions.

This sense that society is an organic whole may also account for a kind of joke that recurs in Jonson's comedies, by which characters see themselves in exalted social or political terms, as though they were public bodies. An obvious example occurs in *The Alchemist*, the '*republique*' (I. i. 110) of cheaters threatened by civil war. Waspe, in *Bartholomew Fair*, thinks of his authority over Cokes in political terms and rebukes Mistress Overdo for interfering: 'you thinke, you are Madam *Regent* still, *Mistress Ouer-doo*; when I am in place? no such matter, I assure you, your *raigne* is out, when I am in, *Dame*' (I. v. 18–20). At the end of the play, he abdicates: 'the date of my Authority is out: I must thinke no longer to raigne, my gouernment is at an end' (V. iv. 97–9). In *The New Inn* the Host speaks of the rules of his house as his '*Magna charta*' (I. ii. 24) and Lady Frampul calls her company 'the body politique' (II. i. 15). The initial effect of such lines is, of course, to show the characters' comically inflated view of themselves. But as they accumulate, they add an extra dimension to the plays, like the dimension created by the layers of connected imagery in Shakespeare. Behind the private actions of the characters we glimpse the shadow of the state.

In the Induction to *The Magnetic Lady* the quarrelling humours are described as 'the root of all Schisme, and Faction, both in Church and Common-wealth' (ll. 115–16). In plays like *The Alchemist*, *The Staple of News* and *The Magnetic Lady*, so many different trades are represented that we seem to be looking at a cross-section of society. When Dapper is promised that he will 'draw you all the treasure of the realme' (I. ii. 102) or Mammon declares that the collapse of his scheme is a loss to the common-wealth (V. v. 75–6) we are reminded that their fantasies, if they ever became reality, would have spread corruption throughout society. Of course neither Dapper nor Mammon nor any of the dupes is a serious threat in reality: their ambitions are safely contained within the little fantasy world that Subtle creates for them. But the idea is there. Through references to the state in the

language, and through the number of times fools and gulls are
brought to book in a formal and public way, Jonson suggests,
again, that society is a whole. Just as seemingly trivial pleasures
can be 'serious actions', so seemingly trivial follies are warning
signals about the health of the state, and need public attention.

When manners are corrupt, society is. Jonson belongs to a
long satiric tradition that regards bad manners and bad taste not
simply as things to be shrugged over but as offences that deserve
the lash. One such offence is indulgence in luxury; Jonson's
sharpest attack on it is in *Catiline*, where we see man, in his
restless search for novelty, transferring his own instability to his
houses, and even to the landscape:

> Their ancient habitations they neglect,
> And set vp new; then, if the eccho like not
> In such a roome, they pluck downe those, build newer,
> Alter them too. . . .
>   letting in of seas
> Here! and, then there, forcing 'hem out againe,
> With mountaynous heaps, for which the earth hath lost
> Most of her ribs, as entrailes! being now
> Wounded no lesse for marble, then for gold.
>
>   (I. 392–5, 399–403)

We recognize here a variation on the shape-shifting that threatens
human identity in other works. The speaker is Catiline himself,
complaining of a luxury he cannot share; and to that extent the
speech is tainted by the motive behind it. But the complaint is
taken up by the Chorus at the end of the first act, who declares
that Rome is engrossing the world: 'Her women weare / The
spoiles of nations, in an eare' (I. 555–6). Even nature is polluted:

> They hunt all grounds; and draw all seas;
> Foule euery brooke, and bush; to please
> Their wanton tasts: and, in request
> Haue new, and rare things; not the best!   (I. 569–72)

In stressing the damage that luxury does, Jonson is not merely
anticipating our twentieth-century concern with the environ-
ment. He is showing his own sense of the inner connections of
life: what may look like a trivial vice is in fact a serious evil. The
vice of a man may involve a whole city; the vice of a city may

pollute the world. And behind all these symptoms is the ultimate disease – an empty mind, without purpose or direction.

But the spectacular luxury of *Catiline* is a more obvious target than Jonson usually aims for. As a satirist, he is more at home with trivia – for example, with the fool who is trying to act well-bred but can produce only a mechanical imitation of breeding. Stephano in *Every Man In* has bought 'a hawke, and a hood, and bells, and all; I lacke nothing but a booke to keepe it by' (I. i. 37–8). The courtiers of *Cynthia's Revels* practise their daily behaviour just as self-consciously; Crites sees them as actors:

> There stands a *Neophyte* glazing of his face,
> Pruning his clothes, perfuming of his haire,
> Against his idoll enters; and repeates
> (Like an vnperfect *prologue*, at third musike)
> His part of speeches, and confederate iests,
> In passion to himselfe.   (III. iv. 55–60)

Like those Jonson characters who create secondary worlds for themselves, the fops have lost their humanity in play-acting. Having no minds of their own, they produce only imitations of behaviour.

But Jonson's attitude to these trivial follies raises an artistic problem. Though we may, in theory, take the point that trivial vices have serious implications, Jonson still needs to embody that idea in a form that persuades the imagination, so as to justify the detail with which folly is anatomized and the indignation it produces. He does not always succeed. We see the problem in *The Devil is an Ass*, where the vices of earth that shock the devils are so trivial we are bound to feel, not that earth is inordinately wicked, but that hell is unduly squeamish. When Satan describes the human iniquities that are keeping the devils on their toes, he seems to be drawing his evidence not from the police news but from the fashion pages:

> Car-men
> Are got into the yellow starch, and Chimney-sweepers
> To their tabacco, and strong-waters, *Hum*,
> *Meath*, and *Obarni*.   (I. i. 112–15)

One is tempted to reply, so what? As for Pug, the junior devil who is sent to ply his trade among men and finds himself sadly out of his depth, he is so easily shocked by the casual, bawdy flirtations of the play's fashionable women that we can only conclude he must have led a very sheltered life: '*Hell* is / A Grammar-schoole to this!' (IV. iv. 170–1). It may be that Jonson is playing an ironic game with his audience here, that our bewilderment at the seeming disproportion of Pug's reaction should lead us to search our own consciences. There are no idle sins. What we regard as squalid peccadilloes are enough to shake a devil, and only our own moral blindness prevents us from seeing this. Perhaps; but if that is Jonson's intention I think the irony misfires. He lays such emphasis on Pug's naiveté that there is no chance of our seeing things from the little devil's point of view, and the mockery that could have been directed at the world is deflected to hell instead – for the satirist, a much less urgent subject.

But the play that raises this problem in its most acute form is *Cynthia's Revels*. This work is one of the severest tests Jonson has set his admirers. On it crawls, scene after scene, anatomizing the trivial follies of the courtiers long past the point when we might have thought the subject exhausted. Jonson does not overwrite (as so many of us do) through haste or carelessness; preparing the play for the Folio, he added long stretches of material that do not appear in the Quarto. Clearly, he thinks it worth while to spend time on these characters. Not only that, but there is a moral earnestness in some of the attacks on them that seems, artistically, out of proportion to their offences. Mercury addresses them in language more suited to crime than to folly: 'Tell to your guiltie brests, what meere guilt blocks / You are, and how vnworthy humane states' (V. iv. 610–11). Crites regards them as a menace to the virtuous; knowing men, he says, are 'Opprest with hills of tyrannie, cast on vertue / By the light phant'sies of fooles, thus transported' (V. iv. 632–3). This is strong language; but the play elsewhere attempts to justify it. Crites asks an important rhetorical question:

> would any reasonable creature make these his serious studies, and perfections? Much lesse, onely liue to these ends? to be the

false pleasure of a few, the true loue of none, and the iust
laughter of all?   (v. iv. 174–7)

The fools have no sense of the priorities of life, and this – not
foppery in itself – is the main offence. Its implications are
serious, even religious. Crites hopes

> That, these vaine ioyes, in which their wills consume
> Such powers of wit, and soule, as are of force
> To raise their beings to aeternitie,
> May be conuerted on workes, fitting men.   (v. iv. 637–40)

Foppery is not just folly but blasphemy: the attention a man
should pay to his immortal soul he pays instead to his wardrobe.
Anaides, according to Mercury, 'neuer kneeles but to pledge
healths, nor prayes but for a pipe of pudding tabacco' (II. ii. 93–4).
(In a similar vein Fungoso, in *Every Man out of his Humour*,
declares 'I'ld aske no more of god now, but such a suit, such a
hat, such a band, such a doublet, such a hose, such a boot' –
II. iii. 143–5.) Yet, ironically, the very disproportion of which
Jonson complains afflicts his play: concern with the set of a
collar, and concern with one's immortal soul, need to be linked
with a more subtle and tactful irony than Jonson has managed
here, where satiric observation of manners and religious
moralizing simply lie side by side, and Jonson's own attitude is
dangerously close to the obsessiveness he satirizes in the Puritans
of *The Alchemist*: 'Thou look'st like Antichrist, in that leud hat'
(IV. vii. 55).

Even when he keeps within a secular context, Jonson has
trouble dramatizing the idea that foppery is a real danger to the
state. It may be true that '*There* is nothing valiant, or solid to bee
hop'd for from such, as are always kemp't, and perfum'd; and
every day smell of the Taylor' (*Timber*, ll. 1415–17), and in some
of the non-dramatic satires – notably 'A Speech According to
Horace' (*The Underwood*, XLIV) he reads persuasive lectures on
the subject. But in comedy he has trouble making us feel that the
danger is real. In order to preserve the comic tone, he keeps the
fops light and amusing, and in order to save his own skin he
keeps them far enough from the centres of real power not to give
offence. (Imprisoned for some mild anti-Scottish jokes in *East-*

ward Ho, dragged before the Council on a charge of treason for
Sejanus, and accused of personal satire through the misreading of
a line in *Epicoene*,[5] Jonson knew all too well the touchiness of the
great.) A character like Fastidius Briske in *Every Man Out* is not
a lost leader but a fool who could never be anything but a fool.
Accordingly, when the voice of serious condemnation is heard –
as it is in *Cynthia's Revels*, or the Induction to *Every Man Out* –
we may understand the theory behind it but we cannot say that
any effective *dramatic* link has been established between that
theory and the fools themselves. The trivial courtiers of *Cynthia's
Revels* are not potentially like the serious ones; they belong to a
different order of being.

The best Jonson can manage is a number of telling local
effects, in speeches in which the fools reveal the disproportion of
their own minds. Sir Politic Would-be discusses religion and
table-manners in the same breath:

> And then, for your religion, professe none;
> But wonder, at the diuersitie of all;
> And, for your part, protest, were there no other
> But simply the lawes o'th'land, you could content you:
> NIC: MACHIAVEL, and monsieur BODINE, both,
> Were of this minde. Then, must you learne the vse,
> And handling of your siluer forke, at meales;
> The mettall of your glasse: (these are maine matters,
> With your *Italian*) and to know the houre
> When you must eat your melons, and your figges.
>
> (IV. i. 22–31)

With the two subjects yoked so calmly together, it is not
surprising that religion becomes as much a matter of local
custom as the timing of meals or the use of cutlery. But while
the potential danger of such thinking is clear, in dramatic terms
Sir Pol hardly seems a menace to society; he endangers nothing
but Peregrine's patience. And in this comedy at least Jonson does
not try to claim more than that.

It is in tragedy that Jonson finds the scope he needs to make
such habits of mind not just ironically amusing but genuinely
menacing, and to show most persuasively the social danger of
triviality. Here he has no need to keep the fops harmless, and

they are anything but. In the interview between Livia and her physician Eudemus in the second act of *Sejanus*, politics, cosmetics and murder are all discussed in the same even tone; and the flattening of value is both comic and alarming. Eudemus applies cosmetics and political advice together, as he lobbies for Sejanus' interest with Livia:

> I like this studie to preserue the loue
> Of such a man, that comes not euery houre
> To greet the world. ('Tis now well, ladie, you should
> Vse of the *dentifrice*, I prescrib'd you, too,
> To cleere your teeth, and the prepar'd *pomatum,*
> To smoothe the skin:). (II. 76–81)

A few lines later the poisoning of Livia's husband becomes just one more item in a busy day:

> EVD When will you take some physick, lady?
> LIV   When
> I shall, EVDEMVS: But let DRVSVS drug
> Be first prepar'd. (II. 121–3)

Here the concern with the trivial business of a beauty treatment reflects, far more directly and convincingly than in plays like *Cynthia's Revels*, a state of mind dangerous to the body politic.

As the ironic devices from this scene are repeated throughout the play, Livia's mentality comes to exemplify the mentality of Rome. There is no longer any sense of the value of things: ordinary spies on a grubby little mission expect to be rewarded with a consulship (IV. 100–1); Sejanus calls Eudemus 'worthy of a prouince, / For the great fauours done vnto our loues' (II. 1–2). There is a parallel effect in *Catiline*: a black-comedy scene in the second act in which politics and cosmetics are discussed in the same breath, symptomatic of a general cheapening of Roman life, in which 'Decrees are bought, and lawes are sold, / Honors, and offices for gold' (I. 579–80), and women-conspirators are bribed with 'states, and empires, / And men, for louers' (III. 540–1).

As values are redefined, so inevitably is language. Jonson called speech 'the Instrument of *Society*' (*Timber*, 1882–3) and connected the health of a society with the integrity of its language:

Wheresoever, manners, and fashions are corrupted, Language
is. It imitates the publicke riot. The excesse of Feasts, and
apparell, are the notes of a sick State; and the wantonnesse of
language, of a sick mind.   (*Timber*, ll. 954–8)

These passages are borrowings from Vives and Seneca respect-
ively; but the idea they express is fundamental to Jonson's work.
Corrupt speech is not only a symptom of a corrupt society: it is
one of the reasons why the rot spreads. Jonson demonstrates this
most powerfully in *Sejanus*, where the doubletalk of the
politicians shows – in a manner with which our century is all too
familiar – how language can be a means of turning the world
upside down. Just as Tiberius practises 'strange, and new-
commented lusts, / For which wise nature, hath not left a name'
(IV. 400–1) Macro, entering the emperor's service, sees himself
going into a trackless jungle where old values have no bearing,
and where the old meanings of words no longer apply:

> He that will thriue in state, he must neglect
> The trodden paths, that truth and right respect;
> And proue new, wilder wayes: for vertue, there,
> Is not that narrow thing, shee is else-where.
> Mens fortune there is vertue; reason, their will:
> Their licence, law; and their obseruance, skill.
> Occasion, is their foile; conscience, their staine;
> Profit, their lustre: and what else is, vaine.   (III. 736–43)

I argued in Chapter 1 that the political corruption in this play
involved the creation of a new, false world. Here we see that to
enter this world one must learn a new language; and the
increasing pace of Macro's speech conveys a sinister excitement
as he comes to realize just what this means. We see the results of
this thinking throughout the play: spying becomes 'honorable
vigilance' (IV. 225); revenge becomes 'iustice' (I. 581). 'A princes
power makes all his actions vertue' (III. 717); Sejanus' favour
makes any action 'honorable' (I. 327–9) and 'crime' too has a
new meaning:

> What are my crimes? Proclaime them.
> Am I too rich? too honest for the times?
> Haue I or treasure, iewels, land, or horses

That some informer gapes for? Is my strength
Too much to be admitted? Or my knowledge?
These now are crimes. (III. 168–73)

The speaker is Silius, who elsewhere ironically rebukes Agrippina
for not having mastered the new jargon: 'You take the morall,
not the politique sense' (II. 435). The master of political doubletalk is Tiberius, and G. R. Hibbard has noted 'the elaborately
obscure and ambiguous manner of speech [Jonson] creates for
him. It is an idiom in which praise sounds like a threat and
approval like the prelude to disaster, as it so often proves to be.'[6]
If 'speech is the instrument of society' it follows that twisted
speech is the instrument of a twisted society.

Sejanus is Jonson's most powerful treatment of this theme; but
it runs throughout his work. The conspirators of Catiline stand
for 'freedom' (I. 421), by which they mean wholesale slaughter
and the engrossing of the commonwealth to themselves. Caesar
advises Catiline, 'Let 'hem call it mischiefe; / When it is past, and
prosper'd, 'twill be vertue' (III. 504–5). The Puritans of The
Alchemist are too law-abiding to engage in 'coyning', but have
no objection to 'casting' (III. ii. 151–3). Corvino defends the
prostitution of his wife to Volpone as 'A pious worke, mere
charity, for physick, / And honest politie, to assure mine owne'
(III. vii. 65–6); but even the word 'prostitute' has no sting for
him, for when Mosca uses it Corvino takes it as a compliment
(III. vii. 75). Certain passages of Bartholomew Fair make much
better sense when one realizes that 'lady' means 'whore' (IV. v.
27–8; v. iv. 49–53).

On the latter point, we are dealing not just with Orwellian
doublethink but with the special, professional jargon of the
pimps Whit and Knock'em. Jonson's fascination with jargon has
frequently been noted; his attitude toward it combines amusement with suspicion.[7] In Every Man In, Bobadill teaches
Matthew the jargon as well as the practice of fencing: 'Venue!
Fie. Most grosse denomination, as euer I heard. O, the stoccata,
while you liue, sir' (I. v. 150–1). John J. Enck has remarked that
the social types who come to Lovewit's house in The Alchemist
'seem to have been selected mainly because they all have special
jargons'[8] and there is of course the special jargon of the alchemist

himself, which Surly calls 'next to canting' (II. iii. 42). The theme
is most elaborately developed in *The Staple of News*, where we go
from the jargon of the Staple itself – '*Emissaries?* stay, there's a
fine new word, *Thom*! / 'Pray God it signifie any thing' (I. ii.
48–9) – to Pennyboy Canter's sour remark that 'All the whole
world are *Canters*, I will proue it / In your *professions*' (IV. i. 56–7).
Doctor, soldier, poet and courtier all have their own special
languages (IV. iv. 36–75).

An obvious function of this jargon is to impress, as when
Matthew tells Bobadill that he has been threatened by Downright:

> MAT He brags he will gi' me the *bastinado*, as I heare.
> BOB How! He the *bastinado*! how came he by that word, trow?
> MAT Nay, indeed, he said cudgell mee; I term'd it so, for my
>   more grace.
> BOB That may bee: For I was sure, it was none of his word.
>   (I. v. 100–7)

Behind this dialogue, however, we can detect a more important
purpose of jargon: to create a little in-group that speaks a
language unknown to the common herd. Bobadill is sure that
Downright – who does not belong to the group – would not use
one of its words. This motive is more openly declared when
Subtle and Mammon defend the jargon of the alchemists:

> SVB   which art our writers
>   Vs'd to obscure their art.
> MAM   Sir, so I told him,
>   Because the simple idiot should not learne it,
>   And make it vulgar.   (II. iii. 199–202)

For the professionals who use it, then, jargon creates a little
world cut off from the big one; and we have seen what such
worlds mean for Jonson. As *Sejanus* amply demonstrates, it is a
small step from an alternative language to an alternative
morality. Therein lies the ultimate social danger of jargon, even
the seemingly harmless jargon we see in *The Alchemist* and *The
Staple of News*.

Shakespeare's depictions of the body politic involve power
struggles at the centre: who loses and who wins, who's in,

who's out. Occasionally he will show the effect of these
struggles on the common people; but he is more interested in
how they affect, and are affected by, the personalities of the
great men themselves. Jonson does not have Shakespeare's
interest in the nuances of personality, or in the life of the
commons. But his interest in the general state of culture in the
society he depicts is greater than Shakespeare's. His concern for
the state of language as an index to the health of society is
characteristic of this; and his interest broadens to include the
state of culture in general: '*I have* ever observ'd it, to have beene
the office of a wise Patriot, among the greatest affaires of the
State, to take care of the *Common-wealth* of Learning' (*Timber*,
ll. 924–6). Learning is not only a little world in its own right
(that might make it unhealthy) but a vital part of the great
world, involved with it and contributing directly to its well-
being. Behind the jocular tribute to King James in *The Gypsies
Metamorphosed* – 'Your *Mercuries* hill too a witt doth betoken, /
Some booke crafte you haue, and are prettie well spoken'
(ll. 293–4) – lies some serious thinking about the importance of
learning to a ruler: 'A *Prince* without letters, is a Pilot without
eyes. All his Government is groping' (*Timber*, ll. 1234–5). In
Epigram XIV, Jonson praises his old master, the historian
William Camden, 'to whom my countrey owes / The great
renowne, and name wherewith shee goes' ('To William Camden',
ll. 3–4). In *Sejanus*, the historian Cordus is arrested and his
books are burned.

If a healthy culture is necessary to a healthy society, it follows
that the role of the poet is of supreme importance. Jonson has
something like Sidney's view of the poet as teacher, but with a
distinctly social emphasis:

> I could never thinke the study of *Wisdome* confin'd only to the
> Philosopher: or of *Piety* to the *Divine:* or of *State* to the
> *Politicke*. But that he which can faine a *Common-wealth* (which
> is the *Poet*) can governe it with *Counsels*, strengthen it with
> *Lawes*, correct it with *Iudgements*, informe it with *Religion*, and
> *Morals*; is all these.   (*Timber*, ll. 1032–8)

The poet, like Tiberius, creates a little world; but unlike the
world of Tiberius it is set up to demonstrate not his own power

but the working of moral and social principles. The study of poetry 'offers to mankind a certaine rule, and Patterne of living well, and happily; disposing us to all Civill offices of Society' (*Timber*, ll. 2386–8). At certain points in the masques, the poets are exalted along with the courtiers. In *The Golden Age Restored* Chaucer, Gower, Lydgate and Spenser are called up 'To waite vpon the age that shall your names new nourish, / Since vertue prest shall grow, and buried arts shall flourish' (ll. 119–20). The movement of the language imitates the ordering of an ideal society, with virtue and art working in parallel.

When Jonson satirizes those who abuse poetry he is not just fighting his own battles but pointing out a threat to the community as a whole. In *Every Man in his Humour* poetry is attacked by Old Knowell, who calls it 'That fruitlesse, and vnprofitable art' (i.i.18) and by Cob and Downright who display a violent, instinctive aversion to it (i.iv.75–6; IV.ii. 19–22); and it is abused by Matthew, whose plagiarisms bring it into disrepute. The issue is taken up publicly at the end of the play. In the Quarto there is a long, solemn speech by Lorenzo Junior in which poetry is defended against those who profane it; the emphasis is less on the usefulness of poetry than on its sacredness; and a touch of ceremony is added by the entrance of torchbearers at the end of the speech. In revising the play for the Folio, Jonson sacrificed this speech in the interests (I suspect) of preserving the play's unity of tone. But he kept the idea, and gave to Justice Clement a defence of poetry that, being brisk and informal, not only fits in much better but allows Jonson to develop a view of the poet that was more important for him than the image of the sacred bard. Justice Clement's defence takes the poet out of the clouds of mystery in which the Quarto speech had wrapped him and puts him firmly in society:

> They are not borne euerie yeere, as an Alderman. There goes more to the making of a good *Poet*, then a Sheriffe, Mr. KITELY. You looke vpon me! though, I liue i' the citie here, amongst you, I will doe more reuerence, to him, when I meet him, then I will to the Major, out of his yeere.
>
> (v.v.38–43)

The poet is still a special being, demanding reverence; but he is also, more clearly than in the Quarto speech, a man among men, part of a community. And when a bad poet is punished, as Matthew is here, the job is done formally, by a justice. The point is made lightly, but the implication is that the whole community is involved.[9]

II

Many of Jonson's ideas about culture and society come together in *Poetaster*. The first purpose of the play may have been to score points in a literary feud with Marston and Dekker, just as the first purpose of *Macbeth* may have been to write a play on a Scottish theme, with a bit of witchcraft in it, to please the King. In both cases the finished product far outstrips that first, small intention. Jonson could not think of the literary world of London without thinking of poetry in general; and – a more significant point – he could not think of poetry without thinking of the society to which it belonged. In the Induction Jonson declares, with the truculence of one who does not really expect to be believed, that the scene is Rome. In fact it is partly Rome, partly London, but mostly an ideal city of the imagination, a working laboratory in which Jonson can try out his ideas of the poet and his community. It is in one sense a close-knit world in which lawyers, poets, citizens and courtiers rub shoulders, in which Caesar and his officers act directly in the community, and ordinary citizens can gain access to the court with surprising ease.[10] But it is also a dangerously fragmented world. The play opens with a basic issue – pressure on a young man to choose his way of life. Ovid wants to be a poet; his father wants him to be a lawyer. There is no suggestion that he could do both, and when he tries to link the two, by turning the law into verse, it seems to be an idle whim rather than a serious idea, and the doggerel that results bears out this impression: '*If thrice in field, a man vanquish his foe, / 'Tis after in his choice to serue, or no*' (I. iii. 5–6). When Jonson writes of the poet's public role, he has something more serious than this in mind.

Most important, the early scenes show us a community in

which poetry is widely despised. The servant Luscus shows a contempt that is simply instinctive, born of a mind in which reason has abdicated:

> These verses too, a poyson on 'hem, I cannot abide 'hem, they
> make mee readie to cast, by the bankes of *helicon*. Nay looke,
> What a rascally vntoward thing this *poetrie* is; I could teare
> 'hem now. (I. i. 8–11)

But his masters are no better. Ovid Senior attacks poetry as materially unrewarding, and speaks in nasty tones of the poverty of Homer (I. ii. 78–93). The braggart captain Tucca resents the way satiric poets show his own vices on the stage (I. ii. 49–52), and the lawyer Lupus has a similar complaint about satire on his trade. Law is offered to Ovid as an alternative to poetry. But law as Lupus embodies it is a lazy, unlearned profession – 'Three bookes will furnish you' (I. ii. 129). In this and other ways it is opposed to poetry; the arguments presented to Ovid come down to saying that law bestows wealth and position, whereas poetry does not. And while poetry is honest with men's faults, law is twisting and opportunistic (I. ii. 130–4). The 'respectable' society that opposes the young poet is in fact a society breaking down, each member concerned with serving his own interests, and with keeping himself covered. It is no surprise when later in the play Lupus appears in the disreputable role of informer.

This is not to say that Ovid himself is Jonson's hero. His concept of poetry is based on inspiration: 'Borne on the wings of her immortall thought, / That kickes at earth with a disdainefull heele' (I. ii. 244–5). But what really inspires him is his love for Julia, a love in which there may be some danger: 'O, in no labyrinth, can I safelier erre, / Then when I lose my selfe in praysing her' (I. iii. 47–8). The loss of self in love may have been a positive idea for Shakespeare and other writers of a romantic bent; but Jonson was much concerned with preserving the integrity of the self, and in Volpone's courtship of Celia we see how pernicious the loss of self in love can be. When he is banished, the passion Ovid feels is not at parting from his community but at parting from his love: 'The court's the abstract of all *Romes* desert; / And my dear IVLIA, th' abstract of the court' (IV. viii. 18–19). The social thinking of the first line is cancelled by the romantic thinking of the second. Jonson allows the sundered lovers pathos in their final scene, and throughout the play he treats Ovid gently. But this is not *Romeo and Juliet*. The weight of the play is against a retreat to the little world of love, and its concern for man's public and social nature requires in the end a different kind of poet-hero.

Ovid is also damaged by his association with Chloe and her circle. She would like to be the centre of an elegant *salon*, but like the courtiers of *Cynthia's Revels* she has no natural breeding and has to learn her courtly behaviour by rote. Crispinus instructs her that when visitors call, 'you must say (A poxe on 'hem, what doe they here?) And yet when they come, speake them as faire, and giue them the kindest welcome in wordes, that can be' (II. i. 145–8). Art has its role in Chloe's circle; but again it is a matter of form and self-display. The musician Hermogenes refuses to sing when entreated, and refuses to stop once he has got started. Crispinus, deciding he wants to be a poet, assumes you have to begin by dressing the part: 'Ile presently goe and enghle some broker, for a *Poets* gowne, and bespeake a garland' (II. ii. 224–5). In Chloe's circle poetry, culture, and social behaviour are connected; but each is superficial in itself, and its superficiality taints the others. Ovid never becomes as flagrantly silly as Hermogenes or Crispinus; but he seems at ease in their company, and this raises doubts about his soundness as a man and a poet.

There is a case for saying that Ovid's poetry, for all its charm, is licentious and requires a public rebuke. This idea comes to a head in the blasphemous banquet of the gods in which a motley assortment of characters, from the genuinely cultivated – Ovid, Julia, Tibullus – to the idiotic pretenders to culture – Chloe, Albius, and the omnipresent Tucca – pretend to be Olympian deities. Jonson's attitude to this strange social occasion is more complex than may at first appear; but he starts with an idea that is never altogether supplanted, namely that the banquet embodies a dangerous and irresponsible view of the poet's function. Gallus defends the occasion by suggesting that the poets have made the gods, not the other way round (IV. ii. 28–31), and Tibullus carries the blasphemy further:

to shew that *poets* (in spight of the world) are able to *deifie*
themselues: At this banquet, to which you are inuited, wee
intend to assume the figures of the Gods; and to giue our
seuerall Loues the formes of Goddesses.   (IV. ii. 38–42)

At the banquet itself Gallus, as Mercury, proclaims a time of
license, allowing the 'gods' to be 'nothing better, then common
men, or women' (IV. V. 20), a license they use to flirt and talk
bawdy. It is a perverted social occasion, a feast that embodies
not order and ceremony but blasphemy and licentiousness, and
it all springs from a tainted view of the poet's function.

The banquet is raided by Caesar Augustus himself; as so often
in Jonson, corrupt manners and perverted art call forth a public
judgement. Denouncing the 'gods', Caesar sees in the blasphemy
of the occasion an abdication of the poet's role as moral teacher;
and when the poet abdicates, the civil authority must step in:

> O, who shall follow vertue, and embrace her,
> When her false bosome is found nought but aire?
> And yet, of those embraces, *centaures* spring,
> That warre with humane peace, and poyson men.
> Who shall, with greater comforts, comprehend
> Her vnseene being, and her excellence;
> When you, that teach, and should eternize her,
> Liue, as shee were no law vnto your liues:
> Nor liu'd her selfe, but with your idle breaths?
> If you thinke gods but fain'd, and vertue painted,
> Know, we sustaine an actuall residence;
> And, with the title of an Emperour,
> Retaine his spirit, and imperiall power.   (IV. vi. 39–51)

The fancies of these poets are licentious and ultimately empty,
'nought but aire', and Caesar uses for them a characteristic
image of false engendering; set against them is the solidity of the
civil power of Rome, the 'actuall residence' of virtue when the
poets abandon her. A few lines later, Caesar banishes Ovid.
There are no trivial offences: what looked like a foolish game is a
crime that calls forth severe punishment; and of all possible
punishments, banishment is the sharpest reminder that man is a
social being. The foolish Olympus, made of gossamer, dissolves; and we become aware of the streets and houses of Rome.

Ovid, for all his romantic charm, takes an irresponsible view of his role. Horace, urbane where Ovid is romantic, is primarily a social being, and around the middle of the play it is Horace who takes over the defence of poetry. Ovid composes in his chamber; Horace, when we first see him, is composing while strolling through the streets. He too belongs to a literary circle, but it is a worthy one, presided over by the patron Maecenas, whose home is a free place where every man finds his own level and is content with it, appreciating others' merits rather than jockeying for position (III. i. 256–9). We may contrast this with the competitive egotism and self-display we see in Chloe's circle. Horace has found his own level. The high heroic strain is not for him – 'when I trie, / I feele defects in euery facultie' (III. v. 19–20); but he can write satire. He sees this art in a public context:

> if they shall be sharp, yet modest rimes
> That spare mens persons, and but taxe their crimes,
> Such, shall in open court, find currant passe;
> Were CAESAR iudge, and with the makers grace.
>
> (III. v. 133–6)

He is careful to distinguish this from personal libel (III. v. 130–2); but the guilty, as we see in the cases of Lupus and Tucca, are bound to object to satire because it touches them, and Horace's friend Trebantius (a distinguished lawyer, and therefore a true representative of the profession Lupus disgraces) has the answer:

> if thou thy selfe being cleare,
> Shalt taxe in person a man, fit to beare
> Shame, and reproch; his sute shall quickly bee
> Dissolu'd in laughter, and thou thence sit free. (III. v. 137–40)

Ovid is caught between poetry and law, each (though to different degrees) tainted with egotism; trying to fuse the two, he produces only doggerel. But Horace's poetry is discussed in language that suggests the workings of the law, and indeed it functions as the law should: in open court, it exposes and punishes the vices of men. It is, as Ovid's is not, a socially responsible art.

That puts it a bit solemnly; and indeed Horace, when defend-

ing himself, can be a bit solemn about his work. But elsewhere
he is a genial figure, capable of relaxed fun and self-deprecation.
Like Sir Henry Goodyere, he has his sporting side, and his
poetry reflects this. But we see enough of him to know that his
moments of relaxation are those of a serious and responsible
man, in whom the spirit of festivity is untainted. This may help
to account for the most surprising moment in the play, when
Horace defends the banquet of the gods. Listening to Caesar's
attack on it, we may feel as we do watching *Cynthia's Revels*:
that the indignation is justified in theory but in practice is a bit
out of proportion. It is simply incongruous to hear figures like
Chloe and Tucca addressed in such solemn tones, and we
cannot help feeling a lingering sympathy for Ovid. His character
may be flawed, but we have not forgotten the grimly philistine
household against which he is reacting. Jonson allows us to feel
this unease, and presents the other side of the case when Horace
attacks the informer Lupus, who led Caesar to the banquet:

> Was this the treason? this, the dangerous plot,
> Thy clamorous tongue so bellow'd through the court?
> Hadst thou no other proiect to encrease
> Thy grace with CAESAR, but this woluish traine;
> To prey vpon the life of innocent mirth,
> And harmelesse pleasures, bred, of noble wit?
>
> (IV. vii. 37–42)

Horace, we may feel, goes too far in the other direction: the
banquet was not altogether innocent. But it could be defended
on the grounds that – like Bartholomew Fair – it was a special
occasion, in which morality could be suspended for the sake of
pleasure, within set limits and therefore safely. Like the false
creations discussed in Chapter One, it has a certain wit and
inventiveness to which Horace responds with sympathy, en-
couraging us to suspend moral judgement. Tactfully, Jonson
directs the blame for failing to perceive this not against Caesar,
whose authority must be kept unquestioned for the end of the
play, but against the informer Lupus, whose motives for acting
as moral censor are clearly tainted. Yet what is most bothersome
is that in defending the banquet Horace draws no distinctions:
for anything he says to the contrary, Tucca and Chloe, as well as

Ovid and Tibullus, seem to be included in his defence. When the Puritans attacked the theatre, Jonson himself was prepared to make common cause with a puppet-show, but even that analogy is not very reassuring. We may conclude that for the sake of his (essentially justified) attack on Lupus Horace – but not Jonson – is simplifying a complex situation.[11]

As a social occasion, the banquet of the gods has a profoundly unsettling effect: we feel uneasy at the banquet itself, at Caesar's attack on it, and at Horace's defence. The false poetic premises from which it starts may or may not threaten Roman society; but they leave the moral underpinnings of the play's world distinctly unsteady. Jonson, I suspect, deliberately creates this effect so that we feel a sharper relief in Act V, when judgements become clear again and we see a reassuring image of a social order in which poetry has its true place. Caesar has calmed down: he forgives two of the participants in the banquet, Gallus and Tibullus, for their services to the state and to poetry. And he is prepared (as a good ruler should be) to be instructed by a poet. Having suggested, tactlessly, that Horace's poverty has likely made him envious, he accepts Horace's rebuke with: 'Thankes, HORACE, for thy free, and holsome sharpnesse: / Which pleaseth CAESAR more, then seruile fawnes' (v.i.94–5). In some of the masques, Jonson (as we have seen) could write like an absolutist, showing the ruler as perfect and all-sufficient; but we are (I think) closer to his most serious political thinking when he depicts the ruler as part of a community, keeping a loose rein on his subjects and ready to appreciate plain speaking. In the *Panegyre* Jonson wrote for the opening of James's first parliament, the King is given a stern lecture by Themis on the responsibilities of kingship and the extreme care with which royal power should be exercised. We are told, 'his eare was ioy'd / To heare the truth, from spight, or flattery voyd' (ll. 93–4). And Jonson was fond of insisting that the real basis for the King's authority was not power but example (*Panegyre*, ll. 125–7; *Epigrams*, xxxv: 'To King James', ll. 1–3). The particular example that Caesar shows in *Poetaster* is his respect for those most valued subjects, his poets. Poetry, attacked in the first act by disreputable spokesmen for ordinary society, abused in the middle scenes by pretenders and social climbers, is defended in the fifth act by the highest authority of the state.

The main subject of this defence is Virgil, whom Jonson holds back for the ending of the play. Ovid's muse was lofty but irresponsible; Horace's was responsible but (by his own wry admission) not particularly lofty; Virgil combines the best of both, together with a modesty about his work that rebukes the self-display of pretenders like Crispinus. He is above the earth,

> refin'd
> From all the tartarous moodes of common men;
> Bearing the nature, and similitude
> Of a right heauenly bodie.   (v. i. 102–5)

And yet the wisdom of his art touches ordinary men, 'distill'd / Through all the needfull vses of our liues' (v. i. 119–20). The jabbering, fragmented society we saw earlier in the play is replaced by a secure community, united in unselfish praise of the man who embodies its highest ideals; the poets' voices chime together as they celebrate their master. What Caesar says early in the scene about poetry in general is particularly true of Virgil: he writes not of his private passions but of his community, and the best of Rome will be preserved and glorified by his work (v. i. 25–7). The parallel between poet and ruler, characteristic of a healthy society, is made by Caesar himself: 'CAESAR, and VIRGIL / Shall differ but in sound' (v. ii. 2–3).

If the banquet of the gods was a perverted social occasion, Virgil's reading from the *Aeneid* is a serious one. It is formally set up: the poet is given the chair of honour, and the doors are barred to keep the profane away. In depicting the great poet reading to an attentive audience, including a ruler who respectfully defers to him, and in placing this reading at the political centre of the community, Jonson is showing us what an ideal society should look like. If Jonson were a lazier or more complacent artist he might have stopped there, feeling he had settled the business of the play. But we cannot help noting that the reading is full of noise and violence; it is the passage in which Dido and Aeneas take shelter in a cave from a storm, and their dangerous affair comes to a crisis. We seem to have reached the still centre of the play's world, and in doing so we find another whirlwind. Formal in itself, Virgil's art speaks of turbulent passions; art must not only celebrate social order, but must give us a clear and understanding view of the forces that threaten that order. The subject has also a more particular relevance; we see here some of the subtle threads that help to bind this seemingly ramshackle play together. Virgil writes of the sort of solipsistic love, neglectful of the world, that Ovid and Julia have embodied. He both understands it and transcends it. If Dido had had her way, the Rome of which Virgil and Caesar are at this moment the twin centres would never have been founded; and we see that Dido, trying to justify her passion, is guilty of the tricky use of language Jonson has identified elsewhere as a basic danger to society: '*She calls this wedlocke, and with that faire name / Couers her fault*' (v.ii.72–3). Jonson does not make the connections between Virgil's reading and the main play crudely direct, any more than he does with the puppet show in *Bartholomew Fair*; but he has not chosen this section of the *Aeneid* by accident.

Towards the end Virgil depicts Fame (i.e. Rumour) as a monster, '*as many tongues shee beares, / As many mouthes, as many listning eares*' (v.ii.88–9); '*As couetous shee is of tales, and lies, / As prodigall of truth: This monster, &c.*' (v.ii.96–7). On the words 'this monster', the monster actually appears.[12] Lupus, Tucca, Crispinus and Demetrius burst into the court, interrupting the reading with their absurd charges against Horace, whose satires they accuse of being libels. As the banquet of the gods was broken up by Caesar, so this more serious occasion, this image of an ideal social and literary community, is smashed, and Caesar and his poets have to deal with the detractors and abusers of art. Caesar complains, 'Our eare is now too much prophan'd (graue MARO) / With these distastes, to take thy sacred lines' (v.iii.165–6) and the reading is postponed to a fitter time. The poets, led by Virgil and using authority bestowed on them by Caesar, do justice on the slanderers and poetasters, purging the latter of their absurd language in a comically literal way. A stupid response to poetry – 'An *embleme?* right: That's *greeke* for a libell' (v.iii.59) – and bad poetry itself are offences that need –

and here receive – the punishment of the state. The tone of the judgement scene is jocular, and it ends the play on a note of lively farce; but there is an undercurrent of sadness here as well. We cannot help noting how hard it is for Caesar and the others to get an hour's peace to listen to true art; they have to spend too much of their time cleaning up the mess created by the enemies of art. And while the illicit love of Dido and Aeneas is contained within Virgil's art, the monster Rumour, in a sense, is not. Like her close relative, Spenser's Blatant Beast, she breaks out of the poem to create havoc in the real world. At the beginning of *Poetaster*, Jonson created for himself an easy triumph over the monster Envy, beaten underfoot by the armed Prologue; but the 'apologeticall Dialogue' appended to the play shows that Envy was not so easily put down. The Author is still being attacked by his enemies, and his conclusion is to withdraw from the arena to a higher, more secluded art:

> There's something come into my thought,
> That must, and shall be sung, high, and aloofe,
> Safe from the wolues black iaw, and the dull asses hoofe.
>
> (ll. 237–9)

We have seen the ideal artist, Virgil, at the centre of his community, surrounded by his admiring peers. But we will also have noted the exclusiveness of the occasion; and the end of the play, supplemented by the 'apologeticall Dialogue', suggests how vulnerable the ideal community is, how hard it is to maintain decent order in the corrupt society the poet has to live in.

Jonson creates another working model of society in a less discursive and more entertaining play, *Epicoene*.[13] In *Poetaster*, positive and negative images of social life are set in opposition, and there are clear lessons to be drawn; the method of *Epicoene* is more devious and ironic. The pattern looks simple at first: Morose is an anti-social egotist, who can stand no noise but his own: 'all discourses, but mine owne, afflict mee, they seeme harsh, impertinent, and irksome' (ii.i.4–5). In his first scene his silent, padded room – his little alternative universe – is invaded by Truewit, blowing a trumpet and calling himself 'a post from the court' (II.i.44), who, through comically inflated language, becomes a representative of social authority: 'be patient, I charge you, in the kings name, and heare mee without insurrection' (II.ii.15–17). If man is properly a social being, then Morose's retreat from the world makes him an enemy of society, whose rebellion must be suppressed. But the effect is very different from Duke Senior asking Jaques to stay for the dance, or Orsino urging that Malvolio be entreated to a peace. Truewit comes, not to reconcile Morose to his society, but simply to torment him. The fact that the ostensible purpose of his visit is to urge Morose *against* marriage suggests how far we are from the traditional pattern of comic reconciliation. And throughout the play the occasions of society are not images of harmony, order and celebration, but ways of tormenting Morose: 'I would make a false almanack; get it printed: and then ha' him drawne out on a coronation day to the *tower*-wharfe, and kill him with the noise of the ordinance' (I.ii.13–16). In romantic comedy, marriage traditionally embodies and cements the social order. Jonson himself, on a more conventional occasion, could write of

> how well it binds
> The fighting *seedes of things*,
> Winnes *natures, sexes, minds*,
> And eu'rie discord in true musique brings.
>
> (*Hymenaei*, ll. 99–102)

Morose's marriage is at every point a reversal of that ideal: he wants a silent wife, whom he can dominate; he finds once the wedding has taken place that he has married a shrew with an active tongue, who will dominate *him*; and he finds in the end that the bride is a boy, and he is not married at all. The banquet that celebrates the wedding also embodies not order but aggression.[14] The play's main fools, Daw and La-Foole, compete for the credit of giving it, and its main purpose is to torment the bridegroom:

> The spitting, the coughing, the laughter, the neesing, the farting, dauncing, noise of the musique, and her masculine, and lowd commanding, and vrging the whole family, makes him thinke he has married a *furie*.
>
> (IV.i.8–11)

Its appropriateness to this particular wedding lies in the way its
clamour matches the revelation that Morose has married a
shrew.

It is not just that social occasions are twisted and perverted in
order to torment Morose. In fact the element of contrivance is
minimal. All the three tricksters Dauphine, Truewit and
Clerimont have to do is bring on the fools and women, and let
them be themselves. L. G. Salingar has demonstrated that
Morose's complaints about the noisiness of his world have some
basis in the reality of overcrowded Jacobean London;[15] and we
might say that Morose is confronted not with a society that
gives the lie to his misanthropy but with a society that confirms
his worst fears. Jonson is trying a special, ironic experiment
here: to a great extent he allows us to see society from Morose's
point of view. We have seen that for Jonson the health of a
society can be measured by the health of its language. If meaning
and value have been corrupted, language will reflect this: words
will be cheapened and lose their meanings. As a corollary of this,
a good society is one that respects culture and learning, and in
which poets in particular have a place of honour; this in turn
places a responsibility on the poets to write well and honestly,
serving not their own egos but the demands of their art and the
moral needs of their fellow men. In all of this, the fundamental
principle is the linking of social life and language. But for
Morose, language is just noise. And if he is right, then social life
is without meaning.

Jonson, as I will argue later, does not commit himself to
Morose's point of view; but for much of the play he toys with it
mischievously, leaving us wondering how far he will go. In a
fairly serious speech in the opening scene Truewit, the most
attractive and intelligent character in the play, speaks of the
emptiness of life as his friend Clerimont lives it:

> Why, here's the man that can melt away his time, and neuer
> feeles it! what, betweene his mistris abroad, and his engle at
> home, high fare, soft lodging, fine clothes, and his fiddle; hee
> thinkes the houres ha' no wings, or the day no post-horse. Well,
> sir gallant, were you strooke with the plague this minute, or
> condemn'd to any capitall punishment to morrow, you would

beginne then to thinke, and value euery article o'your time,
esteeme it at the true rate, and giue all for't.   (I. i. 23–31)

As in the opening scenes of *Poetaster*, the question seems to be,
what should a young man do with his life? But as the tone is
lighter, the implications of the question run deeper. The note of
religious warning is struck less heavily than in *Cynthia's Revels*,
but it is clear enough. When Clerimont says later that he is
willing to repent, but not yet, Truewit replies, 'Yes: as if a man
should sleepe all the terme, and thinke to effect his businesse the
last day' (I. i. 50–1), concluding that the way we waste our time
creates a shifting, varied, ultimately empty life, 'not seeking an
end of wretchednesse, but onely changing the matter still'
(I. i. 54–5). The social round of a young gallant sounds for a
moment like the Protean fantasy-world of *Volpone*. A concern
with trifles distracts man from his real business; his values are
awry. The position is familiar. But for all his moralizing,
Truewit himself does not seem about to take holy orders. To
Clerimont's question, 'Why, what should a man doe?' he offers
only the flippant reply, 'Why, nothing: or that, which when 'tis
done, is as idle. Harken after the next horse-race, or hunting-
match' (I. i. 32–5), and so on through a catalogue of activities as
idle as those he has just accused Clerimont of. His attitude to
social life seems to be a wry acceptance; he can find no meaning
in it, but while he talks vaguely of more serious values, he
cannot himself make the effort to live by them. A few minutes
later he is offering an ironic defence of cosmetics, and by the
fourth act he is telling Dauphine that if he wants a wench, he
must go out and mix with society (IV. i. 55–66).

In the first scene we hear an intelligent young man's ironic,
slightly wistful account of the emptiness of social life. Un-
obtrusively, and without threatening the tone of the play (as do
the more solemn speeches of *Cynthia's Revels*) this forms the
basis for an extravagantly farcical depiction of social life reduced
to emptiness. We have already noted how marriage and feasting,
normally images of social order, have become embodiments of
noisy aggression; and this is not confined to Morose's marriage.
Tom Otter's Fury of a wife, who has imposed on him a pseudo-
political contract 'That I would be a Princesse, and raigne in

mine owne house: and you would be my subiect, and obay me'
(III. i. 33–5), shows that Morose's experience of marrying a
shrew is not a freak occurrence. Mistress Otter belongs to a 'new
foundation' (I. i. 74), a parody of a serious social institution: a
College of ladies

> that liue from their husbands; and giue entertainement to all the
> Wits, and Braueries o' the time, as they call 'hem: crie downe,
> or vp, what they like, or dislike in a braine, or a fashion, with
> most masculine, or rather hermaphroditicall authoritie.
>
> (I. i. 76–80)

The ostensible purpose of the College is to pass judgement on
social and cultural matters; the actual purpose is to allow free
play to the women's voices, to express their arbitrary and
fluctuating opinions. Culture is reduced to senseless noise. For
John Daw, poetry is a means of self-display: 'Nay, I'll read 'hem
my selfe too: an author must recite his owne workes' (II. iii.
23–4); and learning, a means of giving a bit of tone to his
conversation: 'As I hope to finish TACITVS, I intend no murder'
(IV. v. 50–1). In the course of the sadistic practical joke played on
the two knights, Truewit plays ironically on Daw's cultural
pretensions: 'What's six kicks to a man, that reads SENECA?'
(IV. v. 293–4). Yet Daw aspires to fulfil one of Jonson's ideals –
that the man of poetry and culture should be called to the centre
of power: he 'railes at his fortunes, stamps, and mutines, why he
is not made a counsellor, and call'd to affaires of state' (I. iii.
19–20).

Law, like culture, is reduced to noise; Morose flees from the
courts in understandable dismay:

> such speaking, and counter-speaking, with their seuerall voyces
> of citations, appellations, allegations, certificates, attachments, in-
> tergatories, references, conuictions, and afflictions indeed, among the
> Doctors and Proctors! that the noise here is silence too't! a kind
> of calme mid-night!   (IV. vii. 15–19)

In the last act, Otter and Cutbeard – both of whom like to toss
scraps of Latin into their conversations to give themselves a bit
of style – are dressed as civil and canon lawyers for Morose's
further torment. Truewit comments that all they need to make a

reasonable showing in their professions are the right gowns and the right jargon (IV. vii. 43–8). Thus disguised, they subject Morose to a stereophonic babble of noise. Instead of being aided by the law, he is simply talked at.

The comprehensiveness of Morose's misanthropy means that he is occasionally right; when he flees from the law-courts, or from the jabbering women, we recognize a satiric point that does not depend just on his own comic aversion to noise. Nor is he merely a self-centred fool; he has some fragments of social sense, and even some awareness of the possible dignity of social life when properly conducted:

> So that I come not to your publike pleadings, or your places of noise; not that I neglect those things, that make for the dignitie of the common-wealth: but for the meere auoiding of clamors, & impertinencies of Orators, that know not how to be silent.
>
> (v. iii. 55–9)

Lecturing Epicoene on what he expects of his wife, he shows some awareness of the social graces, and we learn later that he was brought up at court (III. vi. 78–81). But lest we be tempted to see him as an intelligent critic of a society that deserves everything he says about it, we have to confront his own social crudeness. Having given a brace of angels to the Parson who, since he has a cold, has given him (literally) a quiet wedding, Morose is angered when the man starts to cough, and demands, 'let him giue me fiue shillings of my money backe. As it is bounty to reward benefits, so is it equity to mulct iniuries' (III. iv. 15–17). He has just been through one of the most important of social and religious ceremonies; and he sees it only in terms of benefit and injury to himself, measured by money. Ian Donaldson, discussing the play as 'festive comedy', has noted Morose's 'hatred of festival and of festival days';[16] in one small, revealing touch, Morose tells us that he has never been a godfather (v. iii. 130–1). Even the small courtesies of daily living seem to him irritating irrelevancies:

> Salute 'hem? I had rather doe any thing, then weare out time so vnfruitfully, sir. I wonder, how these common formes, as *god saue you,* and *you are well-come,* are come to be a habit in

our liues! or, *I am glad to see you!* when I cannot see, what the
profit can bee of these wordes, so long as it is no whit better
with him, whose affaires are sad, & grieuous, that he heares
this salutation.   (v. iii. 25–31)

This is literally true; but in its very literalness there is a crude
reduction of social life to mere advantage.

His retreat from society is a matter of principle:

> My father, in my education, was wont to aduise mee, that I
> should alwayes collect, and contayne my minde, not suffring it
> to flow loosely; that I should looke to what things were
> necessary to the carriage of my life, and what not: embracing
> the one, and eschewing the other.   (v. iii. 48–52)

Like Truewit in the first scene, Morose tries to distinguish
between the necessary and the trivial business of life; but while
Truewit wryly accepts trivialities as the inescapable stuff of
living, Morose tries seriously to reject them. The result is both
ironic and inevitable: he is trapped by them, as Truewit never is.
Whatever the serious business of his life might have been, we
will never know, for he is so concerned to protect himself from
the trivialities that he has no time for anything else. This leads to
an unduly literal measuring of social relationships, and a view
of language that is not qualitative but quantitative:

> EPI   You are not well, sir! you looke very ill! some thing has
>   distempered you.
> MOR   O horrible, monstrous impertinencies! would not one of
>   these haue seru'd? doe you thinke, sir? would not one of these
>   haue seru'd?   (iv. iv. 34–8)

This exchange sums up the dilemma of the play: it is perfectly
true that Epicoene's expressions of concern are not genuine
courtesies but noise-making designed for Morose's torment; yet
in his protest, Morose makes as much noise as she does, and is
just as redundant in his language and as crude in his social sense.
He is ironically bound up with the society he rejects: it makes
empty noises, and he makes empty noises in return.

If this were all that could be said we would have to conclude
that Jonson had reached an impasse. But there are hints throughout the play that a better social life is possible, even if Jonson has

not dramatized it here. Truewit, dressing up Otter and Cutbeard as parody lawyers, is careful to add that he is doing this 'I hope, without wronging the dignitie of either profession, since they are but persons put on, and for mirths sake, to torment him' (IV. vii. 48–50). Quite simply, the satiric fun of the play should not be taken for a definitive comment on society. And if Daw is a poetaster, that does not mean that every writer is:

> CLE   A knight liue by his verses? he did not make 'hem to that ende, I hope.
> DAVP   And yet the noble SIDNEY liues by his, and the noble family not asham'd. (II. iii. 115–18)

The graceful tribute to a real artist catches us by surprise in the midst of a farcical scene; the effect is striking, even moving. There is something positive, too, in the comradeship of the three tricksters Truewit, Clerimont and Dauphine.[17] Jonson does not sentimentalize them: their jokes have an edge of cruelty, and there are times when they get on each other's nerves: 'Looke, you'll spoile all: these be euer your tricks' (IV. v. 144–5). But they are intelligent and engaging; they can criticize each other without breaking their friendship; and the social bond they represent, while it may be less secure than ideal marriage, is much solider than the marriages of this play. When Truewit admits that the reason he engages in the social round is 'for companie' (I. i. 40–1) the casual phrase has a weight of meaning behind it. As the satire on law is put in perspective by the fact that Otter and Cutbeard are dressing up for fun, so the cruelty of the young men's treatment of Morose is put in perspective by constant reminders that it is for one day only; ''Tis but a day, and I would suffer heroically' (III. vii. 12–13). Morose's mock-marriage, and the cacophony that accompanies it, are, like Bartholomew Fair, limited and occasional; according to Ian Donaldson, Morose is subjected to something like a *charivari*.[18] We can enjoy the noise, because we do not have to listen to it all year.

All of this points towards *Epicoene*'s strongest image of social harmony – the play itself. Just as in *Poetaster* the banquet of the gods is replaced by the true social occasion, Virgil's reading, so here the noisy parody-feast that accompanies Morose's wedding is balanced against the feast that Jonson offers his audience (it is also – and this is where *Epicoene* is subtler – a part of that feast; agonizing for Morose, it is entertaining for us):

> Our wishes, like to those (make publique feasts)
> Are not to please the cookes tastes, but the guests.
> Yet, if those cunning palates hether come,
> They shall find guests entreaty, and good roome;
> And though all relish not, sure there will be some,
> That, when they leaue their seates, shall make 'hem say,
> Who wrote that piece, could so haue wrote a play:
> But that, he knew, this was the better way.
>
> (*Prologue*, ll. 8–15)

A good play put on for an intelligent and discriminating public is an important social act. It is a festive occasion that brings a cross-section of society together for a common purpose. As in *Poetaster*, the fools are still hammering at the door: a second Prologue, '*Occasion'd by some persons impertinent exception*', shows Jonson having to answer, even for this play, the old, irritating charge of libel. But if the fools can be kept at bay for a couple of hours, the play can create within the theatre something that Jonson this time refuses to show on the stage: a real sense of community, demonstrating in a light and unsolemn way the social value of art. Truewit's final appeal for the audience's applause is, like Face's or Volpone's, an attempt to make our pleasure part of the meaning of the play. The play's fun has been based on the collision between a crabbed egotist and a noisy, empty society; but if we have *enjoyed* the fun, then our enjoyment – registered, Jonson hopes, in deafening applause – may do for Morose what no one in the play has even thought of doing: 'cure him, at least please him' (v.iv.253).

Looking back from *Epicoene* to *Poetaster*, we can see that Jonson's depiction of the good social occasion in the earlier play was ponderous compared with his engaging view of the play itself as a feast. It is as though Jonson has come to feel that the values he really cherishes must be touched on lightly – not only because too solemn an utterance spoils the pleasure, but because too solid a form attracts the opposition, as we see when the door of Caesar's room bursts open. This may explain why one of Jonson's best known images of the good society, 'To Penshurst', (*The Forest*, II), is so playful. The poem begins with, and at the end circles back to, one controlling idea – the modesty of Penshurst.

The house avoids the ostentatious luxury Jonson attacked in *Catiline* and elsewhere, and this in itself is a guarantee of decent social relations. It is built for pleasure and use, not for pride; and accordingly it inspires not envy but reverence (ll. 1–6). So far, Jonson makes a serious point in a serious way. But the intimacy of the estate leads Jonson's imagination in other directions: it is a tight little community in which, because the scale is so small, all the elements are easily harmonized.[19] Raymond Williams has complained that in this poem, far from man and nature being in harmony, 'this natural order is simply and decisively on its way to the table.'[20] But the point is that it is willing to go:

> The painted partrich lyes in euery field,
>   And, for thy messe, is willing to be kill'd.
> And if the high-swolne *Medway* faile thy dish,
>   Thou hast thy ponds, that pay thee tribute fish,
> Fat, aged carps, that runne into thy net.
>   .   .   .
> Bright eeles, that emulate them, and leape on land,
>   Before the fisher, or into his hand.   (ll. 28–38)

Behind the cheerful fantasy lies a serious idea: that the role of nature is to provide for man, and that in the little world of Penshurst man and nature are so close that that role can be fulfilled naturally, with no effort on man's part. Jonson has a nice sense of how far he can push such fantasy: he does not ask us to imagine fruit leaping off the trees; instead, 'The blushing apricot, and woolly peach / Hang on thy walls, that euery child may reach' (ll. 43–4). There is another kind of fantasy here, one of complete availability, and the reference to children is significant: Penshurst is, if not a womb, a child's dream – a playground-cum-party in which everything is provided.

All this may remind us of the orgiastic dreams of Volpone and Mammon, but the social thinking behind the vision is different.

They were selfish consumers; Jonson implies a reciprocal human kindness at Penshurst. As the fish are willing to be caught, so the local farmers are willing to bring presents, not because they have to – the estate has not exploited them, and they have no need to ask favours of it – but out of love:

> And though thy walls be of the countrey stone,
>   They'are rear'd with no mans ruine, no mans grone,
> There's none, that dwell about them, wish them downe;
>   But all come in, the farmer, and the clowne:
> And no one empty-handed, to salute
>   Thy lord, and lady, though they haue no sute.
> Some bring a capon, some a rurall cake,
>   Some nuts, some apples; some that thinke they make
> The better cheeses, bring 'hem; or else send
>   By their ripe daughters, whom they would commend
> This way to husbands; and whose baskets beare
>   An embleme of themselues, in plum, or peare.
>
>   (ll. 45–56)

If one is used to thinking of society in Morose's terms of need, service and payment, all this must seem deplorably frivolous. Why should the rustics be grateful simply to be left alone, and what good does it do the aristocracy to receive food parcels? But Jonson sees his ideal society in terms of an unforced love whose material signs are genial rather than practical. The playfulness is maintained in the suggestion that the 'ripe daughters' are as delectable as the fruit they bring. Jonson is in fact moving the poem towards more serious thinking about the ideal society; but he still expresses the idea lightly.

The same is true of the presence of culture at Penshurst. It is there, but not so overtly or so solemnly as in Virgil's presence at Caesar's court. Classical figures are worked into the landscape:

> Thou hast thy walkes for health, as well as sport:
>   Thy *Mount*, to which the *Dryads* doe resort,
> Where PAN, and BACCHVS their high feasts haue made,
>   Beneath the broad beech, and the chest-nut shade;
> That taller tree, which of a nut was set,
>   At his great birth, where all the *Muses* met.   (ll. 9–14)

The classical figures are not just graceful decoration but ways of suggesting that this is a place where art and culture matter; the poet whose birth the tree commemorates is Sir Philip Sidney.[21] And there is now another poet at Penshurst:

> And I not faine to sit (as some, this day,
>   At great mens tables) and yet dine away.
> Here no man tells my cups; nor, standing by,
>   A waiter, doth my gluttony enuy.   (ll. 65–8)

Generosity to a representative of the arts takes a form Jonson finds particularly congenial; again the tone is comic. But in the suggestion that there are other places where the show of hospitality to a poet is a hollow form,[22] we see that what Jonson is celebrating is not just the boundless supply of food and drink but the courtesy that lies behind it.

As in other works, poet and King are paralleled; Penshurst is equally courteous to both: 'There's nothing I can wish, for which I stay. / That found King IAMES, when hunting late, this way' (ll. 75–6). In the hospitality that was offered to the King at short notice, Jonson sums up his view of Penshurst as a permanent feast, a social occasion that (unlike other such occasions in Jonson's work) seems to be beyond time: 'not a roome, but drest, / As if it had expected such a guest!' (ll. 87–8). The introduction of the King also implies the ultimate seriousness of the social values this hospitality embodies. This allows a smooth transition to a more sober tone for the ending of the poem. The idea of feeding the children is transformed: 'They are, and haue bene taught religion: Thence / Their gentler spirits haue suck'd innocence' (ll. 93–4). Their education suggests the full range of values Jonson felt necessary for the good society: 'The mysteries of manners, armes, and arts' (l. 98). Compressed in that line is Jonson's sense of the fusion of cultural, moral and religious life in society at its best.[23] The pleasures of Penshurst, celebrated in such a jocular way early in the poem, are not idle ones; in what they imply about decent relations between man and man, they carry a weight of meaning. Nor is the poem itself – as we might be tempted to think – a piece of pure wish-fulfilment, a dream of a great good place that never existed. In an important article, J. C. A. Rathmell has shown how many of

the poem's tributes to the virtues of Penshurst, its master Lord
Lisle, and his wife, are based on reality that can be documented
from other sources. He also suggests that the poem takes greater
account of the troubles of the real world than may at first appear;
Lord Lisle was in desperate financial straits, and Jonson may be
counselling him to make a virtue of his modest means, to
remember that the human decency his estate embodies is more
important than the lavish display of other aristocratic house-
holds.[24] After due allowance has been made for the fun Jonson
has imagining birds and fish coming to their captors' hands, and
for the idealizing natural to a poem of tribute, we may conclude
that Penshurst is not a good place in a dream, but a good place in
the real world.

Jonson also defines the virtues of Penshurst partly by negation,
listing the vices it avoids and thereby reminding us of the
imperfection of the surrounding world.[25] This method is
developed in the companion poem, 'To Sir Robert Wroth' (*The
Forest*, III). Here we are more aware of the circumstances of actual
life: the presence of time, the separateness of man and nature, the
corruption of much social life, and the effort a good man needs
to make to keep his virtue intact. The estate itself is more
realistically conceived. Penshurst seemed beyond time, with no
seasons but a perpetual harvest. Here, we are told of the various
pleasures of spring, autumn and winter (ll. 23–30); the sports are
partly a reaction against nature's occasional harshness: 'Thou
dost with some delight the day out-weare, / Although the
coldest of the yeere!' (ll. 35–6). And there is no question here of
the wildlife of the estate coming willingly to the net or gun. The
separateness of nature is hauntingly evoked in the lines, 'Or, if
thou list the night in watch to breake, / A-bed canst heare the
loud stag speake' (ll. 21–2); and for the rest of this section the
animals and birds of the estate are vigorously hunted.

Wroth himself has made a conscious choice between country
and town, and in the opening of the poem Jonson gives us a
picture of the social life Wroth has decided against:

> How blest art thou, canst loue the countrey, WROTH,
>   Whether by choice, or fate, or both;
> And, though so neere the citie, and the court,

> Art tane with neithers vice, nor sport:
> That at great times, art no ambitious guest
>   Of Sheriffes dinner, or Maiors feast.
> Nor com'st to view the better cloth of state;
>   The richer hangings, or crowne-plate;
> Nor throng'st (when masquing is) to haue a sight
>   Of the short brauerie of the night;
> To view the iewells, stuffes, the paines, the wit,
>   There wasted, some not paid for yet!   (ll. 1–12)

This poem, unlike 'To Penshurst', shows how the spirit of festivity can be tainted. The social occasions of city and court express not harmony and order but the ambition and pretence of the participants. Here the masque is not an expression of true courtly values but an alarming reminder that the courtiers are living beyond their means – unlike Wroth, who lives naturally on what his estate provides, 'with vn-bought prouision blest' (l. 14). The festivity of Wroth's estate is a different matter: it in includes the graces of poetry and music; it shows not social ambition but an easy relationship between the classes; and it suspends temporarily the grubby business of ordinary life:

> APOLLO'S harpe, and HERMES lyre resound,
>   Nor are the *Muses* strangers found:
> The rout of rurall folke come thronging in,
>   (Their rudenesse then is thought no sinne)
> Thy noblest spouse affords them welcome grace;
>   And the great *Heroes*, of her race,
> Six mixt with losse of state, or reuerence.
>   Freedome doth with degree dispense.
> The iolly wassall walkes the often round,
>   And in their cups, their cares are drown'd:
> They thinke not, then, which side the cause shall leese,
>   Nor how to get the lawyer fees.
> Such, and no other was that age, of old,
>   Which boasts t'haue had the head of gold.   (ll. 51–64)

But this golden age is temporary; we are reminded throughout the passage that life is not normally like this. A deliberate condescension is needed to bring the classes together. The rustics' 'rudenesse *then* is thought no sinne' – implying that it is not to be tolerated every day. These rustics are not the scrubbed and idealized figures of 'To Penshurst'; they are the real thing. The lawsuits which normally occupy their lives are forgotten for a moment, but they will matter again tomorrow. Just as the activity of the seasons on the estate reminds us of time, this passage implies that the festive occasion uniting men and smoothing their differences, though it represents serious and important values, is also limited by time.

The presence of time is also felt in Jonson's advice, 'Striue, WROTH, to liue long innocent' (l. 66). The good life must be worked for; there is even a suggestion that it cannot last. The next section itemizes other ways of living – war, litigation, money-making, flattery and luxury – seeing each of them as empty and destructive, and urging Wroth to be content with his own lot. The emphasis is mostly on the privacy of Wroth's integrity, as though he had to withdraw from social life in order to preserve it; but Jonson also tells us that the integrity of such a man is of value to the community: he has 'A body sound, with sounder minde; / To doe thy countrey seruice, thy selfe right' (ll. 102–3). Even that is put in perspective by the final reminder of time that ends the poem: 'but when thy latest sand is spent, / Thou maist thinke life, a thing but lent' (ll. 105–6). This is different, however, from the empty transience of the masque, 'the short brauerie of the night'. Wroth, Jonson hopes, is a man who can live within the flux of time, taking its pleasures and its responsibilities in a spirit of respect for himself and for his fellow men, and remembering his final destiny. As in the parable of the talents, life is 'lent' in order to be used. The feast is not endless, like that of Penshurst. It embodies the same values of social harmony, and it shows once again the importance of seemingly trivial occasions; but, more clearly than in the other poem, it is a special and limited occasion, an island of order in a generally corrupt world.

Jonson's most vivid embodiments of the values he admires are found not in the grand abstractions of Ruler, State and Poet but in particular, though idealized, social occasions. 'To Penshurst' is unusual not in the quality of life it represents, but in the way it is placed beyond the flux of time. Normally the image of order is a temporary achievement, and it has to be worked for. The profane, who like the poor are always with us, have to be excluded for a while, as we see when the doors of Caesar's room are shut before Virgil's reading. This ancient way of beginning a ceremony is found in the masques in particular. Spenser's *Epithalamion* allows the whole community to watch the show; the first song of *Hymenaei* commands, 'Bid all profane away' (l. 67). In *Love's Triumph through Callipolis*, Love itself will not appear '*Till all the suburbes, and the skirts bee cleare / Of perturbations, and th'infection gon*' (ll. 76–7). Even well-meaning buffoons whose hearts are in the right place but who would threaten the tone of the occasion – like the Satyrs in *Oberon* and the wild Irish in *The Irish Masque at Court* – are cleared away.

Jonson was also aware that the conviviality that marks the good occasion had its own dangers. A steady drinker himself, he did not always sentimentalize the pleasures of the bottle. In 'An Epistle Answering to One that Asked to be Sealed of the Tribe of Ben' (*The Underwood*, XLVII) he rejects those 'That live in the wild Anarchie of Drinke, / Subject to quarrell only' (ll. 10–11); and in 'An Epistle to a Friend, to Persuade him to the Wars' (*The Underwood*, XV) – that poem where so much that Jonson despised in social life is gathered together – he complains:

> What furie of late is crept into our Feasts?
> What honour given to the drunkennest Guests?
> What reputation to beare one Glasse more?
> When oft the bearer, is borne out of dore?   (ll. 117–20)

Epigram CI, 'Inviting a Friend to Supper', is one of Jonson's most engaging poems; it is also central evidence for his social ideals, and for his sense of the difficulties that threaten those ideals. The tone is so light that it may seem incongruous to discuss the poem in this way; but that in itself is part of the poem's achievement. The idea of friendship itself was one of the most serious values of Jonson's time; the intelligent friendship of good men was held to be an important binding force in society.[26] The comradeship of the tricksters in *Epicoene* suggests this ideal, though it does not embody it perfectly. Epigram CI shows the particular values Jonson shared with his own circle,

values essential to the ordering of social life. The poem begins
soberly enough, insisting that the worth and mutual respect of
the guests, not the food and drink, are the real basis of the feast,
just as the hospitality of Penshurst is a vehicle for a deeper ideal
of social harmony (ll. 1–6). After this grave opening, the tone
lightens as Jonson gets on to the menu. The jocular quality of
this section, besides setting the tone for the party itself, re-
inforces the idea that it is not the food that matters. Moreover,
Jonson's lodgings are not Penshurst; there is a disparity between
his fantasy of the feast he would like to give and the hard reality
of what he can afford. But the intrusion of reality does not chill
the feast; Jonson's wry admission of the gap between his
shopping list and his budget is part of the fun:

> to these, a coney
>   Is not to be despair'd of, for our money;
> And, though fowle, now, be scarce, yet there are clarkes,
>   The skie not falling, thinke we may haue larkes.
> Ile tell you of more, and lye, so you will come:
>   Of partrich, pheasant, wood-cock, of which some
> May yet be there; and godwit, if we can:
>   Knat, raile, and ruffe too.   (ll. 13–20)

We would expect Jonson's view of a good social occasion
would include a touch of culture, and we are not disappointed:

> How so ere, my man
> Shall reade a piece of VIRGIL, TACITVS,
>   LIVIE, or of some better booke to vs,
> Of which we'll speake our minds, amidst our meate;
>   And Ile professe no verses to repeate.   (ll. 20–4)

Ruefully aware of his own reputation for arrogance about his
art, Jonson promises that he will not make a nuisance of himself
by reciting his own verses. The poetry, unlike that of John Daw
and other poetasters, will not be tainted by self-display. He will
defer to the ancients, as in *Poetaster* Horace and the others
deferred to Virgil. Then, the cultural tone of the occasion having
been established, the pleasures of drink can safely be introduced:

> But that, which most doth take my *Muse,* and mee,
>   Is a pure cup of rich *Canary*-wine,

> Which is the *Mermaids,* now, but shall be mine:
> Of which had HORACE, or ANACREON tasted,
> Their liues, as doe their lines, till now had lasted.
>
> (ll. 28–32)

It is no accident that the drinking is seen in relation to the poetry: Jonson is distinguishing between mere self-indulgence and the conviviality of civilized men.

In the final section other dangers are banished, along with the dangers of drink:

> Of this we will sup free, but moderately,
> And we will haue no *Pooly'*, or *Parrot* by;
> Nor shall our cups make any guiltie men:
> But, at our parting, we will be, as when
> We innocently met. No simple word,
> That shall be vtter'd at our mirthfull boord,
> Shall make vs sad next morning: or affright
> The libertie, that wee'll enioy to night.   (ll. 35–42)

There is the mutual trust of friends, who can drink together without quarrelling. And there is also a promise that there will be no state-spies, 'no *Pooly'*, or *Parrot*',[27] to threaten the liberty of the occasion. Jonson's ideal society is one in which good men are free to 'speake our minds, amidst our meate'. His most scathing depiction of a corrupt society is in *Sejanus*, where Rome is crawling with spies, where a man's most casual words can be taken down and used against him, and where books are not read but burned.

Mutual trust, festivity, culture, and the freedom for an honest man to speak his mind – the supper party embodies all of these. It has to be consciously created; the host has to work against a tight budget, his own tendency to egotism, and the danger of a society in which meddling knaves are always ready to turn a man's words against him. And we might note that Jonson is not describing a party he once held, but preparing one he would like to hold; he is not celebrating an achievement but expressing a hope.

As we have seen, when Jonson dealt with the showy heroism of chivalry in *The Speeches at Prince Henry's Barriers* his imagination kept pulling him back to the civil arts that support the

martial ones. And in his depiction of civil life he is, I think,
happiest when working on a reduced scale. The supper-party of
Epigram CI and the jovial hospitality of 'To Penshurst' carry as
much weight of social meaning as the scene in Caesar's court in
Poetaster; but being less portentous, they are not only more
attractive but closer to the heart of Jonson's social vision. It is in
small things that we measure the real worth of a society: how a
host treats his guests, what a man thinks of poetry, whether
words are used as they ought to be. Jonson's concern with detail
may at times be maddening to a reader in a hurry; but for him
every detail counts, whether it is a trick of language or dress
telling us a whole society is going rotten, or a small gesture of
courtesy reminding us that

> In small proportions, we just beautie see:
> And in short measures, life may perfect bee.

(*The Underwood*, LXX: 'To the Immortal Memory, and Friendship
of that Noble Pair, Sir Lucius Cary and Sir H. Morison', ll. 73–4)

4

VIRTUE'S LABYRINTH

I

The darkness that surrounds the good occasion shows Jonson's awareness that in this world the virtuous live in a state of seige. In the Ode, 'To the Immortal Memory and Friendship of that Noble Pair, Sir Lucius Cary and Sir H. Morison', (*The Underwood*, LXX) the virtue of the two heroes is set off and to a great extent defined by the life that surrounds them. In approaching this virtue, Jonson makes the reader travel a tortuous journey through a fallen world. We begin with the Infant of Saguntum, born as Hannibal is sacking his city, whose virtue – or rather wisdom, which is not quite the same thing – consists in retreating to his mother's womb from the horror of the world he is born into:

> Did wiser Nature draw thee back,
> From out the horrour of that sack?
> Where shame, faith, honour, and regard of right
> Lay trampled on; the deeds of death, and night,
> Urg'd, hurried forth, and horld
> Upon th'affrighted world:
> Sword, fire, and famine, with fell fury met;
> And all on utmost ruine set;
> As, could they but lifes miseries fore-see,
> No doubt all Infants would returne like thee.   (ll. 11–20)

Injustice is active and dominant; faith, honour and right are trampled on; and the only answer seems to be retreat. Virtue has, it seems, nothing to do in the world. Jonson then turns to the worthless lord whose career we considered in Chapter 2. Instead of the violence of history we have something that is if

anything more horrible: the emptiness of ordinary life. As in the
Saguntum passage only the wicked seemed active, now activity
itself looks meaningless.

When Jonson turns to Morison, virtue – with a struggle –
asserts itself at last:

> Alas, but *Morison* fell young:
> Hee never fell, thou fall'st, my tongue.
> Hee stood, a Souldier to the last right end,
> A perfect Patriot, and a noble friend,
> But most, a vertuous Sonne.
> All Offices were done
> By him, so ample, full, and round,
> In weight, in measure, number, sound,
> As though his age imperfect might appeare,
> His life was of Humanitie the Spheare.   (ll. 43–52)

It is as though the poem's grim opening is so daunting about the
prospects of virtue that Jonson has to put forth Morison's claims
carefully, step by step. The first note is lament. Morison's early
death may suggest that he died before he could achieve anything;
that seems at first to be the point of the contrast with the
nameless lord who lived to an old age and wasted his time, as in
Lycidas Milton contrasts the corrupt clergy with the young man
who died before his promise was fulfilled. Then Jonson rebukes
himself, and turns to what Morison did achieve. His virtues are
seen at first as those of being and enduring rather than acting. He
'stood', and exemplified the roles of soldier, patriot and son. But
all these roles require action, and Jonson goes on to credit him
with 'Offices . . . done.' The action is still abstract, but at last
virtue is seen working in the world.

Jonson then returns to the attack, rebuking an unnamed figure
– who may be himself[1] – for his wasted life:

> Goe now, and tell out dayes summ'd up with feares,
> And make them yeares;
> Produce thy masse of miseries on the Stage,
> To swell thine age.   (ll. 53–6)

Once again the contrast is between the great mass of a worthless
life and the short perfect life of Morison; and the same contrast is
drawn in the following stanza, the much-anthologized com-

parison between the old, dry tree and 'the Plant, and flowre of light' (l. 72). Throughout this section Jonson works by opposition, setting Morison's virtue against the emptiness of the life that surrounds him. And when Jonson adds to this an assurance of Morison's immortality, the suggestion is that, like the Infant of Saguntum, he was eager to leave the world: 'Hee leap'd the present age, / Possest with holy rage' (ll. 79–80). Cary and Morison become twin lights of virtue, sundered by death (as the word 'twi-Lights' is split by the line break – ll. 92–3)[2] but still representing the same ideals. Though Jonson does not make this explicit, the suggestion may be that Morison now represents the pure form of virtue in heaven, and Cary the operation of virtue in the world. And what their friendship stood for is defined, characteristically, by exclusion:

> No pleasures vaine did chime,
> Of rimes, or ryots, at your feasts,
> Orgies of drinke, or fain'd protests:
> But simple love of greatnesse, and of good;
> That knits brave minds, and manners, more then blood.
>
> (ll. 102–6)

That passage suggests virtue picking its careful way through the world, avoiding the evil it sees all around; avoiding too the false definition of worth as dependent merely on 'blood', an idea we will see Jonson returning to elsewhere.

In a later passage, the pure form of virtue stands apart from the world, like Morison in heaven – an example that is easier to recognize than to follow:

> And such a force the faire example had,
> As they that saw
> The good, and durst not practise it, were glad
> That such a Law
> Was left yet to Man-kind.   (ll. 117–21)

This is a tough appraisal of our fallen condition, and of the limits to what virtue can do. Even the well-meaning do not always *dare* to practise virtue; the best they can hope for is to know what it is, exemplified in the few men who have the strength to follow it. The poem finally celebrates virtue, not just as a state of mind but as an achievement: 'Who, e're the first downe bloomed on the chin, / Had sow'd these fruits, and got the harvest in' (ll. 127–8). The virtue that Cary and Morison represent is thus more positive than the wisdom of the Infant of Saguntum, who simply retreats from the world.[3] But we see it is limited by more than just the short life of Morison: it is limited by the sheer mass of evil and absurdity that makes up the bulk of life, and that makes good men seem like points of light in a vast darkness. The eagerness of both Morison and the Infant to leave the world suggests that virtue's natural place is not here. This is not to say that the poem is cynical; there is something heroic in the way Jonson constructs his picture of two good men, admitting at every point the presence of the opposition. But it shows that even a virtue whose main terms are private friendship and civil duty is a virtue embattled. Jonson does not imagine Cary and Morison actually struggling with the world; the struggle is rather in his own imagination, and in ours, as we try to get a clear view of what the heroes stand for.

Over and over in Jonson, virtue is depicted in adversity, and is even defined by adversity. We can tell the worth of Lord Salisbury not by the praise of his countrymen (who cannot be counted on to recognize virtue when they see it) but by the resentment of England's enemies abroad: 'Which should thy countries loue to speake refuse, / Her foes enough would fame thee, in their hate' (*Epigrams*, XLIII: 'To Robert Earl of Salisbury', ll. 3–4). Even private, self-contained integrity is imagined against opposition:

> He that is round within himselfe, and streight,
>   Need seeke no other strength, no other height;
> Fortune vpon him breakes her selfe, if ill,
>   And what would hurt his vertue makes it still.
>   (*Epigrams*, XCVIII: 'To Sir Thomas Roe', ll. 3–6)

Envy (personified in the monster beaten down by the armed Prologue at the opening of *Poetaster*) is another adversary of virtue; the presence of envy is in fact one of virtue's touchstones. In the Induction to *Every Man out of his Humour* Mitis expresses misgivings about Asper's confidence: 'I feare this will procure him much enuie'; to which Cordatus replies, 'O, that sets the stronger seale on his desert, if he had no enemies, I should esteeme his fortunes most wretched at this instant' (ll. 224–7). Jonson's own readiness to engage in literary warfare springs not just from personal truculence but from a sense that virtue must expect to be exercised in combat.

He is consistently scornful of the claims of title and ancestry in defining the virtuous man. This may seem ironic in view of the fact that so many of the figures he praises in the Epigrams belong to the aristocracy; but as David Wykes has pointed out, many of them were recently ennobled, so that whatever honour the title bestows has been honestly earned.[4] He declares, 'I a *Poet* here, no *Herald* am' (*Epigrams*, IX: 'To All, to Whom I Write', l. 4); and in *The Staple of News* a good Herald is defined as one who freely admits he cannot bestow honour (IV.iv.155–9). Even a Sidney can be told, 'they, that swell / With dust of ancestors, in graues but dwell' (*The Forest*, XIV: 'Ode to Sir William Sidney, on his Birthday', ll. 39–40). In Jonson's comedies, it is the fools who are concerned with their ancestries, like La-Foole in *Epicoene* (I.iv.37–46), or Cob in *Every Man In*, who can go back to the first red herring eaten by Adam and Eve (I.iv.13–17).[5] Jonson's mockery of ancestor-worship reflects more than just the resentment of a bricklayer's apprentice who had to make his own way in the world; it is consistent with his idea that virtue must be active, and must be defined by its own efforts against adversity.

It is the fate of the virtuous to be surrounded by envy and detraction. Jonson cannot comment on the satisfaction the raising of a virtuous man gives to his friends without noting also the pain it gives his enemies (*The Underwood*, LXXV: 'Epithalamion . . .', ll. 113–20; *Timber*, ll. 1292–7). Complimenting Lord Weston on being created Earl of Portland, Jonson spends most of the poem's energy attacking the envious who are bound to resent the honour, and Weston himself slips into the background (*The Underwood*, LXXIII: 'On the Right Honourable and Virtuous Lord Weston, Lord High Treasurer of England, Upon the Day he was made Earl of Portland; To the Envious'). The same thing happens in the poems on King Charles. The monarch, we are told over and over, is misunderstood and unappreciated by his subjects. Jonson is honestly reporting the King's isolation and unpopularity. But if there is a hint that Charles should re-examine his own policies, it is very deeply buried: all the overt criticism is directed against the ungrateful public: 'How is she barren grown of love! or broke! / That nothing can her gratitude provoke!' (*The Underworld*, LXIV: 'An Epigram. To our Great and Good King Charles on his Anniversary Day', ll. 15–16). Elsewhere Jonson complains of the absence of public rejoicing on royal occasions (*The Underwood*, LXVII: 'An Ode or Song, by All the Muses. In Celebration of Her Majesty's Birthday', ll. 4–12). In *The King's Entertainment at Welbeck*, Jonson – perversely, we might think – has a Gentleman rebuke the rustics for presuming to present the King with an entertainment:

> Give end unto your rudenesse: Know at length
> Whose time, and patience you have urg'd, the *Kings!*
> Whom if you knew, and truly, as you ought,
> 'Twould strike a reverence in you, even to blushing,
> That *King* whose love it is, to be your Parent!   (ll. 292–6)

For a parent, he seems remote and easily offended; but through the rudeness of the rustics Jonson is reflecting on the kingdom's failure to understand and appreciate its King.

Even Cynthia, the ideal monarch of *Cynthia's Revels*, is not immune from envy and detraction. We learn early in the play of 'some black and enuious slanders hourely breath'd against her, for her diuine iustice on ACTEON' (I. i. 92–4). Her entrance in the fifth act is stunning: after all the noisy buffoonery of the court fops, the true Queen enters to one of Jonson's most beautiful lyrics, 'Qveene, *and* Huntresse, *chaste, and faire*' (V. vi. 1–18). The noise of the world is hushed, and we seem to be lifted to a new plane of reality. Yet the song itself suggests a threat to Cynthia's light: '*Earth, let not thy enuious shade, / Dare it selfe to interpose*' (ll. 7–8) and Cynthia's first speech, while responding to the song's plea – 'HESPERVS *intreats thy light, / Goddesse, excellently bright*' (ll. 5–6) – is a bit querulous. Cynthia will indeed shine; but it is more than ungrateful humanity deserves, and she sounds a little tired of its pleas:

Yet, what is their desert?
"Bountie is wrong'd, interpreted as due;
"Mortalls can challenge not a ray, by right,
"Yet doe expect the whole of CYNTHIAS light.
But if that *Deities* with-drew their gifts,
For humane follies, what could men deserue
But death, and darknesse? It behooues the high,
For their owne sakes, to doe things worthily.   (v. vi. 29–36)

The monarch here has divine attributes, favouring by her grace
an undeserving humanity. The play has spent its time on the
fringes of the court, cataloguing the absurdities of its hangers-
on; we have felt, increasingly, the need for some figure of
authority to intervene. Yet Jonson has postponed Cynthia's
entrance until the fifth act is well under way: her appearances are
precious and rare, and her grace is not to be presumed on. Her
light is that of the moon, more beautiful because it shines in
darkness. Putting the song and her opening speech together,
we feel both her beauty and our unworthiness; and this leads us
to feel more poignantly the preciousness of that beauty.

The song, besides asking for Cynthia's light, pleads with her
to '*Lay thy bow of pearle apart, / And thy cristall-shining quiuer*'
(v. vi. 13–14) and the implications of this are pursued later in the
act when Cynthia defends the harshness of her sentences on
Actaeon and Niobe. She has, she complains, been censured as
'too seuere, and sowre' (v. xi. 10); and she answers the charge by
reiterating that she is not to be presumed on:

Seemes it no crime,
To braue a *deitie*? Let mortals learne
To make religion of offending heauen;
And not at all to censure powers diuine.   (v. xi. 21–4)

The song addresses her as '*Qveene, and Huntresse, chaste, and
faire*' (v. vi. 1), and we realize as the sequence develops that there
is more to this than a listing of the goddess's conventional
attributes. The weapons of the huntress are the weapons of
justice, and it is dangerous to cross her. Her chastity makes her
beauty dangerous, as the story of Actaeon shows. Cynthia's
entrance has a masque-like beauty, but as Jonson explores the
implications of that beauty we see a prickly virtue, surrounded

by presumption and detraction, and always ready to hit back at offenders. In the long speech that opens v. xi, Cynthia proclaims a time of revels and a truce to her severity; and yet throughout the speech she keeps returning to the defensive, remembering complaints that have been made of her and rebutting them. In its final act *Cynthia's Revels* seems to turn from satire to celebration, but the change is not absolute, for we see even Cynthia, the ideal ruler, in an unsatisfactory world where she does not receive her due.

There is a certain remoteness about Cynthia, as there is about King Charles; and Jonson often seems tempted by the idea that the world is so irredeemably corrupt the best thing virtue can do is retreat from it. The Infant of Saguntum is only one of many figures in Jonson who express their integrity by withdrawing from the world. The speaker of 'To the World. A Farewell for a Gentlewoman, Virtuous and Noble' (*The Forest*, IV), concludes:

> Nor for my peace will I goe farre,
>   As wandrers doe, that still doe rome,
> But make my strengths, such as they are,
>   Here in my bosome, and at home.   (ll. 65–8)[6]

Jonson begins the 'Epistle. To Katherine, Lady Aubigny' (*The Forest*, XIII) with a rueful suggestion that in this world even the legitimate praise of the virtuous puts one in a beleaguered minority: ''Tis growne almost a danger to speake true / Of any good minde, now: There are so few' (ll. 1–2). He professes misgivings, in other words, about writing poems such as this one; both he and his subject will be exposed to detraction: 'The bad, by number, are so fortified, / As what th'haue lost to'expect, they dare deride' (ll. 3–4). Characteristically, he defies the world and writes the poem; but the note of caution sounded at the beginning returns in his advice to Lady Katherine:

>   what if alone?
>   Without companions? 'Tis safer to haue none.
> In single paths, dangers with ease are watch'd:
>   Contagion in the prease is soonest catch'd.   (ll. 55–8)

This seems to call into question even the value of friendship, which elsewhere in Jonson is a source of strength to the virtuous. Towards the end, after a long catalogue of the vices of the world, Jonson seems to view retreat as the only safe answer:

> You, *Madame,* yong haue learn'd to shunne these shelues,
>   Whereon the most of mankinde wracke themselues,
> And, keeping a iust course, haue earely put
>   Into your harbor, and all passage shut
> 'Gainst stormes, or pyrats, that might charge your peace.
>
> (ll. 89–93)

The image of the ship putting into harbour when its voyage has hardly begun recalls the Infant of Saguntum. In the following lines, Jonson sets against that idea the fertility of Lady Katherine: 'For which you worthy are the glad encrease / Of your blest wombe, made fruitfull from aboue' (ll. 94–5). Both by her posterity and by her example, Lady Katherine can still make her mark on the world in the name of virtue: 'you are truly that rare wife, / Other great wiues may blush at' (ll. 110–11). But it is virtue seen in opposition to a great mass of folly and sin, virtue that must remain aloof to preserve its integrity.

The good man should learn to want nothing, and to fear nothing, from the world:

> A man should study other things, not to covet, not to feare,
> not to repent him: to make his Base such, as no Tempest shall
> shake him: to be secure of all opinion; and pleasing to himselfe,
> even for that, wherein he displeaseth others.
>
> (*Timber*, ll. 1459–63)

If he wants anything from the world, it is the satisfaction of knowing he has given offence to the unworthy. Yet that may suggest his retreat is not absolute; he is still keeping one eye on the world for signs that his virtue has made an impression. Jonson frequently identified himself with the image of the virtuous man in retreat: 'high, and aloofe, / Safe from the wolues black iaw, and the dull asses hoofe' (*Poetaster*, 'To the Reader', ll. 238–9). He did this particularly when his art was under attack; those words from the postscript to *Poetaster* are echoed in an ode on the detraction he has suffered in the theatre (*The Underwood*, XXIII: 'An Ode. To Himself', ll. 35–6). But for him the retreat

can never be final; there is always something for the retired man
to *do*:

> Well, with mine owne fraile Pitcher, what to doe
> I have decreed; keepe it from waves, and presse;
> Let it be justled, crack'd, made nought, or lesse:
> Live to that point I will, for which I am man,
> And dwell as in my Center, as I can,
> Still looking to, and ever loving heaven;
> With reverence using all the gifts thence given.
>
> (*The Underwood*, XLVII: 'An Epistle Answering to One that Asked
> to be Sealed of the Tribe of Ben', ll. 56–62)

The last line of that passage is an important reservation about
everything that has gone before. Jonson is no mere sensitive
plant, and the purely contemplative life is not for him. It is
natural for him to describe his retirement, not as a state of being
but as an opportunity to use his gifts. And within a few lines he
is getting in a kick at Inigo Jones, specifying that friendships
should be 'Such as are square, wel-tagde, and permanent, / Not
built with Canvasse, paper, and false lights' (ll. 64–5). For
Jonson there was something combative in the very act of
writing. Even the poems that appear to advocate retreat alternate
that advice with fierce attacks on the world. In Jonson, when
virtue retreats it is not to a monastic cell but to a fortified tower
with plenty of ammunition.

Nor is retreat always a virtue. We have seen already that
retiring from the world is a necessary condition for creating a
false, fantasy life. Tiberius, Volpone, and Morose have all in
their different ways retreated. And the most striking stage-
picture in Jonson of a character in hiding is Sir Politic Would-be
under his tortoise-shell.[7] Against the value Jonson puts on
self-sufficient integrity, we may set the value he puts on social
intercourse.

The good occasions in Jonson, as we have seen, centre on
the virtue of one man – Virgil, Sir Robert Wroth, Jonson himself inviting a friend to supper. But they are also *social* occasions,
involving a small – and sometimes a large – community. As
Isabel Rivers has pointed out, a good part of the audience to
whom Jonson preached withdrawal consisted of aristocrats,

who by their very position had to move in society.[8] The young
men of *Time Vindicated to Himself and to his Honours* have been
withdrawn from the world, and their withdrawal has been
complained of. But Diana defends it as necessary for their
education, which has a social purpose: '*To make them fitter so to
serve the* Time' (l. 495). Jonson's advice to Sir Robert Wroth is
characteristically mixed: 'To doe thy countrey seruice, thy selfe
right' (*The Forest*, III: 'To Sir Robert Wroth', l. 103). The good
friend must balance self-respect with an outgoing nature:

> looke, if he be
> Friend to himselfe, that would be friend to thee.
> For that is first requir'd, A man be his owne.
> But he that's too-much that, is friend of none.

> (*The Underwood*, XLV: 'An Epistle to Master Arthur Squib',
> ll. 21–4)

The image of the compasses, that Donne made famous as a way
of describing the unity of parted lovers, Jonson uses for the man
who can travel in the world and yet remain centred in himself
(*The Underwood*, XIV: 'An Epistle to Master John Selden',
ll. 29–33).

Jonson's tendency in the poems is to describe ideal states, and
here the two interests can be held in balance. In the plays – and
particularly in the figure of Crites in *Cynthia's Revels* – Jonson
uses the dramatic form to explore the problems inherent in
reconciling private integrity with involvement in the world. The
dramatic form itself, which by its very nature shows man
interacting with his fellows, resists any simple depiction of the
self-contained man. Crites is described as such a man, 'Who (like
a circle bounded in it selfe) / Contaynes as much, as man in
fulnesse may' (V. viii. 19–20). He seems not to care about the
world: 'Hee striues rather to bee that which men call iudicious,
then to bee thought so: and is so truly learned, that he affects not
to shew it' (II. iii. 131–4). That this self-contained virtue is by its
very nature irritating to the envious is demonstrated by Hedon
and Anaides:

HED   How confidently he went by vs, and carelessly! neuer
      moou'd! nor stirr'd at any thing! did you obserue him?

ANA   I, a poxe on him, let him goe, dormouse: he is in a dreame
now. He has no other time to sleepe, but thus, when hee
walkes abroad, to take the ayre.   (III. ii. 13–18)

But when we see into Crites' mind he seems much less aloof
from the play's fools than these descriptions would indicate.
Having asked, 'And who'd be angry with this race of creatures?'
(III. iii. 32) he goes on to reveal that he is sensitive to their
hostility, and that even his indifference is a way of getting back
at them:

And I doe count it a most rare reuenge,
That I can thus (with such a sweet neglect)
Plucke from them all the pleasure of their malice.
For that's the marke of all their inginous drifts,
To wound my patience, howsoe're they seeme
To aime at other obiects.   (III. iii. 37–42)

Elsewhere he complains that he cannot take his eyes off the
world:

I suffer for their guilt now, and my soule
(Like one that lookes on ill-affected eyes)
Is hurt with meere intention on their follies.
Why will I view them then? my sense might aske me.
                                              (I. v. 40–3)

He never really answers that question.

An answer may be suggested, however, at the opening of the
play, in Jonson's handling of the Narcissus myth. Eccho laments
the waste of Narcissus' beauty in mere self-contemplation:

O, hadst thou knowne the worth of heau'ns rich gift,
Thou wouldst haue turn'd it to a truer vse,
And not (with staru'd, and couetous ignorance)
Pin'd in continuall eying that bright gem,
The glance whereof to others had beene more,
Then to thy famisht mind the wide worlds store.
                                              (I. ii. 45–50)

Jonson does not make the connection explicit; but what is said
here of Narcissus' beauty could equally be said of Crites' virtue –
it should not be hoarded, away from the world. It is right that
Crites, for all his apparent indifference, should in the last
analysis be affected by the life around him. He is involved with

his fellow men, and his anguish at their folly is a sign of his
moral health. But anguish is not enough. Where Crites is
contemplative, and suffers for it, Mercury is active against the
fools. And in the last act he urges Crites to join him. Crites is at
first reluctant: 'I could be willing to enioy no place / With so
vnequall natures' (v. i. 8–9). He fears that if he attacks the fools
he will simply suffer detraction himself, as the virtuous usually
do: 'Th'offence will be return'd with weight on me, / That am a
creature so despisde, and poore' (v. i. 26–7). For once, his self-
confidence seems shaky. But Mercury assures him that the good
will approve, and that in asking him to act he is not asking him to
compromise his integrity:

> And good men, like the sea, should still maintaine
> Their noble taste, in midst of all fresh humours,
> That flow about them, to corrupt their streames.
>
> (v. i. 13–15)

The corrupt and the virtuous come as close as water flowing into
water, but the one does not taint the other. Finally, under the
guidance first of Mercury and then of Arete, Crites becomes an
active figure, not just suffering the folly of the world but
mocking, exposing, and correcting it. He is withdrawn from the
world, in that he remains uncorrupted by it; but he is made to
learn that absolute withdrawal is neither possible nor desirable.

Jonson had some of Milton's sense that virtue is not only
defined and clarified but actually strengthened by its confrontation with vice. Our adversaries keep us on our toes: 'To make
Arguments in my Study, and confute them, is easie; where I
answer my selfe, not an Adversary' (*Timber*, ll. 427–9). Even
detraction has its value:

> I am beholden to *Calumny*, that shee hath so endeavor'd, and
> taken paines to bely mee. It shall make mee set a surer Guard
> on my selfe, and keepe a better watch upon my *Actions*.
>
> (*Timber*, ll. 206–9)

Above all, 'He knowes not his own strength, that hath not met
Adversity' (*Timber*, 7–8). But if Jonson cannot praise a fugitive
and cloistered virtue, he is less sanguine than Milton about

virtue's chances in the arena. There is a chill behind his advice to
Sir Robert Wroth, 'Striue, WROTH, to liue long innocent' (*The
Forest*, III: 'To Sir Robert Wroth', l. 66). 'Long', not 'ever': the
struggle to preserve innocence seems ultimately doomed. Merit
is acquired slowly, and with constant effort:

> 'Tis by degrees that men arrive at glad
> Profit in ought; each day some little adde,
> In time 'twill be a heape; This is not true
> Alone in money, but in manners too.
> (*The Underwood*, XIII: 'An Epistle to Sir Edward Sackville,
> now Earl of Dorset', ll. 131–4)

And there are traps along the way, one of the most insidious
being the desire to impress the world with one's virtue. Praise is
a dangerous but necessary spur:

> though Ambition it selfe be a vice, it is often the cause of great
> vertue. Giue me that wit, whom praise excites, glory puts on,
> or disgrace grieves: hee is to bee nourish'd with Ambition,
> prick'd forward with honour; check'd with reprehension; and
> never to bee suspected of sloath.   (*Timber*, ll. 1687–92)

And yet, 'Hee that would have his vertue published, is not the
servant of vertue, but glory' (*Timber*, ll. 1465–7). Virtue is not
only set about with adversity: when it acts in the world it may
contain the seeds of vice in itself.

II

The clarity with which Jonson distinguishes virtue and vice in
the Epigrams, and the satisfaction he takes in exposing and
punishing fools in the early comedies, might suggest a writer
with a confident moral vision. Jonson may indeed be confident
about virtue in its ideal form; but he is honest enough to admit
that virtue in this world can seldom take its ideal form, and he is
enough of an artist to see the possibilities for drama in that
admission – the drama of a virtue in tension not only with a
hostile world but with the weakness of the forms virtue itself can
take in that world. We find this mostly in the plays, as we might
expect; but there is one remarkable poem, the 'Epode' (*The*

Forest, XI), that explores the problem closely, generating considerable tension in the process. It is a slow-moving and difficult poem, and its form reflects the difficulty of drawing an image of virtuous life in a fallen world. It is preceded by a short, untitled poem (*The Forest*, X) whose opening words are 'And must I sing?' The first note struck is one of reluctance, even if the reluctance is at this point more coy than sincere. As Jonson warms to his task, he seems to do so only by deciding which images of virtue he will *not* use. The result is a satiric debunking of classical mythology, not far in spirit from the coarse fun of the puppet show in *Bartholomew Fair*. The Epode, once it gets under way, will be much concerned with love, but Jonson rejects the classical figures of love as unworthy of his muse:

> Goe, crampe dull MARS, light VENVS, when he snorts,
> Or, with thy *Tribade* trine, inuent new sports,
> Thou, nor thy loosenesse with my making sorts.

> Let the *old boy,* your sonne, ply his old taske,
> Turne the stale prologue to some painted maske,
> His absence in my verse, is all I aske.   (ll. 16–21)

Venus and Mars are sensual in a vulgar way; he is asleep and snoring, and Venus has to pinch him awake. The Graces are Lesbians, and Cupid a tired old actor.

What Jonson is doing, I think, is proclaiming the independence of his own muse. He will not depend on a worn-out literary past; his poetry must be free to set its own terms (ll. 25–30). As the virtuous must make their own way in the world, free from a lazy dependence on title or ancestry, so the poet must establish his own images of virtue and beauty. This untitled poem, which looks at first neither tasteful nor relevant, is Jonson's characteristically rough way of clearing the ground. There must be in the workings of virtue a free and experimental quality; it must establish itself on its own terms in a hostile and dangerous world. How dangerous, the Epode itself shows.

There is a distinct wariness in the slow, difficult movement of the opening lines:

> Not to know vice at all, and keepe true state,
>   Is vertue, and not *Fate:*
> Next, to that vertue, is to know vice well,
>   And her blacke spight expell.   (ll. 1–4)

In the first two lines in particular language and even logic seem
to be strained by the attempt to imagine a virtue so invulnerable
it does not know vice at all. And perhaps the definition of this as
'vertue, and not *Fate*' means that such a pure condition is not
bestowed by Fate on anyone. The next best state is more familiar
and more easily imagined – to know vice and to expel it. Dealing
with this idea the verse relaxes, becoming more clear and easy in
its movement. But already we notice that some ground has been
surrendered. Compared with innocence, this state of combatting
vice – usually virtue's proper stance in Jonson – is second best.
And the words 'Next, to that vertue', while they may suggest
that this is another type of virtue, may equally suggest that it is
not virtue at all; some other term must be found for it. In fact
when Jonson goes on to describe this state, he does so without
using the word 'virtue'. We must, he argues, keep a close watch
on the senses, 'taste the treason' (l. 15) in order to reject it: ' 'Tis
the securest policie we haue, / To make our sense our slaue'
(ll. 17–18). It is the safe, the careful thing to do.

Yet even this course of action, second-best though it may be,
is more than we can expect from men in the world we live in:

> But this true course is not embrac'd by many:
>   By many? scarse by any.
> For either our affections doe rebell,
>   Or else the sentinell
> (That should ring larum to the heart) doth sleepe,
>   Or some great thought doth keepe
> Backe the intelligence, and falsely sweares,
>   Th'are base, and idle feares
> Whereof the loyall conscience so complaines.   (ll. 19–27)

Even this limited virtue – so limited that 'securest policie' seems
a better term for it – fails us. Our reason is overwhelmed from
without and subverted from within, betrayed by that lethargy
whose pervasiveness in Jonson's world we examined in Chapter 2.

Jonson abandons trust in one's own strength as a hopeless

cause, and turns to the virtue that finds its strength outside itself, in the ideal of love. But in doing so he has to distinguish between love and

> blinde Desire,
>   Arm'd with bow, shafts, and fire;
> Inconstant, like the sea, of whence 'tis borne,
>   Rough, swelling, like a storme:
> With whom who sailes, rides on a surge of feare,
>   And boyles, as if he were
> In a continuall tempest. Now, true Loue
>   No such effects doth proue;
> That is an essence, farre more gentle, fine,
>   Pure, perfect, nay diuine;
> It is a golden chaine let downe from heauen,
>   Whose linkes are bright, and euen,
> That falls like sleepe on louers, and combines
>   The soft, and sweetest mindes
> In equall knots: This beares no brands, nor darts,
>   To murther different hearts,
> But, in a calme, and god-like vnitie,
>   Preserues communitie.   (ll. 37–54)

In this rejection of impure desire in favour of pure love, we seem to be on familiar territory. The issue looks an easy one. And we see one reason why Jonson rejected the worn-out deities of classical mythology in the introductory poem: the Lesbian Graces, Venus and the snoring Mars, Cupid with his arrows – these are images of blind desire, not true love. And yet we are warned that the word 'love' is confused in the world we live in by being applied to desire. As we saw in Chapter 3, virtue must watch its language. Nor is true love, as depicted here, altogether without sensuality. There is that reference to the golden chain 'That falls like sleepe on louers'. The suggestion, inevitably, is of the sleep that comes after physical love-making. For all the talk of 'calme, and god-like vnitie' there is a suggestion here that as desire sometimes uses the name of love, so love can take to itself the satisfactions of desire. We remain, as always in the poem, creatures of sense even in our highest moments. And we are, perhaps, closer than we expected to be to Venus and the snoring Mars.

What the poem now celebrates is the possession of a woman who combines virtue and beauty (ll. 57–61). But as we reach this apparently secure vision, there is a sudden flash of danger:

> Who (blest with such high chance)
> Would, at suggestion of a steepe desire,
>   Cast himselfe from the spire
> Of all his happinesse?   (ll. 62–5)

The danger is, once more, internal treason, with the suggestion this time of a death-wish, an irrational compulsion to leap from a high place. In the imagery of the poem, the 'high chance' becomes dangerous precisely because it is high. The question is apparently rhetorical – who would be such a fool as to betray such virtue and beauty? – but the compelling movement of the verse makes the danger seem very real.

Rather than face the problem directly, Jonson turns to an easier kind of danger, the familiar Jonsonian danger of detraction:

> But soft: I heare
> Some vicious foole draw neare,
> That cryes, we dreame, and sweares, there's no such thing,
>   As this chaste loue we sing.   (ll. 65–8)

There is a fine suggestion here of physical irritation, as the mysteries are broken in on by the jarring voice of the fool; we recall, from *Poetaster*, the invasion of fools who interrupt Virgil's reading in the closed room. However, in rebutting the fool, Jonson is less confident and aggressive than we might have expected – perhaps because the fear of the 'steepe desire', having been admitted, has not been expelled, and has shaken our confidence in the security of the vision. After a quick counter-attack of the expected kind ('Peace, Luxurie') Jonson suddenly changes his tone, carefully and patiently separating from the vision of chaste love everything that might discredit it:

> And yet (in this to'expresse our selues more cleare)
>   We doe not number, here,
> Such spirits as are onely continent,
>   Because lust's meanes are spent:
> Or those, who doubt the common mouth of fame,

> And for their place, and name,
> Cannot so safely sinne. Their chastitie
> Is meere necessitie. (ll. 75–82)

The image of chaste love is refined by removing from it all the wrong reasons for chastity; but in the process we are reminded how many wrong reasons there are. Jonson rounds off this section of the poem by deploring the sort of virtue that is merely negative, not loving goodness but fearing the penalty for sin:

> He that for loue of goodnesse hateth ill,
> Is more crowne-worthy still,
> Then he, which for sinnes penaltie forbeares.
> His heart sinnes, though he feares. (ll. 87–90)

With such a neat formulation, we might suppose that danger to be identified and disposed of. But the ending of the poem shows this is far from the case.

Once again the beautiful, virtuous lady is celebrated; and once again, in the form of a rhetorical question, the fear of betrayal returns:

> O, so diuine a creature
> Who could be false to? chiefly, when he knowes
> How onely shee bestowes
> The wealthy treasure of her loue on him;
> Making his fortunes swim
> In the full floud of her admir'd perfection?
> What sauage, brute affection,
> Would not be fearefull to offend a dame
> Of this excelling frame? (ll. 102–10)

The fear of betrayal has now been stated three times, becoming more nagging and insistent with each repetition. And as the fear repeats itself, the reasons for the lover's loyalty become more dubious. If natural love of goodness is not enough to stop betrayal, he must think more possessively, remembering that he has been singled out for special favour, 'the wealthy treasure of her loue' bestowed on him alone. And here the image of the flood gets dangerously close to the rough sea imagery of the vision of desire, the sea from which Venus was born. Finally, he will be 'fearefull to offend' her. We seem to have fallen back on

one of the wrong reasons for virtue, as identified earlier – fear.
This is sadly confirmed by the end of the poem:

> He will refraine
> From thoughts of such a straine.
> And to his sence obiect this sentence euer,
> *Man may securely sinne, but safely neuer*.   (ll. 113–16)

We are back not to virtue but to 'securest policie'. And perhaps
we are further back still, to the admission that it is not *safe* to sin.
The lover becomes one 'which for sinnes penaltie forbeares', and
we have to remember how the rhyme was completed: 'His heart
sinnes, though he feares.' Jonson at first rejects fear as a ground
of virtue, only to return in the end to a grim admission that it
may be the only ground that works. We end with the image of a
lover who remains loyal to his ideal because he is afraid not to. It
is a tactical retreat to a safe position, but a position that seems
hardly worth defending.

All too often in Jonson's world, virtue is comprised by the need
to defend itself. Nowhere is this clearer than in *Volpone*. Celia's
name implies heavenly virtues, and her besieged chastity carries
with it piety, honesty and integrity; Jonson does not dismiss her
as a ninny, and it would be wrong for the reader or audience to
do so.[9] But she is placed in dramatic situations in which her
virtue cannot operate effectively. Her pleas to Corvino and
Volpone fall on deaf ears, as she appeals to decent feelings that
simply do not exist.[10] When at the end of the play she is
vindicated, she does the proper thing and asks the court for
mercy on her enemies. Once again the plea falls on deaf ears:
'You hurt your innocence, suing for the guilty' (v. xii. 106). One
cannot accuse Celia – as one can certainly accuse the Avocatori –
of hypocrisy or gullibility. But she is trying to defend chastity
and mercy in a world that does not know what those words
mean, and she is reduced to despair by the results: 'I would I
could forget, I were a creature' (IV. v. 102). We may even think
that her pleadings are themselves inadequate. Instead of making
a positive case for chastity, she expresses a horror at Volpone's
intentions and a masochistic loathing of her own beauty:

> punish that vnhappy crime of nature,
> Which you miscal my beauty: flay my face,
> Or poison it, with oyntments, for seducing
> Your bloud to this rebellion. Rub these hands,
> With what may cause an eating leprosie,
> E'en to my bones, and marrow: any thing,
> That may disfauour me, saue in my honour.

(III. vii. 251–7)

Chastity can be depicted as a positive, active virtue, as we see in Spenser's Britomart; but Celia's chastity is so much on the defensive that it comes down to mere rejection, countering Volpone's offer of sensual pleasure with an equally sensual disgust.

Her one supporter is Bonario, and he too is vulnerable, not through any weakness in himself – though we may think he is too easily taken in by Mosca – but through the dramatic situations he is placed in. His great moment comes when he rescues Celia from the Fox: 'Forbeare, foule rauisher, libidinous swine, / Free the forc'd lady, or thou dy'st, impostor' (III. vii. 267–8). Heroic in theory, this moment is explosively funny in practice, and not just because modern audiences see it as nineteenth-century melodrama.[11] Jonson, in the writing of Act III, has set up a comic pattern of which this moment is the natural climax. Volpone begins III. iii. impatient for Celia. He gets instead Lady Politic Would-be, who nearly drives him crazy with her noise, and poses an even more basic threat, 'that my loathing this / Will quite expell my appetite to the other' (III. iii. 28–9). Hurried away by Mosca, she makes a false exit and returns almost at once, to Volpone's dismay. Then, when he is finally rid of her, there is a long slow build-up to the seduction of Celia, as the encounter is delayed by Celia's argument with Corvino. When at last Volpone is alone with her, further delays are caused by his own protracted wooing and her resistance. Finally, his impatience explodes: 'I should haue done the act, and then haue parlee'd. / Yeeld, or Ile force thee' (III. vii. 265–6). Just when the audience is most keyed up, Bonario bursts from his hiding place – another interruption, another frustrating reversal for Volpone. It is as though Lady Pol had returned for the third

time; the repetition of the effect, like the sudden breaking of
tension, makes the moment comic.

Bonario fares no better in the trial scenes, where he is
reduced to *ad hominem* attacks on Voltore – 'This fellow, / For
six *sols* more, would pleade against his maker' (IV. v. 96–7) –
attacks that are entirely justified but create the impression
Bonario has no case. Voltore twists Bonario's suspicions of
Volpone – again, perfectly justified – to make the young man
look cruel:

> Perhaps, he doth dissemble?
> BON   So he do's.
> VOLT   Would you ha' him tortur'd?
> BON   I would haue him prou'd.
> VOLT   Best try him, then, with goades, or burning irons.
>   (IV. vi. 29–31)

The most desperate moment for Celia and Bonario comes when
they are asked to produce their own witnesses, and one can hear
the unimpressed silence into which their replies fall:

> AVO I   What witnesses haue you,
>   To make good your report?
> BON   Our consciences.
> CEL   And heauen, that neuer failes the innocent.
> AVO 4   These are no testimonies.
> BON   Not in your courts,
>   Where multitude, and clamour ouercomes.   (IV. vi. 15–20)

Lest we dismiss Bonario and Celia as laughably naive, we should
notice a passage in Jonson's preface, the Epistle to the two
Universities. Of the standard charge that his satire is personal
libel, Jonson writes, '*whil'st I beare mine innocence about mee, I
feare it not*' (l. 64). Jonson's treatment of these two figures of
virtue could have been simply idealistic, or merely cynical.
Instead, he shows us genuine virtue adrift in a hostile world,
made vulnerable and even laughable by its context, but not
despicable in itself. It is in the end a comic effect, but a subtle and
provocative one.

It may also be a guide to Jonson's more elaborate treatment of
the same problem in *Sejanus*.[12] The Germanican faction, standing for the virtues of old Rome, can do nothing in the corrupt

world of Tiberius but protest, retreat, or die. One of the state's
henchmen remarks, 'They all lock vp themselues a'late; / Or
talke in character' (II. 333–4). The only way to be safe in Rome is
to hide. They even seem to speak a private language; though
what that probably means is that they speak an uncorrupted one,
which the rest of Rome no longer recognizes. Agrippina's advice
to her friends is 'stand vpright; / And though you doe not act,
yet suffer nobly' (IV. 73–4). One who seems at first prepared to
do more than this is Arruntius. He is constantly heckling from
the sidelines, denouncing the state and praising those who resist
it. He can be witty and pointed, and he says many things the
audience wants to hear; but he is also capable of futile bluster, as
when he says of one particular criticism of Tiberius, 'He should
be told this' (I. 425). The use of the passive voice is a betrayal of
weakness (though it is fair to add that a few lines later he seems
about to address the Emperor, and is restrained by Sabinus –
I. 430–1). He shows a wry awareness of his own futility when he
says of the role he and his friends play in the Senate:

> We,
> That are the good-dull-noble lookers on,
> Are only call'd to keepe the marble warme.   (III. 15–17)

Sejanus' contempt is simple and devastating: 'And ther's
ARRVNTIVS too, he only talkes' (II. 299). Finally, the authorities
subject him to what for them is the ultimate insult: they spare his
life.

One whose life is not spared is Silius. He takes the classic way
of resisting a tyrant, a Stoic suicide that proclaims his own
independence of his persecutors:

> SILIVS hath not plac'd
> His guards within him, against fortunes spight,
> So weakely, but he can escape your gripe
> That are but hands of fortune.   (III. 321–4)

This idea is one for which the Renaissance had considerable
respect, and I think it would be wrong to dismiss Silius' suicide
as a futile and despairing gesture. As in *Volpone*, it is on the
theatrical level rather than on the level of ideas that Silius'
achievement is blunted. The suicide itself is a grand stage effect,

but Arruntius' aside 'My thought did prompt him to it' (III. 342)
breaks our concentration on it in a curiously irritating way, as
the great talker seems to be trying to get some of the credit for
himself. But what really destroys the effect is Tiberius' reaction:

> We are not pleas'd, in this sad accident,
> That thus hath stalled, and abus'd our mercy,
> Intended to preserue thee, noble *Romane:*
> And to preuent thy hopes.   (III. 344–7)

The shameless hypocrisy of this is more striking than the
suicide, because it is less expected. This gives Tiberius a
theatrical edge over Silius, and dissipates the power of his death.

Others defend a policy of simple passiveness. Sabinus, in a
speech that gives a Tudor colouring to this Roman play,
declares:

> No ill should force the subiect vndertake
> Against his soueraigne, more then hell should make
> The gods doe wrong. A good man should, and must
> Sit rather downe with losse, then rise vniust.   (IV. 163–6)

Behind what to Jonson's audience would be the familiar idea of
submission to authority may lie a deeper despair about the evil
of action itself. If only wrong can subdue wrong, it is better to
submit. Using language Jonson himself used for his retreats
from the world, Lepidus proclaims his own policy as that of
survival:

> > Arts, ARRVNTIVS?
> None, but the plaine, and passiue fortitude,
> To suffer, and be silent; neuer stretch
> These armes, against the torrent; liue at home,
> With my owne thoughts, and innocence about me,
> Not tempting the wolues iawes: these are my artes.
>
> > > > > (IV. 293–8)

The image of the swimmer who surrenders to the flood puts this
dangerously close to the state of living death examined in
Chapter 2. And it can be objected that the passivity of the
virtuous is actually culpable, for it allows Sejanus and the others
to flourish.[13] Looking elsewhere in Jonson, we see that while he

is sometimes attracted by the idea of retreat from the world, he also has a powerful impulse to go on fighting.

However, I think there is more to the virtuous figures in *Sejanus* than mere futility. Like Celia and Bonario, they remain uncorrupted in a world where evil is contagious. The more aggressive figures, Silius and Arruntius, may never dominate whole scenes but they do score points. The historian Cordus – significantly, a spokesman for culture and free speech in a dark age – does more. The eloquence of his defence seems to cow his accusers – 'He puts 'hem to their whisper' (III. 463) – and though his books are burned action against the man himself is postponed. The virtuous represent a variety of approaches to the problem of living in an evil world – satiric mockery, stoic defiance, politic inaction. The fact that none of these achieves political results underlines the futility of virtue; but the variety of this group has its own value. Tiberius, Sejanus and Macro are striking figures, but their dupes and agents have a grim sameness; the virtuous succeed in keeping simple human variety alive.[14] With this in mind we can see a value even in the unheroic Lepidus. He emerges late in the play, after a good deal of lurid action; it is a relief to hear a quiet voice at last. The fourth act begins with Arruntius alone, his allies either killed or banished; but Lepidus joins him and for the rest of the play they work together. There seems to be an irreducible minimum of virtue that cannot be stamped out. As in *Volpone*, the figures of virtue are powerless in a corrupt world, and Jonson dramatizes their plight with the tough honesty we expect of him. But this toughness includes a refusal to allow mere cynicism: even a helpless virtue can still command respect.

Figures of authority and moral correction also have their difficulties in Jonson, not only because they are coping with a world in which folly and vice are out of control, but because of the inherent weakness of their own natures. In some cases – the Avocatori in *Volpone*, Waspe and Busy in *Bartholomew Fair* – the authority figures are obviously foolish or tainted, and the comic effects are broad. But Jonson's treatment of Old Knowell in *Every Man in his Humour* and Justice Overdo in *Bartholomew Fair* is a bit more delicate. The comedy here is based not on simple folly but on the sight of genuine and attractive virtue compromised partly by the world it deals with and partly by its own weakness. Old Knowell could have been a stock comic father, but Jonson complicates the picture by giving him touches of genuine wisdom and good nature.[15] Controlling what he sees as the wantonness of his son, he plans to exercise his authority gently:

> Force workes on seruile natures, not the free.
> He, that's compell'd to goodnesse, may be good;
> But 'tis but for that fit: where others drawne
> By softnesse, and example, get a habit.   (I. ii. 131–4)

This strikes a nice balance between recognizing the intractability of youth and trusting its inherent good nature to be brought around in time. The tone is a bit magisterial; but one can detect behind it the old man's affection and respect for his son.

The rather dry and abstract lecture on reason Jonson gives him in the Quarto version of the play is replaced in the Folio by a much racier attack on the corruption of manners, particularly in education:

> We make their palats cunning! The first wordes,
> We forme their tongues with, are licentious iests!
> Can it call, whore? crie, bastard? ô, then, kisse it,
> A wittie child! Can't sweare? The fathers dearling!
> Giue it two plums.   (II. v. 19–23)

Here again there is a delicate balance: we are listening to an old man fussing over trifles: yet we know that for Jonson small matters like these really were an index to the health of a society. As Old Knowell's lecture on degenerate manners proceeds, it becomes virtually indistinguishable from many of Jonson's own strictures on the same subject in his non-dramatic satires. Yet it rests on a perilous basis. There is one sign above all that the world is going to the dogs, and that begins the speech:

> When I was yong, he liu'd not in the stewes,
> Durst haue conceiu'd a scorne, and vtter'd it,
> On a grey head; age was authoritie
> Against a buffon: and a man had, then,

A certaine reurence pai'd vnto his yeeres,
That had none due vnto his life.   (II. v. 5–10)

While Old Knowell's lecture on manners contains several points
that are well taken, the obvious self-interest with which it begins
gives us a comic detachment from it. But our response is further
complicated by Old Knowell's admission that the respect paid to
age in the old days was not always deserved. We are listening, in
short, not to a wise authority figure or a doddering old fool, but
to something more human than either: a well-meaning and
good-natured spokesman for virtue, whose authority is delicately
qualified by his own fussiness and self-importance, but who
never becomes the butt of simple mockery.

The treatment of Justice Overdo is somewhat broader. For
those who like to see authority figures in trouble, Overdo is as
satisfying a character as Jonson ever created. His disguise as a
mad ranting beggar compromises his dignity from the start. His
moral lectures draw crowds, to the benefit of the cutpurse
Edgeworth; and Overdo is beaten as an accomplice. He takes it
into his head that Edgeworth, one of the Fair's most hardened
criminals, is a civil young man who needs to be rescued from
evil company. He spends some time in the stocks, the perfect
figure of authority overturned; and when in the end he reveals
his identity and tries to impose his authority on the Fair, he is
stunned into silence by the sight of his own wife dressed as a
harlot, drunk and vomiting. Setting himself up as the scourge of
the Fair, he becomes first one of its sights and finally one of its
victims. Throughout the play, his fussiness and self-importance
exceed Old Knowell's, as we find him furiously taking notes
about trifles he calls 'enormities'. Yet his first speech is a volatile
mixture of pomposity – 'And as I began, so I'll end: in Iustice
name, and the Kings; and for the Common-wealth' (II. i. 48–9) –
with genuine good sense:

> For (alas) as we are publike persons, what doe we know? nay,
> what can wee know? wee heare with other mens eares; wee see
> with other mens eyes; a foolish Constable, or a sleepy Watch-
> man, is all our information, he slanders a gentleman, by the
> vertue of his place, (as he calls it) and wee by the vice of ours,
> must beleeue him.   (II. i. 27–33)

Overdo's solution may not be the wisest, and we see very soon that he is capable of making his own mistakes without the help of foolish constables; yet he has put his finger on a real problem,[16] and in his attempt to solve it, foolish though it may be, it is hard to separate self-importance from genuine public spirit.

Overdo, though he seems suspicious of poetry and thinks, like Old Knowell, that it is no fit occupation for a young man (III. v. 3–9) nonetheless speaks familiarly of his 'friends' Ovid, Horace, and Persius (II. iv. 67; IV. vi. 95–101) and consoles himself in the stocks with snatches of Latin. This is more delicate fun than the obvious literary pretensions of John Daw; Overdo really seems to have made the classics part of his life, and to be close to Jonson's ideal of the cultivated public man. Most important, he is capable of learning from his mistakes. He learns quite early in his search for enormities not to take the insults the Bartholomew-birds hurl at each other too literally (II. iii. 25–42). When beaten as a bawd of the cutpurses, he accepts his responsibility for the mistake, and is willing to take his misfortunes in good part and make an after-dinner joke of them: 'And they shall ha'it i'their dish, i'faith, at night for fruit: I loue to be merry at my Table' (III. iii. 20–1). His self-importance comes out when he describes the mad Troubleall, who will do nothing but by Justice Overdo's warrant, as 'a sober and discreet person' (IV. i. 27); but when he learns that his own dismissal of Troubleall was responsible for his derangement, and when he hears himself described by the officers as a testy and bad-tempered magistrate, his eyes are opened: 'I will be more tender hereafter. I see compassion may become a *Iustice*, though it be a weaknesse, I confesse; and neerer a vice, then a vertue' (IV. i. 82–4). We see here a fussy sententiousness struggling with genuine good nature. At the end of the play, the other mock-authority figures, Waspe and Busy, simply collapse, but Overdo is more resilient:

> I inuite you home, with mee to my house, to supper: I will haue none feare to go along, for my intents are *Ad correctionem, non ad destructionem; Ad aedificandum, non ad diruendum:* so lead on.   (V. vi. 110–13)

He does not get the last word of the play; that belongs to Cokes, who insists that the puppets come too. All the same, Overdo's final speech, with its note of genial authority, of correction tempered by festivity, is a statement that might have belonged to the playwright himself. And while Overdo has hardly been born again – one wonders what Ursula and her cronies will make of his Latin – there is a definite softening of the pomposity of his earlier speeches. Sententious, self-important, and for most of the play completely out of his depth, Overdo is still no mere buffoon. His folly is mixed with genuine good intentions, and through his fool's coat we glimpse – somewhat distorted, to be sure – the image of a cultivated public man who takes his responsibilities seriously.

One thing that prevents Overdo from being an effective agent of virtue is his innocence, a quality he shares with Celia and Bonario in particular. In some of Jonson's later plays we see that those who want to achieve virtuous ends in a crooked world must be prepared to deal with that world on its own terms. And the ends of virtue often include frank material self-interest. In *Bartholomew Fair*, Quarlous and Winwife are out to save Grace from an intolerable marriage with Bartholomew Cokes – and incidentally to win a desirable match for themselves. In the process they are prepared to employ a cutpurse and to play fast and loose with legal documents. In *The Devil is an Ass*, Wittipol and Manly rescue Mistress Fitzdottrel from the worst consequences of her marriage to a fool by gaining control of her husband's estate. Their end, though worthy, is limited and material, and their approach to it is tortuous to say the least. It begins with Wittipol's tempting Mistress Fitzdottrel to an adulterous affair, combining high-minded appeals to her noble nature with more basic methods of persuasion: '*He growes more familiar in his Courtship, playes with her paps, kisseth her hands, &c.*' (II. vi. 71). The lady herself, seconded by Manly, persuades Wittipol that she needs, not a lover but '*Counsell . . . and honest aides*' (IV. vi. 25). Wittipol submits, and the two young men gain control of the lady's estate, using chicanery similar to that Wittipol had used in his seduction attempt. Throughout,

Wittipol employs the rogues of the play, Ingine and Meercraft, for his own interests. He is in the main a sympathetic figure; but his love (like the love described in the Epode) sinks a bit too easily to the sensual; the help he gives Mistress Fitzdottrel is financial, and to that degree limited; and since he operates in a crooked world he has to use crooked means to gain even his most virtuous ends.

He is in many ways similar to Compass, the central character of *The Magnetic Lady*. While his brother Ironside attacks the fools of the play directly, Compass works on them in a devious, ironic way, mocking and flattering them in the same breath. The lawyer Practice, whose name sufficiently indicates his nature, appreciates Compass's devious methods:

> I now doe crave your pardon, Mr. *Compasse:*
> I did not apprehend your way before,
> The true *Perimeter* of it: you have Circles,
> And such fine draughts about!   (III. iv. 96–9)

Compass's ends are limited and material: not to reform the world, but to get a good marriage for himself with the heiress Placentia. He achieves this by being one step ahead of his rivals in a complicated intrigue. He is also associated with the sort of business enterprise Jonson had satirised through Meercraft in *The Devil is an Ass*, since he has the reversion of an office – Surveyor of the Projects. The ostensible business of the play, announced in its subtitle, is to reconcile the humours, and while Compass sometimes works for that end, he is, once more, limited and ironic in the way he sets about it. The reconciling of Interest and Bias, which he presides over, is a matter of mutual self-interest, as Compass comments:

> Foure hundred is the price, if I mistake not,
> Of your true friend in Court. Take hands, you ha'bought him,
> And bought him cheap.   (IV. iii. 45–7)

The Magnetic Lady is Jonson's last finished play, and the Induction suggests it will be his final statement, since he is 'now neare the close, or shutting up of his Circle' (ll. 104–5). If this leads us to expect a grand conclusion we are disappointed, for the circle Compass draws is a small one. He seems to expect very little from the world, and far from reforming it he accepts its folly in a spirit of irony, and gets what he can out of it by whatever means will work.

The Staple of News looks like a more confident work, in which moral correction operates effectively in the world. But it too presents the conclusion that the world must be dealt with on its own terms. Its moral pattern, embodied in the three Pennyboys, looks simple – too schematic, in fact. Pennyboy Senior is a usurer, who keeps the Lady Pecunia locked up, or debases her for gain. His nephew Pennyboy Junior is a prodigal who abuses Pecunia by squandering her favours. In the middle is Pennboy Canter, the prodigal's father, who has arranged a fake death for himself and then returned in disguise to spy on his son's use of his fortune. Towards the end of the play, he removes his disguise and lectures the other two on their misuse of Pecunia; he seems to be the mean between extremes. On the whole, the characters function obedient to this moral design, behaving exactly as we would expect; yet they are all capable, in different ways, of surprising us. Pennyboy Senior is mostly a stock usurer, crabbed and miserly.[17] But he attacks the luxury of the world (III.iv.45–64) in language very close to one of Jonson's own borrowings from Seneca in *Timber* (ll. 1386–1412). And while Pennyboy Junior is mostly a fool, he speaks some home truths about the usurer's abuse of Pecunia (IV.iii.24–7). Each has a partial view of the world, but each view contains some of the truth. Pennyboy Canter seems to have the whole truth, as he lectures both of them on the right use of money. But for all that, he is not altogether capable of dealing with the world himself. As part of his plan to test his son, he has allowed the lawyer Picklock to get his hands on the estate, and he soon finds that his trust is misplaced. Pennyboy Junior has to rescue him, regaining the estate by using Picklock's own technique of double dealing. Pennyboy Canter says all the right things; but his brush with Picklock shows that it takes more than fine speeches to deal with this world: you have to meet it on its own terms, as his son does in cheating Picklock. The use of the same basic name for all three characters may suggest an ideal figure split in three; not one of the Pennyboys is by himself adequate to confront the world.

The fullest treatment in Jonson's drama of the problems of
virtue – its strength and weakness, and the compromises it has to
make with reality – is found in the character of Cicero in
Catiline. He may be thought to represent an ideal for Jonson –
the philosopher–statesman, the writer as magistrate.[18] But the
way this ideal works in practice as Cicero smashes the Catiline
conspiracy is more complicated and ironic. Cicero has to use not
just ideal means – the power of truth, embodied in his great
oration to the Senate – but any means that will work. As Catiline
complains of the conspirators he has to work with –

> What ministers men must, for practice, vse!
> The rash, th'ambitious, needy, desperate,
> Foolish, and wretched, eu'n the dregs of mankind,
> To whores, and women!   (III. 714–17)

– Cicero in order to save Rome has to use the same shabby
material: deserters from Catiline's side, Curius and the courtesan
Fulvia. He unconsciously duplicates Catiline's complaint when
he laments that Rome's safety must depend on

>   a base
> And common strumpet, worthless to be nam'd
> A haire, or part of thee? Thinke, thinke, hereafter,
> What thy needes were, when thou must vse such meanes:
> And lay it to thy brest, how much the gods
> Vpbraid thy foule neglect of them; by making
> So vile a thing, the author of thy safetie.   (III. 450–6)

Even more significant, he has to treat his instruments as Catiline
does his – soothing and flattering them. He appeals to Curius as
'A person both of bloud and honor, stock't / In a long race of
vertuous ancestors' (III. 329–30) though he himself, as we will
see, makes a special point of having a virtue that does not depend
on lineage, and of scorning ancestry as a basis of worth. He
bribes Fulvia with a promise of fame:

> What voices,
> Titles, and loud applauses will pursue her,
> Through euery street! What windores will be fill'd,
> To shoot eyes at her! What enuy, and griefe in matrons,
> They are not shee!   (III. 345–9)

In this, he plays shrewdly on the kind of mentality Fulvia reveals
when she declares:

> Come, doe you thinke, I'ld walke in any plot,
> Where madame SEMPRONIA should take place of me,
> And FULVIA come i'the *rere*, or o'the *by?*   (III. 375–7)

And he promises them both 'titles' and 'rewards' (III. 401) from
the Senate. His fellow consul Antonius (whom he despises) he
enlists by bestowing a province on him. Antonius cheerfully
admits to having been bought:

> There is some reason in state, that I must yeeld to;
> And I haue promis'd him. Indeed he has bought it,
> With giuing me the *Prouince.*   (IV. 111–13)

Both Cicero and Catiline, in short, have to deal pragmatically
with human nature as they find it in order to gain their ends. As
Cicero remarks, 'So few are vertuous, when the reward's away'
(III. 480). Each suffers some loss of dignity in the process; but in
a sense the damage to Cicero is greater. It is hard to say which is
more embarrassing: that the guardian of public virtue should
resort to bribery and flattery, or that he should be so surprisingly
good at it.

But the most complex irony surrounding Cicero is that the
roots of his civic virtue, and the roots of his vulnerability, are so
twisted together. He is a 'new man'; this means his virtue is his
own, not spuriously derived from his ancestors. His political
debts are not to this party or that, but to Rome itself. He takes
his own career as a sign that virtue, cut free of the established
political machinery, can make its own way in Rome, seeking
only the good of the state:

> I haue no vrnes; no dustie moniments;
> No broken images of ancestors,
> Wanting an eare, or nose; no forged tables
> Of long descents; to boast false honors from:
> Or be my vnder-takers to your trust.
> But a new man (as I am stil'd in *Rome*)
> Whom you haue dignified;   (III. 14–20)

We have seen already how insistent Jonson is that mere ancestry
is no guarantee of virtue. But the lack of it makes Cicero terribly
vulnerable to criticism. Even before he appears, we hear the
gossips of Rome attacking him for his low birth (II. 119–33).
Since he is a new man, he must be constantly proving himself. In
proclaiming his own virtue, he is bound to look vain; in carving
out a niche for virtue he is bound to look as though he is carving
out a niche for himself. Caesar, a more subtle and dangerous
antagonist than Catiline, exploits this. His wry aside, 'O confidence! more new, then is the man!' (III. 46) shows the line this
clever Machiavel will take in the play as a whole. In complaining
of Cicero's boasts, he attacks him at a point on which he is
genuinely vulnerable. In speeches like the one quoted above,
there is an undeniable note of self-congratulation. And there is
something compelling in Caesar's claim that Cicero is inventing
a conspiracy in order to advance his own credit:

> Doe you not tast
> An art, that is so common? Popular men,
> They must create strange monsters, and then quell 'hem;
> To make their artes seeme something. Would you haue
> Such an HERCVLEAN actor in the scene,
> And not his HYDRA?   (III. 95–100)

The charge, we know, is a lie; but it is a lie whose power we are
bound to recognize. It appeals so compellingly to one of our
most basic needs, the need to believe that our fears are ground-
less. The fact that Caesar is given some of the sharpest and most
expressive writing in this frequently turgid play helps to
strengthen the effect.

The price that Cicero pays for being virtuous is to be
surrounded by envy and detraction; that, in Jonson, is the
standard price virtue pays. The price he pays for being a new
man is that the detraction is genuinely dangerous. Throughout
the play, he is a beleaguered man. His first words express not
buoyant confidence but an anxiety about what people will say of
him, an anxiety that is never far from his mind as the action
progresses:

> Great honors are great burdens: but, on whom
> They'are cast with enuie, he doth beare two loades.

His cares must still be double to his ioyes,
In any dignitie; where, if he erre,
He findes no pardon: and, for doing well
A most small praise, and that wrung out by force.   (III. 1–6)

It is a curiously negative note for Cicero to begin with; but it can
be paralleled in the opening speeches of Cynthia in *Cynthia's
Revels*, and in the poems on King Charles. In a later scene, we
see him barricaded in his house, speaking from the safety of a
position above the stage. Even at his moment of triumph over
the conspiracy, Cicero sounds the same note:

I do not know whether my ioy or care
Ought to be greater; that I haue discouer'd
So foule a treason: or must vndergoe
The enuie of so many great mens fate.   (IV. 816–19)

In the balancing of the lines the care outweighs the joy, and
spoils the victory.

Connected with Cicero's fear of envy is a constant concern
that the rightness of his actions should be obvious to the public;
detraction must have nothing to feed on. This results in a
persistent and (it sometimes appears) excessive caution in taking
action against the conspirators. Cicero explains to the Senate
why he has let Catiline go so far rather than having him seized:

But when there are in this graue order, some,
Who, with soft censures, still doe nource his hopes;
Some, that with not beleeuing, haue confirm'd
His designes more, and whose authoritie
The weaker, as the worst men, too, haue follow'd:
I would now send him, where they all should see
Cleere, as the light, his heart shine; where no man
Could be so wickedly, or fondly stupide,
But should cry out, he saw, touch'd, felt, and grasp'd it.
                                           (IV. 402–10)

We realize the practical force of the argument, for we have heard
much in this play of the lethargy of Rome. Yet we are bound to
feel also the danger to the state in letting Catiline go so far as he
does. And by the end of the play another danger has become

apparent, against which Cicero's caution makes him powerless.
Cato demands that proceedings be taken against Caesar and
Crassus. For him the issue is simple: 'Why dare we not? What
honest act is that, / The *Roman Senate* should not dare, and doe?'
to which Cicero replies,

> Not an vnprofitable, dangerous act,
> To stirre too many serpents vp at once. . . .

> They shall be watch'd, and look'd too. Till they doe
> Declare themselues, I will not put 'hem out
> By any question. There they stand. Ile make
> My selfe no enemies, nor the state no traytors.   (IV. 526–37)

Above all, the magistrate must not suffer detraction – as he
would do if he acted before all could agree on the justice of his
actions. This kind of thinking serves Cicero well enough in his
dealings with Catiline; but against the more subtle and long-
range threat posed by Caesar he is helpless and immobile.[19]
Though not unaware of the danger, he is reduced to tolerating
and even placating Caesar. He rejects accusations made against
Caesar and Crassus as libels, and when Caesar demands that
Curius – Cicero's instrument against Catiline, who is now ready
to strike at Caesar – should not be given the reward he was
promised, Cicero seems to acquiesce. It may appear that Cicero
is starting to participate in the very lethargy of which he accused
the Romans earlier in the play (III. 438–44). But the irony is that
he has been immobilized by the very political tactics he has
evolved to protect himself from envy and to ensure that the state
supports his efforts. As a new man, with no established party
behind him, he needs not only to be right but to be *seen* to be
right; and this need finally cripples him.

Eliot called *Catiline* 'that dreary Pyrrhic victory of a tragedy'[20]
and whether it is itself a Pyrrhic victory, it certainly shows one.
Cicero defeats Catiline; but his caution, and his concern with
acting only on truths that are firmly established, leave him
helpless before his next and more powerful adversary. Virtue
cannot take a straight and simple course (as Cato, for one, would
have it do); it has many enemies, the complacent as well as the
evil, and it must work with care if it is to work at all. Yet that

very care hampers its effectiveness. We cannot write Cicero off as a fool, a braggart, or a bumbler; he has skill and eloquence, and embodies values Jonson deeply admires. But his career shows with painful clarity the paradoxes of virtue's operation in a fallen world.[21]

The masque is normally a chance to present an unfallen world, to show virtue triumphing as simply and decisively as light over darkness. And that is usually what we get. But in one masque in particular, *Pleasure Reconciled to Virtue*, Jonson seems to have incorporated some of his thinking about virtue's difficulties in the world, and the result is a more rich and complex vision. In the antimasque Hercules, having routed the followers of Comus, is invited to rest only to find himself menaced by pygmies. We are reminded – lightly and comically, to be sure – that to be the servant of virtue is to be committed to a never-ending struggle in which the moments of relaxation can only be temporary. And there are, as in *Catiline*, some ironic parallels between the figures of vice and virtue. The bowl that Comus' followers bear in their celebration of the bouncing belly is Hercules' own bowl – a sly reminder that this warrior of virtue is not exactly a figure of temperance. Prominent on the side of virtue is the great inventor Daedalus; but the belly is also an inventor, '*that found out the excellent ingine, the spit*' (l. 16) not to mention the plough, the flail, the mill and the other apparatus of what we now call the food industry.

Daedalus' chief invention, for the purposes of the masque, is the labyrinth. The labyrinth, which is also a dance, is the masque's central image. Through it, virtue becomes involved in the fallen world, not in a manner that taints and compromises it, but in a manner that shows virtue's skill. The masquers, significantly, must descend from a mountain to engage in the dance. The song that invites the descent specifically tells the masquers there is nothing to fear:

> Descend,
> descend,
> though pleasure lead,
> feare not to follow:

> *they who are bred*
> *within the hill*
> *of skill,*
> *may safely tread*
> *what path they will:*
> *no ground of good, is hollowe.*   (ll. 226–35)

The suggestion is that the descent would normally have been a treacherous one, and pleasure a dangerous guide. But on this occasion opposites are reconciled, virtue's skill makes its followers safe, and the winding path becomes a graceful dance. Daedalus' song, introducing the first dance, shows virtue not as a pure and simple force but as a force in complex interaction with the world, an interaction that has a beauty of its own:

> *Come on, come on; and where you goe,*
> *so enter-weaue the curious knot,*
> *as eu'n th'obseruer scarce may know*
> *which lines are Pleasures, and which not.*
>
> *Then, as all actions of mankind*
> *are but a Laborinth, or maze,*
> *so let your Daunces be entwin'd,*
> *yet not perplex men, vnto gaze.*   (ll. 253–64)

To say that the actions of mankind are 'a Laborinth, or maze' is normally to stress the darkness of our fallen condition. But here, as in Spenser's Mutabilitie cantoes, the vicissitudes of life are accepted, even celebrated, as part of a formal and beautiful pattern.

The song introducing the third dance, the Labyrinth of Beauty, is more specific. Here, the young men are invited to dance with the ladies. Like the Epode, the song rejects ordinary fallen love, while at the same time its language flirts with it:

> *And so let all your actions smile,*
> *as if they meant not to beguile*
> *the Ladies, but the howres.*
> *Grace, Laughter, & discourse, may meet,*
> *and yet, the beautie not goe les:*
> *for what is noble, should be sweet,*
> *but not dissolu'd in wantonnes.*

> Will you, that I giue the law
>   to all your sport, & some-it?
> It should be such shold envy draw,
>   but euer ouercome-it.   (ll. 306–16)

There is a delicate fusion here of high courtesy and ordinary flirtation, suggested in words like 'beguile'. The internal enemy is wantonness (as in the Epode or *The Devil is an Ass*); the external enemy is envy (as in *Catiline*). Both are faced – envy is even *invited*, for its presence is a touchstone of virtue – and this time both are expelled.

It looks as though the problems raised in other works we have examined have been resolved, by transforming painful complexity into beautiful patterning, the interaction of virtue with fallen nature into a graceful dance. Up to a point that is just what has happened. It is a solution peculiarly appropriate to the genre of the masque, with its stylization, its deliberate creation of a simplified and beautiful world. But another peculiarity of the masque is that it belongs to a single occasion. Like the good social occasions examined in Chapter 3, it is by definition transient. Morning comes, the dance is over, the scenery and costumes are packed away. *Pleasure Reconciled to Virtue*, like many of Jonson's masques, admits its own transience. The reconciliation of the 'noted opposites' is not a permanent achievement. It is something that has happened on this one occasion by 'working of the stars' (l. 188) and as a compliment to the King: '*Pleasure*, for his delight / is reconcild to *Vertue*' (ll. 200–1). At the end, the young men who are virtue's pupils are told that the party is over:

> An eye of looking back, were well,
>   or any murmur that wold tell
>   your thoughts, how you were sent,
>   and went,
> to walke with Pleasure, not to dwell.
> Theis, theis are howres, by Vertue spar'd
>   hirself, she being hir owne reward,
>   But she will haue you know,
>   that though
> hir sports be soft, hir life is hard.

> *You must returne vnto the Hill,*
> *   and there aduaunce*
> *with labour, and inhabit still*
> *   that height, and crowne,*
> *from whence you euer may looke downe*
> *   vpon triumphed Chaunce.*   (ll. 323–39)

The masquers dance for the last time, and return to the
mountain, 'which closeth, and is a Mountaine againe, as before'
(ll. 350–1). As Stephen Orgel puts it, 'we are left not . . . in a
golden age, but rather in a craggy landscape'.[22] It may not be
altogether mischievous to say that the argument of *Pleasure
Reconciled to Virtue* is that virtue and pleasure cannot finally be
reconciled. This is a masque, not a tragedy, and its final note is
celebration – but celebration of virtue as exclusive and independent. She belongs to Heaven, and her final relation with
the lower world is one of opposition:

> *She, she it is, in darknes shines.*
> *   'tis she that still hir-self refines,*
> *   by hir owne light, to euerie eye,*
> *more seene, more knowne, when Vice stands by.*
> *   And though a stranger here on earth,*
> *   in heauen she hath hir right of birth.*   (ll. 339–44)

That virtue is indeed 'a stranger here on earth' is, I think, the
burden of the works examined in this chapter. Those who
follow virtue find themselves in conflict with a hostile world,
having to deal with it somehow while preserving their own
integrity. Sometimes, they are simply helpless. Their victories,
when they come, tend to be limited and temporary, or compromised by the means used to win them. The robust moral
confidence seen in some of Jonson's works (most of the
Epigrams, for example) does not tell us the whole story. But in
presenting figures of virtue as in various ways compromised,
Jonson is not mocking or cynical. The virtue they represent is
genuine and important, and the interplay between the ideal and
the fallen world gives rise to tense drama, or to a wry and
complex comedy, touched with pain.

5
JUDGEMENT AND TRANSFORMATION

I

Jonson's respect for facts led him to depict an intractable world where the operations of virtue are tortuous and not always satisfactory. But his respect for ideals led him to imagine worlds in which virtue could operate perfectly, and in which truth and right could assert themselves with the swift, irresistible force of natural law. The court masque was a proper medium for such visions. The presence of the real world was acknowledged by constant references to – and the occasional involvement of – the aristocratic audience. That audience was invited to look into a mirror in which they saw not what they were but what they ought to be: the gaudy, frequently disreputable court was translated into a world of ideal forms. And within that world, there could be discovery within discovery, depth within depth. The drawing of a curtain or the turning of a stage machine could bring fresh revelations in a moment. The immediate effect might be striking and picturesque rather than significant; but even in moments that look like pure spectacle a kind of significance could be implied.

At the opening of one of the earliest court shows, *An Entertainment of the King and Queen at Theobalds*,

> there was seene nothing but a trauerse of white, across the roome: which sodainely drawne, was discouered a gloomie obscure place, hung all with black silkes, and in it only one light, which the GENIVS of the house held, sadly attir'd; his Cornucopia readie to fall out of his hand, his gyrland drooping on his head, his eyes fixed on the ground. (ll. 3–8)

The Genius laments that the house is to change masters; then the voice of Mercury speaks out of the darkness, 'Despaire not, GENIVS, thou shalt know thy fate' (l. 25) and there is a fresh discovery: '*the black vanishing, was discouered a glorious place, figuring the* Lararium, *or seat of the household-gods*' (ll. 26–7), full of bright colours. Then, discovery within discovery: '*Within, as farder off, in* Landtschap, *were seene clouds riding, and in one corner, a boy figuring* Good Euent, *attyred in white, houering in the ayre*' (ll. 32–4). The occasion of the entertainment is the Earl of Salisbury's turning over his house to King James. The mood changes with the simplicity of the colours, from white to black to white, exemplifying the mixed emotions of the occasion. The discoveries turn the show into a series of surprises. An entertainment begins in gloom; then the gloom turns to glory. The second revelation puts into simple theatrical form the education of the Genius of the house, who must be reconciled to the change of masters. This is not as simple as the 'discoveries' might suggest, for he is inclined to argue, and Mercury has to tell him, 'GENIVS, obey, and not expostulate' (l. 91). But by the end the Genius is won over and rebukes himself for mourning. The final song celebrates the house's destiny:

> O blessed change!
> And no lesse glad, then strange!
> Where, wee, that loose, haue wunne;
> And, for a beame, enioy a Sunne.   (ll. 130–3)

The transfer of the house is a practical transaction, essentially political in its significance. But Jonson strikes through the practical surface to an inner reality, a pattern of apprehension, surprise, and delight, by which the house itself, through the Genius, learns and understands its fate. In the dialogue of the Genius, Mercury and the Fates, this happens slowly, through question and argument – 'But is my Patron with this lot content, / So to forsake his fathers moniment?' (ll. 74–5). In the stage effects it happens swiftly and cleanly. The dialogue complicates the issue and the stage effects simplify it; in that respect the two kinds of revelation seem to be in tension. But in the long view they work for the same end, and support each other. The

argument explores the significance of the scenic revelations, and
the scenic revelations show the essential pattern behind the
argument.

At times the moral significance of the discovery is obvious: a
world of darkness is transformed, in a satisfyingly decisive way,
into a world of light. *The Masque of Queens* opens with an
antimasque of hags, who threaten to bring disorder by their
magic spells:

> In the heate of their *Daunce*, on the sodayne, was heard a sound
> of loud Musique, as if many Instruments had giuen one blast.
> With which, not only the *Hagges* themselues, but their *Hell,*
> into which they ranne, quite vanishd; and the whole face of the
> *Scene* alterd; scarse suffring the memory of any such thing:
> But in the place of it appear'd a glorious and magnificent
> Building, figuring the *House of Fame*.   (ll. 354–60)

Jonson's stage direction emphasizes the suddenness of the transformation. The evil of the hags is not only dark and disordered,
as we might expect: it is so evanescent it hardly seems real; one
blast of Fame's trumpet can disperse it, and the transformation is
so complete that when the hags are gone we wonder if we ever
saw them.[1] The imperfect creatures of *Mercury Vindicated from
the Alchemists at Court* are replaced by a vision of the Bower of
Nature, false art by an art that celebrates reality. In *The Masque
of Augurs*, the '*straying, and deform'd Pilgrims*', reflecting the crazy
pseudo-art of Vangoose, are frightened away by '*the opening of
the light above, and breaking forth of* Apollo' (ll. 271–3), the god of
true art.

In moments like these the vision revealed by the dispersal of
the antimasque is presented as the true one, the antimasque as
false. It follows that the audience is not only seeing something
different, but seeing more clearly. In *The Vision of Delight* the
cheerful nonsense of Phant'sie (who breaks forth from a cloud) is
succeeded by the revelation of the bower of Zephyrus, and by a
further discovery of the masquers themselves, as the Glories of
the Spring. The nature of these transformations is suggested by
the song that accompanies the revelation of the Bower: 'We see,
we heare, we feele, we taste, / we smell the change in every
flowre' (ll. 136–7). As the revelations take place, we feel more

vividly and see more clearly. We are brought from harmless but nonsensical fantasy to true dreams that reflect reality.[2] In *Hymenaei* (ll. 212–15) and *The Haddington Masque* (ll. 41–5) clouds part and the sky clears; the effect is not to transform the world but to reveal the truth that was always there. And as our perceptions clear, there are fresh revelations within the world of truth itself, like the height beyond height in a Baroque ceiling. This happens in *Oberon*:

> *There the whole* Scene *opened, and within was discouer'd the* Frontispice *of a bright and glorious* Palace, *whose gates and walls were transparent. . . . There the whole palace open'd, and the nation of* Faies *were discouer'd, some with instruments, some bearing lights; others singing; and within a farre off in perspectiue, the knights masquers sitting in their seuerall sieges: At the further end of all,* OBERON, *in a chariot, which to a lowd triumphant musique began to moue forward, drawne by two white beares, and on either side guarded by three* Syluanes, *with one going in front.*
>
> (ll. 138–40, 291–8)

As our eyes become accustomed to the light, we can see more and more clearly into it; finally the figure at the heart of the vision is revealed, and comes forward into closer view.

Machines open, clouds part, caves vanish and bowers appear; but the one constant is the presence of King James in the audience, and he is the focus of the occasion. In *The Masque of Blackness*, as we have seen, he is the sun who can 'blanch an AETHIOPE' (l. 255). This transformation is promised rather than performed, and we have to wait for the sequel *The Masque of Beauty* to see the results. But in *News from the New World Discovered in the Moon* the King's sun-like power to transform is seen at work directly, when a herald tells him that the masquers, who are bound up in ice,

> have their ends in your favour, which alone is able to resolve and thaw the cold they have presently contracted in comming through the colder Region.
> *They descend and shake off their Isicles.*   (ll. 315–18)

In *The Irish Masque at Court* James settles the Irish Question at a stroke, as the masquers, at a glance from the King, let fall the mantles that concealed their finery and 'come forth new-borne

creatures all' (l. 182). While the transformation is in two senses
an illusion – an idealized vision, produced by a technical trick –
the power to which it is attributed is a living man sitting in the
audience. The King is both an idea, the centre of an inner reality,
and a real man, the centre of a particular social occasion.

In Chapter 1, we saw Jonson's paradoxical attitude to artificial
creations, both his characters' and his own. The same paradox is
at work here: the moments of transformation are clever technical
tricks, sleight of hand creating a world that never was; but they
are also a means of creating perfect forms, more 'real' in a
Platonic sense than the surface of reality. I have been stressing
the second part of the paradox, the use of transformations to
reveal truth and to help the spectators see more clearly. But
Jonson was also aware of the first part, the element of sheer
gimmickry. After all, the transformations were worked to a
large extent by mechanical rather than dramatic means, and –
while in a work like *The Masque of Queens* the mechanism is
fully in the service of the moral statement[3] – Jonson became
increasingly edgy about the importance of the mechanical side of
the masque. In 'An Expostulation with Inigo Jones' (*Ungathered
Verse*, XXXIV) he complains that the spectacle is commanding
attention for its own sake:

> And I haue mett with those
> That doe cry vp the Machine, and the Showes!
> The majesty of Iuno in the Cloudes,
> And peering forth of Irish in the Shrowdes!   (ll. 31–4)

He concludes bitterly, 'Painting and Carpentry are the Soule of
Masque' (l. 50). This is easy enough to say in a poem; but we
may wonder if Jonson (who did not shrink from challenges) was
ever tempted to make such a complaint in a masque. There
would be the difficulty of getting it past his collaborator; and
(for Jonson) the greater difficulty that it might damage whatever
serious statement he wanted the masque itself to make. In the
more lightweight masques, however, Jonson could acknowledge
the frivolity of the transformation effects. In *Neptune's Triumph*
the move from the antimasque to the main masque is announced
by the Poet's line, 'Well, now, expect the *Scene* it selfe; it opens!'

(l. 333), a line that seems to drain from the moment of revelation any significance it may have possessed. Later, the discovery of the Fleet seems to be variety for its own sake: "'Tis time, your eyes should be refresh'd at length, / With something new, a part of *Neptunes* strength' (ll. 508–9).

At such moments Jonson seems to greet the transformation itself with a shrug. But in his most entertaining masque, *The Gypsies Metamorphosed*, the trickery of the metamorphosis is made part of the fun. The Gypsies vanish suddenly, as if by miracle (ll. 900–3); but when the Patrico promises to show them to us again, transformed, the device seems simply one of his gypsy tricks, 'more of my skill' (l. 1256). Finally, the means of transformation are revealed:

> But least it proue like wonder to the sight,
> To see a *Gipsie* (as an *Aethiop*) white,
> Know, that what dide our faces was an oyntment
> Made and laid on by Mr. *woolfs* appointment,
> The Courtes *Lycanthropos:* yet without spelles,
> By a meere Barbor, and no magicke elles,
> It was fetcht of with water and a ball;
> And, to our transformation, this was all,
> Saue what the Master *Fashioner* calls his.
> For to a *Gypsies* metamorphosis
> (Who doth disguise his habit and his face,
> And takes on a false person by his place)
> The power of *poesie* can neuer faile her,
> Assisted by a *Barbor* and a *Taylor*.   (ll. 1479–92)

In the epilogues to some of his comedies, Shakespeare gracefully acknowledges that it was all a play. Jonson is more brutal with the illusion, giving us the backstage details, making sure there is no 'wonder' left. But this does not spoil the tone of the masque, for in this case the illusions were never very serious in the first place; the illusions of the artist and the trickery of the gypsies are easily yoked together, and there is no discomfort when they are joined by the skill of the make-up man. There may, however, be an extra kick in the last line, if we remember the tension between Jonson and Jones: for this transformation, the mechanical devices that aid the poet are supplied by unpretentious tradesmen.

Lightning transformations are acceptable within the conventions of the masque; but if one chooses to question the conventions, they become suspect at once. In *The Gypsies Metamorphosed* Jonson's scepticism is deliberately comic, and is simply part of the fun of the occasion. We will see later that in some of his plays Jonson uses masque-like transformations but allows the different conventions of drama to call their effectiveness into question. And in *Lovers Made Men*, Jonson for once uses a serious masque to depict a transformation that is not as simple as it looks. It is significant that in dramatizing this particular transformation, Jonson relies more on dialogue and less on stage machinery than is usual in the genre. Moreover, this masque is untypical in that it was not devised for the Court; this time there is no King to change the vision at a stroke. The title suggests that the masquers need to be rescued from love in order to recover their full humanity, and when Mercury leads the young men on at the beginning, he confirms this idea. He tells Lethe that they were 'tost upon those frantique seas, / Whence VENVS sprung' (ll. 43–4), where they were 'Drown'd by love' (l. 56). Like the characters examined in Chapter 2, who sank into the 'dead sea of life', they have lost their humanity and been dissolved into elements:

> Another sighing, *vapour forth his soule,*
>   A third, to *melt himselfe in teares,* and say,
>
> O Love, I now to salter water turne
>   Then that I die in; then, a fourth, to crie
> Amid the surges, *oh! I burne, I burne:*
> A fift, laugh out, *it is my ghost, not I.*   (ll. 64–9)

But the phrases in italics suggest that Jonson is mocking the conventions of love poetry; and the idea of dying for love is one of those conventions. The Fates then declare that the young men, despite what Mercury has said, are not dead at all. While Mercury objects, 'They say themselves, *they' are dead*' (l. 95), the mischievous paradox merely confirms what the Fates have said, and Mercury himself is finally persuaded: 'they onely thinke / That they are ghosts' (ll. 107–8).

Just as the state from which they need to be rescued is a

paradoxical state of living death, and finally an illusion, so the transformation itself contains a number of paradoxes. They are saved from water by water: drowned in the sea of love, they are made to drink the water of Lethe 'to forget / LOVES name' (ll. 113–14). When they do so, the transition is deliberately blurred:

> Here they all stoope to the water, and dance forth their Antimasque
> in severall gestures, as they liv'd in love: And retyring into the
> Grove, before the last person be off the Stage; the first couple appeare
> in their posture between the trees, readie to come forth, changed.
>
> (ll. 122–6)

The dance that shows their former bondage to love appears to take place *after* the cure, and the change in manner that signals the cure has taken effect moves through the party gradually, so that as some are ready to display their new state, others are still trapped in the old one. This is very different from the instantaneous transformations of other masques. The actual significance of the transformation, however, seems clear: 'now they'are substances, and men' (l. 130). Rescued from the dead sea, they are ready to resume full human identity and to warn the rest of the world 'how they prove / Shadowes for *Love*' (ll. 150–1). But after the dance that shows their recovered state, Cupid appears and offers quite a different interpretation:

> Why, now you take me! these are rites
> That grace *Loves* dayes, and crowne his nights!
> These are the motions, I would see,
> And praise, in them that follow mee!
> Not sighes, nor tears, nor wounded hearts,
> Nor flames, nor ghosts: but ayrie parts
> Try'd, and refin'd as yours have bin,
> And such they are, I glory in!   (ll. 156–63)

In being made true men, they have been made true lovers. They needed to be rescued not from love but from a false version of it; having been tried by this experience, they are now ready for love itself for the first time.

Mercury has presided over the transformation, and – like the Genius in the Theobalds entertainment – he is inclined to argue. He sees Cupid's reading as a temptation the young men must

resist (ll. 165–8). But Cupid retorts by offering a fuller re-
valuation of what we have seen:

> Come, doe not call it CVPIDS crime,
>   You were thought dead before your time.
> If thus you move to HERMES will
>   Alone; you will be thought so still.
> Goe, take the Ladies forth, and talke,
>   And touch, and taste too: Ghosts can walke.
> 'Twixt eyes, tongues, hands, the mutuall strife
>   Is bred, that tries the truth of life.
> They doe, indeed, like dead men move,
>   That thinke they live, and not in love!   (ll. 171–80)

The state of living death was in a sense imposed on the young
men by Mercury's interpretation, which Cupid mocks in the
ironic invitation to the dance, 'Ghosts can walke'. The true
living death is not to be in love at all, and they can still avoid
that. The men respond to Cupid's invitation by dancing with the
ladies, and it is for the sake of the ladies that Mercury agrees to a
compromise:

> FATE is content, these Lovers here
>   Remaine still such: so LOVE will sweare
> Never to force them act to doo,
> But what he will call HERMES too.   (ll. 208–11)

Cupid agrees, and in the final destiny of the young men,
announced in the last line, the interests of the two gods are fused:
'they still shall loue, and loue with wit' (l. 219). The title of
Lovers Made Men appears to promise a simple transformation;
but as one considers the implications of that title, an awkward
question arises: can a lover not be a man? The masque itself
raises the same question, and we might say that the transformation itself is transformed, as we are made to see its
paradoxical quality and to adjust our view of its significance. As
Jonson would likely have been the first to point out, none of this
could have been done by simply drawing a curtain or turning a
machine.

The masque might appear to present Jonson with his best
opportunity for showing a world in which the true forms of

things could be revealed. But its dependance on machinery was a source of irritation to him, and though he used the form more creatively than any other English writer he was not always happy with it. For a steady vision of the world's inner reality we have to look elsewhere. Jonson called the *Epigrams* 'the ripest of my studies' (Epistle to the Earl of Pembroke, l. 4). The description is at first glance surprising; the conventional view would be that the ripest of Jonson's studies are *Volpone* and *The Alchemist*. But in one sense the description is just, for the collection read as a whole creates (with occasional reservations and disturbances) an ideal moral universe in which the poet is fully in command, giving the virtuous and the wicked each their due, and above all calling things by their true names. Jonson evokes here a sense of the power of names that lies very deep in the human imagination, and that links these polished and sophisticated poems with magic and primitive ritual.[4] Epigram x, 'To My Lord Ignorant', reads in its entirety: 'Thou call'st me *Poet*, as a terme of shame: / But I haue my reuenge made, in thy name'. This is name-calling at its most basic level, a contest for power in which the one who finds the true name wins. Ignorant has misused the name of poet by turning it into a term of abuse; in doing so he has revealed his own true name, which Jonson seizes on, and with which he pins him like a butterfly, fixed forever in the poet's collection. He may, to the world, be Lord this or that, but to the discerning eye his true name is Ignorant. The same is true of the other specimens Jonson pins and labels: Sir Voluptuous Beast, Groome Idiot, Court-Parrat, Groyne, Gut. Whatever face they present to the world, their natures have been reduced by vice and their names reflect that reduction.

The virtuous, on the other hand, are not so reduced. Labels such as 'Charity' and 'Chastity' will not do for them, for they have full human identities that cannot be summarized by any one virtue. It is part of their merit that the names they present to the world are their true names, and are all the poet needs to identify them and evoke their virtues. Those names, revealing as they do family, position, and background, place the virtuous in a real world, as opposed to the fantasy world of vice.[5] Epigram cii, 'To William Earl of Pembroke' begins,

> I doe but name thee PEMBROKE, and I find
>> It is an *Epigramme*, on all man-kind;
> Against the bad, but of, and to the good. (ll. 1–3)

That summarizes neatly the power of a good man's name. But if the name itself *were* the Epigram the poem would not go on, as it does, for twenty lines. The significance of the name must be analysed and expounded: in this case the point is that Pembroke has a secure identity, as opposed to the majority of mankind, who are unreliable in the struggle between vice and virtue because they have no self-knowledge or integrity (ll. 7–10). Finally, as Pembroke's name reveals the man he is, so in turn the man shows the commonwealth everything it needs for its salvation: 'they, that hope to see / The common-wealth still safe, must studie thee' (ll. 19–20). The poem attributes no specific action to Pembroke; simply the virtue of being himself.

Epigram CIII, 'To Mary Lady Wroth', shows the power of a *family* name:

> Forgiue me then, if mine but say you are
>> A SYDNEY: but in that extend as farre
> As lowdest praisers, who perhaps would find
>> For euery part a character assign'd. (ll. 9–12)

We have seen that Jonson had no reverence for aristocracy as such; but he reverenced the Sidneys as a family of proven virtue, and to identify Lady Mary as one of them is sufficient praise. The third poem in the group, 'To Susan Countess of Montgomery', explores another (and perhaps narrower) way in which a name can be significant:

> Were they that nam'd you, prophets? Did they see,
>> Euen in the dew of grace, what you would bee?
> Or did our times require it, to behold
>> A new SVSANNA, equall to that old? (ll. 1–4)

A Christian name, no less than a family name, may carry with it the virtues of those who have previously borne it. We should note, however, that her godfathers were not creating her virtue but prophesying it. Her name did not make her virtuous; her virtue makes the name a true one.

The game of finding a person's true name is an ancient one,

and survives in folktales and riddles. We have seen Jonson play it with Lord Ignorant, and win. The game is played in some of the masques: the Ethiopes of *The Masque of Blackness* will be transformed if they can find a land whose name ends in TANIA, ruled by a greater sun than Sol (ll. 188–95). 'BRITANIA' and 'James' are the answers that save them. In *Love Freed from Ignorance and Folly* Love rescues himself from the bondage of the Sphinx by answering a similar riddle. In *The Gypsies Meta-morphosed*, the Captain of the Gypsies tells the fortune of a member of the audience; each attribute he sees makes the character clearer, and the speech comes to a climax when his true identity is discovered: 'But stay! in your *Iupiters Mount,* what's here! / A Kinge! a Monarch! what wonders appeare!' (ll. 295–6). The fortune-telling speech does in a jocular way what is done more solemnly at the endings of *News From the New World Discovered in the Moon* – '*Joyne then to tell his name,* / *And say but* JAMES *is he*' (ll. 374–5) – and *Love's Triumph Through Callipolis:*

> And who this King, and Queene would well historify,
> Need onely speake their names: Those them will glorify.
> MARY, *and* CHARLES, CHARLES, *with his* MARY, *named are,*
> And all the rest of Loues, or Princes famed are.　　　(ll. 218–21)

The ultimate revelation is that of the true identity of the monarch, whose name is itself sufficient cause for celebration.

Perhaps the most significant instance of finding a true name occurs in Epigram LXXVI, 'On Lucy Countess of Bedford'. Like the opening poem of Sidney's *Atrophel and Stella*, this describes a poet in trouble, rescued by his Muse:

> This morning, timely rapt with holy fire,
> 　I thought to forme vnto my zealous *Muse,*
> What kinde of creature I could most desire,
> 　To honor, serue, and loue; as *Poets* vse.
> I meant to make her faire, and free, and wise,
> 　Of greatest bloud, and yet more good then great;
> I meant the day-starre should not brighter rise,
> 　Nor lend like influence from his lucent seat.
> I meant shee should be curteous, facile, sweet,
> 　Hating that solemne vice of greatnesse, pride;
> I meant each softest vertue, there should meet,

Fit in that softer bosome to reside.
Onely a learned, and a manly soule
  I purpos'd her; that should, with euen powers,
The rock, the spindle, and the sheeres controule
  Of destinie, and spin her owne free houres.
Such when I meant to faine, and wish'd to see,
  My *Muse* bad, *Bedford* write, and that was shee.

(ll. 1–18)

The poet tries to construct a perfect woman, using a collection of abstract virtues and conventional poetic devices.[6] The location of this in the past suggests failure, and the description of the enterprise shows the reasons for that failure. The poet is not yielding to reality but trying to construct an abstraction from his own ideas: words like 'faine' and 'wish', coming towards the end of the poem, suggest a wistful artifice, a daydream. In the words 'as *Poets* use' there is a wry admission that he is following one of the routines of poetry. He is also, as the second line implies, trying to dictate to his Muse instead of submitting to inspiration. In the 'Epode', the unnamed perfect woman – 'What kinde of creature I could most desire' – was threatened by the impurity of the surrounding world, including the impurity of the lover's own feelings. But in this Epigram the abstract ideal is empty and the real world is not the place of imperfection but the place where true virtue is to be found. The opening words 'This morning' locate the action at a particular time, and thus undermine the abstraction. The final intervention of the Muse completes the poem by giving the poet a particular name from the real word, a name that is all he needs to express the ideas he has been struggling with. Jonson here reverses the normal view that the real world is imperfect and that perfection is to be found in the abstractions of the mind. Here, virtue is to be found not in abstraction but in concrete reality; and the poet's struggle to discover that, which ends when the Muse dictates a particular woman's name to him, gives the poem its tension.

    The names of the virtuous are revealed with a flourish, and the excitement with which Jonson loads such moments is matched by the satisfaction he takes elsewhere in revealing impostures and stripping away disguises. This is partly a matter, once again,

of finding the true names; this in turn means correcting the
slippery misuse of language through which (as we saw in Chapter
3) vice does its work: 'Then, *The townes honest Man*'s her
errant'st knaue' (*Epigrams*, CXV: 'On the Town's Honest Man',
l. 34). The reality masked by euphemism is exposed:

> Where lately harbour'd many a famous whore,
>   A purging bill, now fix'd vpon the dore,
> Tells you it is a hot-house: So it ma',
>   And still be a whore-house. Th'are *Synonima*.
>   (*Epigrams*, VII: 'On the New Hot-House', ll. 1–4)

In an interesting variation on his normal use of names in the
Epigrams, Jonson warns 'Person Guiltie': 'Beleeue it, GVILTIE,
if you loose your shame, / I'le loose my modestie, and tell your
name' (*Epigrams*, XXXVIII: 'To Person Guiltie', ll. 7–8). What
Jonson threatens to tell, I think, is not that Person Guiltie is
really Mr X, but that Mr X is really Person Guiltie. In the
masques and plays, the problem posed is often solved by
removing a disguise or exposing an imposture, as in *Hymenaei*,
where Opinion masquerades as Truth; or *Love Restored*, where
Plutus pretends to be Cupid. At the end of *Epicoene*, a number of
revelations are compressed into a single moment. When
Epicoene's peruke is removed, this one gesture reveals – with
the swiftness of a masque transformation – that the lady is a boy,
that Morose's marriage is a sham, that (despite the apparent
dominance of Truewit) Dauphine is the cleverest of the
tricksters, and that Daw and La-Foole, who claim they have
slept with Epicoene, are liars. There is dramatic excitement in a
moment like this; and a similar excitement is implied, I think, in
the Epigrams, in the game of finding the true name and
revealing the virtuous and vicious for what they are.

In the plays, the final moment of revelation can also be a
moment of judgement, exposing and fixing a character's true
nature. Often a figure who has seemed full of noise and energy is
revealed as empty at the core, and lapses into silence. Morose
leaves the stage without a word; Sir Politic Would-be is reduced
to politic silence inside his tortoise-shell.[7] Sejanus has no great
Last Speech in the manner of Marlowe or Webster. In the Senate

scene in which Tiberius' letter destroys him he seems flat and stunned; for over twenty-five lines before he is dragged off he has nothing to say. As his statue is melted down, his own body is torn apart, and as the events are described he and his statue seem interchangeable: 'The great SEIANVS crack, and piece, by piece, / Drop i' the founders pit' (v. 775–6). Of the man himself, once the mob is finished with him, 'there is not now so much remayning / As would giue fastning to the hang-mans hooke' (v. 840–1). Jonson is more daring with Catiline, who seems literally turned to stone:

> And as, in that rebellion 'gainst the gods,
> MINERVA holding forth MEDVSA's head,
> One of the gyant brethren felt himselfe
> Grow marble at the killing sight, and now,
> Almost made stone, began t'inquire, what flint,
> What rocke it was, that crept through all his limmes,
> And, ere he could thinke more, was that he fear'd;
> So CATILINE, at the sight of *Rome* in vs,
> Became his tombe: yet did his looke retayne
> Some of his fiercenesse, and his hands still mou'd,
> As if he labour'd, yet, to graspe the state,
> With those rebellious parts.   (v. 677–88)

The transformation is made more horrible by the fact that enough consciousness and movement remain, for a moment, to remind us that this was a man. The punishment is appropriate for one who tried to reverse creation, and spoke of digging his way back into the 'stony entrailes' (1. 93) of his mother's womb. In a sense he is revealed as the dead thing he always was; even his still twitching hands lose their names, becoming 'those rebellious parts'.

The hags of *The Masque of Queens* vanish as though they had never been; and in general the stylization of the masque allows figures of disorder to be reduced even more than Catiline is, and to disappear altogether: 'Die all, that can remaine of you, but stone, / And that be seene a while, and then be none' (*The Golden Age Restored*, ll. 75–6). The figures of the antimasque in *The Fortunate Isles* likewise vanish completely, and there is a further revelation about them:

MERE-FOOLE.

What! are they vanish'd! where is skipping *Skelton?*
Or morall Scogan? I doe like their shew
And would haue thankt 'hem, being the first grace
The Company of the *Rosie-Crosse* hath done me.

IOHPHIEL.

The company o' the *Rosie-crosse!* you wigion,
The company of *Players.*   (ll. 425–32)

The illusion is not gently surrendered – 'These our actors, / As I foretold you, were all spirits, and / Are melted into air, into thin air' – but brusquely smashed. The most comprehensive vanishing trick, however, is in the Cock-lorell song in *The Gypsies Metamorphosed*, in which the Devil consumes a huge banquet of comic type-figures – a Puritan, a Promoter, a usurer, and so on:

Then from the Table he gaue a start,
   Where banquett and wine were nothing scarce,
All which he flirted away with a fart,
   From whence it was calld the *Devills arse*.   (ll. 1122–25)

To produce these moments of judgement and transformation, Jonson sometimes evokes the figure of the ideal judge, who can spy out the truth, fix men's true names, and devise appropriate rewards and punishments. In the masques King James is credited with an all-seeing eye and the ability to transform. In the *Panegyre* written for the opening of his first parliament, we are told:

these his searching beams are cast, to prie
Into those darke and deepe concealed vaults,
Where men commit blacke incest with their faults.

(ll. 8–10)

To this all-seeing eye is wedded the ability to do justice with God-like speed and simplicity: 'we haue now no cause / Left vs of feare, but first our crimes, then lawes' (*Epigrams*, xxxv: 'To King James', ll. 5–6).

By implication, and sometimes directly, Jonson himself plays the same role in the Epigrams. If the Epigrams, read as a group, add up to a coherent world – and I think they do – this is because

of what Bruce R. Smith calls 'the assured and fixed perspective
of the observing persona . . . a self-assured legislator and
judge.'[8] The world may be fooled by Lady Would-be, but
Jonson is not:

> Fine MADAME WOVLD-BEE, wherefore should you feare,
>   That loue to make so well, a child to beare?
> The world reputes you barren: but I know
>   Your 'pothecarie, and his drug sayes no.
>
>   · · ·
>
> What should the cause be? Oh, you liue at court:
>   And there's both losse of time, and losse of sport
> In a great belly. Write, then on thy wombe,
>   Of the not borne, yet buried, here's the tombe.
>   (*Epigrams*, LXII: 'To Fine Lady Would-be', ll. 1–4, 9–12)

If he can detect and name the unworthy, he can also celebrate the
worthy as they deserve. Not content with simply praising the
great, the Epigrams call attention to the act of praising. The
country has not given William Lord Mounteagle his due for
helping uncover the Gunpowder Plot; but Jonson has:

> Loe, what my countrey should haue done (haue rais'd
>   An obeliske, or columne to thy name,
> Or, if shee would but modestly haue prais'd
>   Thy fact, in brasse or marble writ the same)
> I, that am glad of thy great chance, here doo!
>   (*Epigrams*, LX: 'To William Lord Mounteagle', ll. 1–5)

In the ideal world of the Epigrams, true justice is done.

The plays present larger and more complex invented worlds,
and accordingly their judgement scenes are more variable in
effect. A multitude of characters engaged in a developing action
cannot always be disposed of as simply as a single figure in a
short poem. Sometimes Jonson invests his judgement scenes
with the same light, playful quality we have seen in the ideal
social occasions of 'To Penshurst' and 'Inviting a Friend to
Supper'. There are a number of reasons for this. The follies of a
comedy cannot bear a really solemn judgement without damaging the play's tone (a problem we have already examined in
Chapter 3); and in a play that purports to be a mirror of life as it
is, the intrusion of a vision of life as it ought to be (a firm ending

in which the characters are satisfactorily disposed of) ought not
to be insisted on too heavily.

One such play is *Every Man in his Humour*, whose prologue
declares an intention to 'shew an Image of the times, / And sport
with humane follies, not with crimes' (ll. 23–4). Sporting with
folly is a precise description of the actions of Justice Clement, in
whose hands the play's final judgement scene rests. His manner
is eccentric; but there is logic in what he does. Hearing Bobadill
is a soldier, Clement arms to meet him, soldier to soldier;
finding he is really a coward, Clement disarms again. He
pretends that this is to avoid frightening Bobadill; but the
gesture also presents a mocking mirror image in which the
pretences of the false soldier are stripped away. Hearing that
Matthew is a poet, Clement responds in a similar fashion,
meeting doggerel with doggerel:

> A *poet?* I will challenge him my selfe, presently, at *extempore.*
> *Mount vp thy Phlegon muse, and testifie,*
> > *How* SATVRNE, *sitting in an ebon cloud,*
> *Disrob'd his podex   white as iuorie,*
> > *And, through the welkin, thundred all aloud.*   (V.V.9–14)

This also suggests a parody of the last trumpet; and what follows
is a mocking judgement scene in which the little world of
Matthew's poetry – 'a whole realme, a common-wealth of
paper' (V.V.21) – is consumed by fire. Passing sentence,
Clement suggests – in characteristic Jonson fashion – that the
burning of bad poetry is necessary for the health of the whole
community:

> Bring me a torch; lay it together, and giue fire. Clense the aire.
> Here was enough to haue infected, the whole citie, if it had not
> beene taken in time! See, see, how our *Poets* glorie shines!
> brighter, and brighter! still it increases! ô, now, it's at the
> highest: and, now, it declines as fast. You may see. *Sic transit*
> *gloria mundi.*   (V.V.28–34)

The poems vanish as quickly as the world of an antimasque; and
through it all Matthew stands silent. His own nothingness, like
the nothingness of his creations, has been exposed. But the tone
remains comic, and the inflation of scale is largely mocking.

When Jonson revised the conclusion for the Folio he allowed Clement to preside over the ending in a more purposeful and comprehensive way than in the Quarto version. He also provided a simpler punishment for Matthew and Bobadill. In the Quarto, they suffer public exposure and ridicule, their appearances transformed to reveal them for the fools they are:

> first you signior shall this night to the cage, and so shall you sir, from thence to morrow morning, you signior shall be carried to the market crosse, and be there bound: and so shall you sir, in a large motlie coate, with a rodde at your girdle; and you in an old suite of sackcloth, and the ashes of your papers (saue the ashes sirha) shall mourne all day, and at night both together sing some ballad of repentance very pitteously, which you shall make to the tune of *Who list to leade and a souldiers life.*   (v. v. 356–65)

The tune is carefully picked; so are the emblems of their folly.[9] It is a mocking punishment, not a solemn one; but even so it must have seemed too heavy for Jonson, as he replaced it in the Folio with:

> But, to dispatch away these, you signe o'the Souldier, and picture o'the *Poet* (but, both so false, I will not ha' you hang'd out at my dore till midnight) while we are at supper, you two shall penitently fast it out in my court, without; and, if you will, you may pray there, that we may be so merrie within, as to forgiue, or forget you, when we come out.   (v. v. 48–54)

The tone is lighter – they are left out of the party – but the judgement in fact cuts deeper. They are empty men, mere signs and pictures; there is not enough in them to be worth punishing. Instead of suffering the elaborate and purposeful exposure of the Quarto version, they are dismissed, either to forgiveness or oblivion – Clement does not seem to care which.

The judgement that ends *Cynthia's Revels* may seem sharper in tone: Jonas A. Barish has called this 'Jonson's most punitive, least festive play'.[10] Certainly the judgement scene is the most decisive and systematic in Jonson's drama; but the masque-devices that allow it to be so may also give the occasion a touch of revelry. The fools are dressed as ideal court virtues – Natural Affection, Delectable and Pleasant Conversation, Well Con-

ceited Wittiness, Simplicity – in other words, as the opposite of
their true selves. In these disguises they are allowed to dance
before Cynthia; but when at her command they unmask, she
sees their true natures at once, and imposture melts. She then
removes her veil 'that shadowes may depart, / And shapes
appeare' (v. xi. 71–2), and sees through the remaining disguises
of the play, such as those of Cupid and Mercury. Having seen
true images, she proceeds to judgement: 'we must lance these
sores, / Or all will putrifie' (v. xi. 68–9).

The seriousness of that last remark is typical of the risk Jonson
takes throughout the play, passing solemn judgements on trivial
vices. Yet in the punishments themselves, the tone suddenly
lightens.[11] Cynthia turns the matter over to Arete and Crites:

> impose what paines you please:
> Th'incurable cut off, the rest reforme,
> Remembring euer what we first decreed,
> Since reuells were proclaim'd let now none bleed.
>
> (v. xi. 96–9)

Crites sentences them to undergo a masque-like transformation:
they are to go

> to the well of knowledge, *Helicon;*
> Where purged of your present maladies,
> (Which are not few, nor slender) you become
> Such as you faine would seeme.   (v. xi. 153–6)

In other words, they are to undergo a true form of the transformation they have merely pretended, becoming figures in an
ideal Platonic reality. The play throughout has combined satiric
observation with Lylyesque artifice, and of the two manners the
punishment obviously belongs to the second. This may not
blunt the point of the judgement, but it does lighten the tone.
Crites himself summarizes the effect at the end of the speech in
which he passes sentence: 'The scope of wise mirth vnto fruict is
bent' (v. xi. 160). The mirth is 'wise', and purposeful, but it is
still mirth. Jonson was enough of a moralist in this play to want
a reformation of folly; but he was enough of a dramatist to know
that a serious psychological transformation of the court butter-
flies would not work. And so he took the route of playful

artifice, starting with Cynthia's reminder that 'reuells were proclaim'd', and concluding with the 'Palinode' in which the fops sing their repentance in a parody of the Litany:

AMO *From* spanish *shrugs,* french *faces, smirks, irps, and all affected humours:*
CHORVS Good MERCVRY defend vs.
PHA *From secret friends, sweet seruants, loues, doues, and such phantastique humours.*
CHORVS Good MERCVRY defend vs. (Palinode, ll. 1–6)

At the end of this frequently oversolemn play, Jonson manages a judgement scene that is part ritual, part game. In the stripping away of pretence and the identification of the true faces beneath the masks, it has the clarity of the masques and Epigrams. It has also some of their occasional sportiveness: in the Palinode the vices of the court are identified and dismissed in a playful manner that suits their triviality, and that gives the play (not before time) a lively ending.

II

There may be in the artifice of *Cynthia's Revels* a rueful admission that true judgement is not so easily performed in reality. The more fantastic a judgement scene is the more it concedes (tacitly, to be sure) that it's an unjust world and virtue is triumphant only in theatrical performances. Just as virtue's exemplars in Jonson's drama are often flawed, so judgements and the figures who carry them out are often imperfect – or simply wrong. In Epigram LXV, 'To My Muse', even the ideal judge of that special world acknowledges he has slipped: his muse has 'betray'd me to a worthlesse lord' (l. 2). (It may be no accident that this epigram appears after two poems in praise of Robert Earl of Salisbury, of whose meanness Jonson complained to Drummond of Hawthornden.)[12] There is also some jocular questioning of the judgement of the gods. By a curious irony Jonson himself suffered the same treatment from the god of fire that Matthew suffers at the hands of Justice Clement: his papers were burnt. 'An Execration upon Vulcan' (*The Underwood,*

XLIII) complains of the speed and the injustice of the judgement:

> And why to me this, thou lame Lord of fire,
>   What had I done that might call on thine ire?
> Or urge thy Greedie flame, thus to devoure
>   So many my Yeares-labours in an houre?   (ll. 1–4)

The speed of the destruction seems to quicken later in the poem – 'ravish'd all hence in a minutes rage' (l. 56); the disaster is given greater resonance by being compared with the fate of the Globe: 'raz'd, e're thought could urge, This might have bin! / See the worlds ruines!' (ll. 136–7). Jonson ruefully admits that his papers may have included 'parcels of a Play, / Fitter to see the fire-light, then the day' (ll. 43–4); even so, he complains that Vulcan should have had the decency to wait for public opinion to pass sentence on them. And in the poem as a whole he complains that the punishment has been visited, not on a library that would have deserved it, full of libels or trashy romances, but on one full of solid literature undeserving of the flame. In this, one of his most engaging poems, Jonson turns a grave personal misfortune into a rueful joke: and part of the joke's subtlety is that in its speed and comprehensiveness, and in particular its destruction of an author's papers, Vulcan's action is like a parody of one of Jonson's own judgement scenes.

A sadder joke is the fate of Solomon Pavy, recorded in Epigram CXX, 'Epitaph on S.P., a Child of Queen Elizabeth's Chapel', who

> did act (what now we mone)
>   Old men so duely,
> As, sooth, the *Parcae* thought him one,
>   He plai'd so truely.
> So, by error, to his fate
>   They all consented;
> But viewing him since (alas, too late)
>   They haue repented.   (ll. 13–20)

The balancing of pathos and irony is surprisingly delicate; and once again an important part of the irony is that the mistake of the Fates is a parody of one of Jonson's judgement scenes. They think they have seen Solomon Pavy's true form, and act accordingly; in fact he is disguised, and they have failed (unlike the true judge – Cynthia, for example) to penetrate the disguise. Perhaps the fanciful absurdity of the explanation is a way of registering a deeper absurdity – there seems no good reason why a boy like this should die. But the end of the poem suggests a consolation. It may be the Fates were not so wrong after all: 'But, being so much too good for earth, / Heauen vowes to keepe him' (ll. 23–4). The issue is no longer his talent but his virtue; and there is a slight shift from classical to Christian language. This brings a light but perceptible suggestion that the final judgement on the young actor is made by a divine power higher than the Fates.

In these two poems the idea of divine misjudgement is partly a joke. But it is a joke with serious implications, and Jonson's jokes are often signals of his most fundamental concerns. The idea of misjudgement – even the misjudgement of Heaven itself – is the subject of Jonson's most sombre poem. 'To Heaven' (*The Forest*, xv):

> Good, and great GOD, can I not thinke of thee,
>   But it must, straight, my melancholy bee?
> Is it interpreted in me disease,
>   That, laden with my sinnes, I seeke for ease?
> O, be thou witnesse, that the reynes dost know,
>   And hearts of all, if I be sad for show,
> And iudge me after: if I dare pretend
>   To ought but grace, or ayme at other end.
> As thou art all, so be thou all to mee,
>   First, midst, and last, conuerted one, and three;
> My faith, my hope, my loue: and in this state,
> My iudge, my witnesse, and my aduocate.
> Where haue I beene this while exil'd from thee?
>   And whither rap'd, now thou but stoup'st to mee?
> Dwell, dwell here still: O, being euery-where,
>   How can I doubt to finde thee euer, here?
> I know my state, both full of shame, and scorne,
>   Conceiu'd in sinne, and vnto labour borne,
> Standing with feare, and must with horror fall,
>   And destin'd vnto iudgement, after all.
> I feele my griefes too, and there scarce is ground,
>   Vpon my flesh to'inflict another wound.

Yet dare I not complaine, or wish for death
  With holy PAVL, lest it be thought the breath
Of discontent; or that these prayers bee
  For wearinesse of life, not loue of thee.   (ll. 1–26)

The opening suggests an appeal from men's false judgements
to the true judgement of God. Jonson's acquaintances have mis-
interpreted his religious zeal, but God, who knows all, will judge
him truly. That is our first impression; but is it in fact his fellow
men who accuse him of mere melancholy at the beginning and
end of the poem? Whose misjudgement does Jonson feel so
deeply that he 'dare' not complain? Normally, he defends
himself without hesitation against any attack. As William
Kerrigan has suggested, the poem opens up the terrible possibility that the injustice is God's.[13] Jonson has obviously been
through a period of spiritual exile; he has been whipped until
further punishment seems impossible, and the full horror of the
last judgement is still to come. He is – or claims to be – sincerely
asking for God's grace, yet God continues to strike him. To
accuse God of injustice is of course to commit a fundamental
absurdity; but the poem explores with terrible honesty the state
of mind in which such an absurdity is possible. At the same
time, Jonson invites God to be what He truly should be, 'My
iudge, my witnesse, and my aduocate'. In his account of his
sufferings, complaint struggles with a genuine desire to submit:
'destin'd vnto iudgement, after all' conveys both resentment at a
seemingly excessive punishment and resignation to it. If Jonson
is accusing God, then it is he himself who is guilty of misjudgement, and the poem admits that too, by its tone: 'The querulous
despair . . . reveals both Jonson's conception of himself (unjustly
accused) and God's conception of Jonson (unjustly accusing).'[14]
Thus, the spiritual exile – 'Where haue I beene this while exil'd
from thee?' – can be seen as self-inflicted; the suffering of the
second part of the poem, as a just punishment for a deep spiritual
crime. The ironic phrasing, 'But it must, straight, my melancholy bee' leaves open the possibility that he *is* melancholy, that
the accusation is just.

Jonson was always complaining of being misjudged by the
world, and at first glance the opening and closing sections of the

poem may suggest only that. But the idea of misjudgement becomes, I think, more profound. The ultimate judge of the world is God; the ultimate judge of the artistic world that Jonson creates is Jonson; and in this poem the two judges confront each other. If this were a poem by Herbert, God's judgement would prevail, clearly, within the poem itself – as in 'The Collar', where God's intervention at the end forces the rest of the poem to admit its own folly. But this is not a poem by Herbert; its folly, if it can be called that, is made of more stubborn metal. The confrontation of God's judgement with Jonson's remains unresolved; partly because (unlike Herbert) Jonson does not clearly admit that he is accusing God unfairly. To do so would bring a collapse of his right to judge; and in the poem there is a firm, tense balance between self-accusation and self-justification. Herbert is always willing to surrender his right to judge; Jonson, in refusing to do so, paradoxically allows the whole business of judgement to be called into question, with an irony that reflects impartially on himself and on his Maker.

The dramatic possibilities of a judgement that does not quite work are explored in a number of Jonson's plays, the most obvious instance being *Bartholomew Fair*. Justice Overdo aspires to be the ideal Jonson judge, discerning the truth through imposture and passing sentence with god-like power (v. ii. 3–6). What actually happens is rather different. When Overdo removes his disguise and starts to denounce the enormities of the Fair, the result is not a repetition but a parody of the moment when Cynthia unveils and sees through the disguises of the others. He has barely warmed to his task when '*Mistresse Ouerdoo is sicke: and her husband is silenc'd*' (v. vi. 67). The true identity of one of the whores in the gathering he is about to denounce is revealed not by Overdo's act but by her own queasy stomach; and the revelation shows how far Overdo is from being able to control the world around him. Like Morose and other characters he is reduced to silence. But this effect is temporary: he is then judged by Quarlous as he had expected to judge others, and made to confront his own true nature, as revealed by his name: 'remember you are but *Adam*, Flesh, and blood!' He is further enjoined to reform, by dispensing with that part of his name that suggests his claim to be better than other men: 'you haue your frailty, forget your other name of *Ouerdoo*, and inuite vs all to supper' (v. vi. 96–8). The judge himself becomes subject to judgement, and to transformation.

The revelation of characters' true natures that Overdo intended to accomplish is in fact accomplished in several devious ways by the Fair itself: characters who enter it stand revealed for what they are. Overdo's disguise as a ranting fool reveals more than he intends about his own nature, as does Mistress Overdo's labelling him an enormity (III. v. 205–7). As we have seen, the relatively intelligent characters Grace, Winwife and Quarlous have their own basic, practical desires revealed by the matches they make. The ease with which Win Littlewit and Mistress Overdo slip into the roles of prostitutes suggests a similar revelation about them. Waspe, like Overdo a pretender to authority, finds his true level as a brawler and loses his authority in the stocks. Like Overdo, he collapses at once when the truth comes out. But the most elaborate case is that of Zeal-of-the-Land Busy. The animal greed beneath the Puritan dress is obvious enough from the beginning, and Jonson hardly needs to bring Busy to the Fair to make the point. But he has a more fundamental revelation to make, and it comes when Busy attacks the puppet Dionysus. Having revealed its own sexlessness – and therefore its lack of real humanity – by hoisting up its garment, the puppet goes on to point out its affinities with Busy himself:

> PVP Nay, I'le proue, against ere a Rabbin of 'hem all, that my stand-
> ing is as lawfull as his; that I speak by inspiration, as well as he;
> that I haue as little to doe with learning as he; and doe scorne her
> helps as much as he.
>
> BVS I am confuted, the *Cause* hath failed me.
> PVP Then be conuerted, be conuerted.
> LAN Be conuerted, I pray you, and let the Play goe on!
> BVS Let it goe on. For I am changed, and will become a beholder
> with you!   (v. v. 109–17)

As Quarlous has already remarked, 'I know no fitter match, then a *Puppet* to commit with an Hypocrite!' (v. v. 50–1).

(Eugene M. Waith has reminded us that 'hypocrite' originally meant 'actor'.)[15] Claiming the right to judge, Busy finds the figure he is denouncing is a mocking image of himself; like Bobadill and Matthew when Clement parodied them, he is looking into a mirror. As speedily as Waspe or Overdo, he is silenced and transformed.

The ending of *Bartholomew Fair* parodies a conventional Jonson judgement scene: the figures who claim authority are judged themselves, and their true natures are revealed. Elsewhere Jonson presents conventional judgement scenes that go more or less the way the judges intended; but he leaves a residue of unfinished business that complicates the main effect, and forces us – as in *Lovers Made Men* – to think more fully about what we have seen. Caesar's raid on the banquet of the gods in *Poetaster* is a case in point. It is dramatically sudden, like the breaking forth of light in a masque. It exposes imposture: confronted with a true authority figure, the false gods suddenly look very foolish, and their disguises are stripped away by Caesar's sharp question, 'I aske not, what you play? but, what you are?' (IV. vi. 26) – a question that resonates through all the judgement scenes in Jonson's work. Yet the harshness of Caesar's attack, as we have seen, raises disturbing questions. Horace later rebukes the informer Lupus for exaggerating the danger of the banquet, and Maecenas pleads with Caesar, 'O, good my lord; forgiue: be like the Gods' (IV. vi. 60). He has been a human ruler rebuking false gods; but he can, Maecenas suggests, do better than that, by showing godlike virtue himself. Later, Caesar's wrath cools and he forgives some of the participants because of their past records. While the actual moment of Caesar's intervention has a masque-like clarity and sharpness, the affair of the banquet demands a more complex and balanced judgement, and in the later scenes, stage by stage, Jonson provides it. On the whole the machinery of judgement operates more confidently in the game-like trial of the poetasters at the end of the play; in a manner recalling *Cynthia's Revels* the culprits are exposed, mocked and comically 'cured'. But here too the effect is slightly blurred, by Tucca's enthusiastic participation as one of the judges. It leads to his own exposure as a two-faced knave; but it goes on just long enough to break our concentration on the image of perfect judgement.

The Staple of News, the most masque-like of the late plays, contains a similar judgement with reservations. Pennyboy Junior undergoes a transformation at the beginning of the play: as the clock signals his coming of age, he discards his gown of wardship and is dressed in the rich clothes of an heir. But the transformation is bogus, for his father Pennyboy Canter is still alive, spying on him in disguise to see how he will use the money. He squanders it, surrounding himself with parasites. At the climax of Act IV, Pennyboy Canter strips off his disguise, denounces his son, and declares the parasites – soldier, courtier, herald and the rest – to be false exponents of professions that in their true forms have real dignity: 'If thou had'st sought out good, and vertuous persons / Of these professions: I'had lou'd thee, and them' (IV.iv.135–6). As in a masque a true vision supplants a false one, so Pennyboy Canter's lecture evokes an ideal social world in which these professions are honourably followed, as opposed to the parody of true society with which Pennyboy Junior has surrounded himself. The prodigal is then uncased, and given his father's disguise, a ragged beggar's cloak, to wear. His retinue, stylized and caricatured, were like the figures of an antimasque; and they vanish just as completely.[16] The Staple of News itself vanishes, with the suddenness of a transformation scene:

> Our *Emissaries, Register, Examiner,*
> Flew into vapor: our graue *Gouernour*
> Into a subt'ler ayre; and is return'd
> (As we doe heare) grand-*Captaine* of the *Ieerers.*
> I, and my fellow melted into butter,
> And spoyl'd our Inke, and so the *Office* vanish'd.
> The last *hum* that it made, was, that your Father,
> And *Picklocke* are fall'n out, the *man o' Law.*   (v.i.45–52)

The Staple disappears like the dream it always was, and it seems to take its employees with it.

But one of them is telling the tale; he reports that Cymbal, having vanished, has reappeared in a new role, and the last piece of news the Staple gives out before it expires introduces the extra

complication of the fifth act. Pennyboy Canter was not an
all-seeing judge after all; he trusted Picklock and Pennyboy
Junior has to rescue him. We may have thought the prodigal's
true emptiness was revealed when he was dressed in rags; but the
words with which his father restores him suggest that that too
was only a disguise: 'Put off your ragges, and be your selfe
againe' (v. iii. 22). Pennyboy Junior's final transformation into a
sensible young man, wordly-wise and loyal to his father, seems
to be the ultimate truth about him; the apparently decisive
judgement of the fourth act was only one step towards it.

The Argument prefixed to *The Alchemist* summarizes the
play's ending with the words '*all in* fume *are gone*' (l. 12). This
sounds like the vanishing of the Staple or the dispersal of an
antimasque. There is a small explosion in the opening line – 'I
fart at thee' (I. i. 1) – anticipating a much larger one in Act IV
when the alchemist's apparatus blows up. Ostensibly this is a
judgement on Mammon, whose attempt to seduce Dol
Common (disguised as a mad gentlewoman) has revealed him to
be unworthy of the Stone. But the exploding furnace is also 'an
objectification of what happens to the plot'[17] as the intrigue is
wound up and the little world of the cheaters vanishes. The play
is much concerned with language; as a prelude to the explosion
language starts to overheat as Dol enters '*In her fit of talking*'
(IV. v. 1) and her babble cuts across the frantic dialogue of Face
and Mammon. Then there is '*A great crack and noise within*'
followed by Face's announcement:

> O sir, we are defeated! all the *workes*
> Are flowne *in fumo:* euery glasse is burst.
> Fornace, and all rent downe! as if a bolt
> Of thunder had beene driuen through the house.
>
> (IV. v. 57–60)

The alchemists themselves seem destroyed with their machine.
Subtle falls in a dead faint, and Face declares, 'My braine is quite
vn-done with the fume, sir, / I ne'er must hope to be mine owne
man againe' (IV. v. 69–70). The image of the thunderbolt
suggests divine judgement, as does Mammon's cry, 'O my
voluptuous mind! I am iustly punish'd' (IV. v. 74).

But this judgement-and-transformation scene is not what it

appears; it is engineered by the cheaters themselves as part of their duping of Mammon. And while it suggests an ending of the fake world of the alchemists, there is in fact a good deal of tidying up to do. When in Act V the dupes return to the house to claim their property, Lovewit and Jeremy the butler are in possession and it is as though everything that went before had no reality at all – until the voice of Dapper is heard crying from the privy, 'For gods sake, when wil her *Grace* be at leisure?' (v. iii. 65). There is one dupe left over; and Face-Jeremy, who has been trying to convince Lovewit that nothing has happened in the house, is forced to confess the truth. But what follows is not an ordinary stripping away of imposture. Two false Spanish Counts have been competing for the hand of Dame Pliant – Surly in fact, Drugger in anticipation – and Lovewit becomes the third, replacing imposture not with truth but with more effective imposture. Face, reduced to Jeremy, is working for his master rather than his confederates, but he is still playing the old game. Jeremy would appear to be his 'real' name; but the speech headings continue to call him Face, and that is how we still think of him. His alias is in a deeper sense his true name. Subtle and Dol are discomfited, but they have more resilience than the victims of other Jonson judgement scenes. Unlike Morose, Busy, or for that matter Sejanus, they go out fighting:

> DOL   Poxe vpon you, rogue,
> Would I had but time to beat thee.
> FAC   SVBTLE,
> Let's know where you set vp next; I'll send you
> A customer, now and then, for old acquaintance:
> What course ha' you?
> SVB   Rogue, I'll hang my selfe:
> That I may walke a greater diuell, then thou,
> And haunt thee i' the flock-bed, and the buttery.
>
>   (v. iv. 142–8)

Even Face's ironic dismissal suggests that somewhere in London the old confidence game will go on – as his epilogue, with its promise 'To feast you often, and inuite new ghests' (v. v. 165) suggests that it will go on in the theatre itself. The explosion seemed to bring the game to an end; in fact it merely starts it on a new phase.

It is also, I should reiterate, produced by the cheaters themselves. Just as in *Bartholomew Fair* the judge himself is judged, so in *The Alchemist* the culprits take over the machinery of judgement. And the chief culprit of *Volpone* does the same, in grand style. The Epistle to the two Universities, Jonson's preface to the play, appears to endorse the punishments meted out by the court, '*my speciall ayme being to put the snaffle in their mouths, that crie out, we neuer punish vice in our* enterludes' (ll. 115–16). Up to a point the punishments are appropriate: Voltore, who has disgraced his profession, is 'banish'd from their fellowship, and our state' (v. xii. 128); Corbaccio, who has tried to deny his age, will be 'learn'd to die well' (v. xii. 133); and Corvino, who has disgraced the marriage bond, will be publicly shamed and must send Celia 'Home, to her father, with her dowrie trebled' (v. xii. 144). Mosca, who has pretended to social rank (a pretence the Avocatori happily endorsed when they thought he had money) will be put in his place as a galley-slave; and Volpone will be forced to repeat his performance forever 'crampt with irons, / Till thou bee'st sicke, and lame indeed' (v. xii. 123–4). Yet the effect of all this is not quite so decisive as it may at first appear. The three dupes are not treated quite consistently – Voltore is to be banished, Corbaccio reformed, Corvino disgraced – and there seem to be no compelling reasons for the differences in treatment. The punishment on Mosca for his imposture is bound to make us think of the ease with which the court accepted that imposture – 'A proper man! and were VOLPONE dead, / A fit match for my daughter' (v. xii. 50–1). The punishment of Volpone seems the soundest and most logical of the judgements; yet it is the one that meets the greatest resistance from our imaginations, for while the other prisoners merely grumble, Volpone sets up a powerful counter-judgement of his own.

The court, all along, has been singularly gullible, unable to identify truly the figures before it. Volpone is 'the old gentleman' (iv. vi. 56), Celia and Bonario (whose names reveal their true natures) are 'two such prodigies' (iv. vi. 55), and the judges cannot bear to think of Mosca as being what his name proclaims him to be: he is 'Him, that they call the parasite' (v. x. 38). In this cloud of confusion, Volpone acts as a true judge, revealing his own identity and confidently pinning labels on the other characters:

> I am VOLPONE, and this is my knaue;
> This, his owne knaue; this, auarices foole;
> This, a *Chimaera* of wittall, foole, and knaue.

> (v. xii. 89–91)

His egotism is apparent here: he is the only figure with a proper name; the others are labelled as types. But the labels are largely just, and we may feel that Volpone, as the character with the greatest vitality, is entitled to a name of his own. The revelation has the suddenness of a transformation scene, and strips away all the deceptions at a single blow: 'The knot is now vndone, by miracle!' (v. xii. 95). It also gives Volpone an authority that is carried over into the Epilogue, when he appeals to us to judge him not for his crimes but for the pleasure he has given. In the masques and Epigrams, transformations could be decisive in their moral significance, and judgements could be confidently administered. But in the plays Jonson views such effects with greater scepticism. There is unfinished business to tidy up; there are reservations about the judgements themselves; and in some cases the authority of the judge himself is challenged. In this respect *Bartholomew Fair* and *Volpone* represent complementary extremes: in one, the judge is in the dock; in the other, the criminal is on the bench.

Every Man out of his Humour, the first of Jonson's 'comicall satyres', is also his most elaborate experiment with the linked devices of judgement and transformation. The leading character of the play proper is the envious railer Macilente, who judges the other characters by his sardonic commentary on them, and who assists at most of the transformations by which the others are taken out of their humours. But Macilente is not the one true man in a false world. For one thing, the Induction identifies him as a role played by the satirist Asper. Asper in turn is identified as the 'author' of the play; but this does not mean that Macilente is simply the author's spokesman. Jonson prefaces the play with character sketches of the cast, beginning with Asper and Macilente, whom he treats not just as separate figures but as opposed and complementary ones. Asper has a proper, judicial detachment from the world – nothing to fear, and no axes to grind – while Macilente, driven by envy, is too much a creature of the world, emotionally dependent on it (ll. 1–13). Alvin Kernan has suggested a Jeckyll-and-Hyde relationship between them, in which Macilente 'has every twisted impulse, every dark and unpleasant characteristic of the satirist' while Asper 'has all of the virtues of the satirist with none of his defects'.[18] But if we think this makes Macilente the dark shadow of the perfect man who is Asper, we have to consider the dramatic effect of the Induction. Asper is not given full authority here, but is set in debate with Cordatus, who is described as '*The Authors friend; A man inly acquainted with the scope and drift of his Plot: Of a discreet, and vnderstanding iudgement; and has the place of a Moderator*' (ll. 111–13). The 'author' whose friend Cordatus is may be Asper; but at this point Asper has not yet been identified as the author of the play, and it is more natural to assume that Cordatus is presented as Jonson's friend. Not, we should note, Jonson himself or even his spokesman; rather, his friend, who understands the play and can act as a moderator. He has a special and important role; but he too is not given final authority. Passages from the Induction taken out of context suggest that Jonson is lecturing his audience; but the effect of the Induction as a whole is of a conversation among dramatic characters, with the author himself standing back.

At its opening we find Asper – with a violence quite contrary to the cool detachment suggested in his 'character' – denouncing the world, and Cordatus and Mitis trying to restrain him. They fear his anger will simply be dissipated in useless frenzy (Induction, 45–50). Unfocussed emotion will not do as the starting point for a work of art: Asper has to discipline his mind. And the disciplinary exercise he sets himself, encouraged by his friends, is characteristic of Jonson – the close definition of a word, in this case the key word of the play's title. 'Humour' is not a matter of trivial eccentricity, but

> when some one peculiar quality
> Doth so possesse a man, that it doth draw
> All his affects, his spirits, and his powers,
> In their confluctions, all to runne one way,
> This may be truly said to be a Humour.

> (Induction, ll. 105–9)

This definition helps introduce Asper's play, in which the fools exemplify ruling passions of this kind, and the generalized, overblown attack on the corruption of the world is replaced by a precise, concrete depiction of particular follies. The clear definition of a word leads to a clear definition of the characters whom the word describes. Part of the business of the Induction is to get Asper away from mere railing into the identification of particular offences that stamps the true judge in Jonson's work.

Within the play, a large cast of characters display their humours, commented on by their fellow characters, and by Cordatus and Mitis from the sidelines, so that their natures are established as clearly as possible. Then, one by one, they are brought out of their humours, as the play's title promises. Jonson rings the changes on the themes of punishment, self-discovery and transformation. The first to be dishumoured is the grasping farmer Sordido. Like his counterpart who is welcomed to Hell by Macbeth's porter, he hangs himself on the expectation of plenty; a rustic cuts him down, but repents his action when he realizes whom he has rescued; and his fellow rustics curse him for saving 'so damn'd a monster' (III. viii. 35–6). Sordido is shocked into repentance, and goes off with the sententious conclusion, 'No life is blest, that is not grac't with loue' (III. viii. 57). We may be bothered by the solemn tone of this; and in the ensuing conversation of the rustics Jonson allows the sense of miracle to be touched with parody, in an attempt to restore the comic quality of the scene:

> RVST 2   O miracle! see when a man ha's grace!
> RVST 3   Had't not beene pitty, so good a man should haue beene
> cast away?
> RVST 2   Well, I'le get our clarke to put his conuersion in the *Acts*,
> and *Monuments*.   (III. viii. 58–62)

The conversion of Sordido is the most fully dramatized of the play's transformations, and it does not altogether benefit from this. We are asked to look too closely at an episode that would benefit from greater stylization, and the combination of black comedy and solemn moralizing is unsteady. Swift though the conversion is, it is not quite swift enough.

Jonson deals with other characters more briskly, justifying the speed of the transformations through Cordatus' remark, 'How tedious a sight were it to behold a proud exalted tree lopt, and cut downe by degrees, when it might bee feld in a moment?' (IV. viii. 169–71). The speed may also make us think of the masques that are still to come; but Jonson varies the nature of the transformations. The fine court lady Saviolina is exposed by her failure to detect the rusticity of Sogliardo; she believes the story that he is a gentleman pretending to be a clown, and claims she can detect his true gentility beneath the imposture. When told he really *is* a clown, she goes off in a huff; she has been not so much cured as embarrassed and put out of countenance. In particular, she has pretended to the ability to penetrate a disguise, an ability Jonson gives only to his true judges, and this pretence is exposed. Shift, who has pretended a colourful life of crime, collapses when accused of a real crime, and confesses 'I ne're rob'd any man, I neuer stood by the high-way-side, sir, but only said so, because I would get my selfe a name, and be counted a tall man' (v. iii. 64–7). The special irony of this exposure is that Shift is humiliated by confessing not guilt but innocence. Fungoso suffers a very practical ordeal: abandoned by his friends and presented with an enormous tavern bill, he repents the money he has spent on fine clothes.

As the play draws toward an end, the various dishumourings start to interlock: Puntarvolo's dog, involved in his travelling venture, is poisoned, and when Puntarvolo first misses it he makes the accusation that humiliates Shift. Macilente gets the doting citizen Deliro to bail Fungoso out of his difficulty, promising this will earn the gratitude of his peevish wife Fallace – who is Fungoso's sister, and whom Deliro has been trying without success to please. In fact Macilente draws Deliro away in order to give Fallace a chance to meet the courtier Fastidius

Briske, with whom she is infatuated. The speed of the transformations has been increasing by this point, and when Deliro
confronts Briske and Fallace the doting husband and the peevish,
domineering wife are dishumoured in a total of five words:

FALL   Sweet husband:
DELI   Out lasciuious strumpet.   (V. xi. 16–17)

These are their last words in the play. The scurrilous jester Carlo
Buffone is also silenced, more forcibly, by having his lips sealed
with hot wax. He is not so much reformed as punished and
suppressed. Fastidius Briske, unlike the others, is reduced by
stages. After he has been revealed as a person of no account at
court, Deliro remarks, 'his masking vizor is off' (IV. ii. 57), but
he is not finally put down until the end of the play, when
Macilente warns him that Deliro is about to enter substantial
actions against him: 'Now, Monsieur, you see the plague that
treads o' the heeles of your fopperie' (V. xi. 49–50). Briske has no
answer; he is reduced to silence.

The treatment of the fools varies from one to another: some
repent, some are merely beaten; some suffer exposure, others
loss or damage. But they share a common destiny, to be in some
way driven out of their humours. They are bound together in a
single plot rhythm, or to use Jonson's own image, they float on
the same tide in the dead sea of life. Cordatus and Mitis discuss
Briske's first, temporary setback:

MIT   . . . this gallants humour is almost spent, me thinkes, it
      ebbes apace, with this contrarie breath of his mistresse.
COR   O, but it will flow againe for all this, till there come a
      generall drought of humour among all our actors, and then, I
      feare not but his wil fall as low as any.   (III. ix. 146–50)

The flood-table includes Mitis himself, whose function in the
first part of the play is to raise objections: from the repentance of
Sordido onwards, he objects less and less, and begins to follow
the proceedings with interest and approval. Part of the effect is
to build a structure of irony around the fools; most of the dishumourings take place in public, and the fools have a chance to
laugh at each other; but no one can laugh for long, for his turn

may be next, as Macilente warns Puntarvolo when he crows over the exposure of Saviolina:

PVNT   Come, on mine honour wee shall make her blush in the
presence: my splene is great with laughter.
MACI   Your laughter wil be a child of a feeble life, I beleeue, sir.

(V. ii. 132–5)

But Macilente himself is subject to the same irony. He tries to stand back from the group, as a satiric commentator; but just as Overdo is himself one of the enormities of the Fair he seeks to correct, so Macilente is as trapped in the tide of humour as are any of his victims.

His ruling passion, envy, is as much in need of cure as are the follies of the others. He envies the wealth and position of fools and undeservers, as opposed to his own miserable state; and this envy clouds his judgement. While he sometimes speaks of Fallace with the contempt she deserves, he cannot help envying Deliro's possession of her: 'How long shall I liue, ere I be so happy, / To haue a wife of this exceeding forme?' (II. iv. 135–6). He envies Sordido for the wrong reasons, 'not as he is a villaine, a wolfe i'the common-wealth, but as he is rich, and fortunate' (I. iii. 163–4). He can even envy the worthless Shift for his reputation with the other fools: 'I dare doe more then he, a thousand times: / Why should not they take knowledge of this? ha?' (IV. v. 31–2). In a curious way he is like Sordido, the first character to be dishumoured, as Macilente is the last. Both are driven to distraction by other men's good fortune.

Macilente is not an ideal judge, seeing through the characters and disposing of them from a position of detached wisdom. He is in the grip of his own humour, which swells as the others lose theirs; we see this in his mounting excitement at the success of his plots against them. But having swollen, his humour breaks; with the inevitability of natural law, his envy vanishes when there is nothing more for it to feed on. Dishumouring others, he is instrumental in dishumouring himself. After disposing of Briske, the last of his victims, he suddenly declares:

Why, here's a change! Now is my soule at peace.
I am as emptie of all enuie now,

As they of merit to be enuied at.
My humour (like a flame) no longer lasts
Then it hath stuffe to feed it.   (v. xi. 54–8)

Something more is revealed here. Macilente's dominance of the
play has not always been obvious; he has frequently been absent,
or reduced to grumbling from the sidelines while other characters take the stage. But we now realize that in a sense the play has
been *about* Macilente. The varied dishumourings of the other
characters have in the end one thing in common: they all
contribute to the dishumouring of Macilente. When that is
achieved, the play ends. Macilente dismisses the importance of
the other characters; it might be as well if they could be not just
discomfited but reformed – but it hardly matters:

I could wish
They might turne wise vpon it, and be sau'd now,
So heauen were pleas'd: but let them vanish, vapors.
                                          (v. xi. 63–5)

Like Volpone, he sees himself as the only real character in the
play.[19]
A further revelation accompanies this, when he steps back
into the Induction world of Cordatus and Mitis:

Wel, gentlemen, I should haue gone in, and return'd to you, as I
was ASPER at the first: but (by reason the shift would haue
beene somewhat long, and we are loth to draw your patience
farder) wee'le intreat you to imagine it. And now (that you
may see I will be out of humour for companie) I stand wholly
to your kind approbation, and (indeed) am nothing so per-
emptorie as I was in the beginning: Mary, I will not doe as
PLAVTVS, in his *Amphytrio,* for all this *(Summi Iouis causa,
Plaudite:)* begge a *Plaudite,* for gods sake; but if you (out of the
bountie of your good liking) will bestow it; why, you may (in
time) make leane MACILENTE as fat, as Sir IOHN FAL-STAFFE.
                                          (v. xi. 75–87)

Is he Macilente, or Asper? The speech heading calls him
Macilente, and he appears to accept that role at the beginning of
the speech; but as he talks, Asper comes more to the fore, and
Macilente slips back into the third person. And which, we might
ask, is the essential character, which the role? The character who

speaks of Macilente in the third person is still costumed and made up as Macilente. Jonson's apology for the fusing of the characters on technical grounds is, I suspect, ironic. Like the ending of *The Gypsies Metamorphosed* it calls our attention to the technicalities of theatre; in this case the effect is not to explain a transformation but to explain why no transformation will take place. But there is a deeper reason than the technical one. Asper and Macilente are not as sharply distinguished as we might have thought from the opening character descriptions.[20] We now suspect that Macilente is not just a role played by Asper; Macilente *is* Asper. Through this impersonation Asper has purged himself of the violent emotion that bothered us in the Induction.[21] He defers to the audience as judges who will assess the merits of the play; but if the audience notices the trick of the last speech, they will be judges of another kind, piercing through the disguise of Macilente and seeing Asper beneath.

We also have the power, by our applause, to transform Macilente, to make the lean satirist as fat as Falstaff. That jocular touch is the one suggestion in the final version of the play that Asper–Macilente is not just purged, but positively reformed. It is also the only suggestion of a power outside himself working on the character. But in the original version of the play, Macilente was not cured simply by having his envy drained away. His humour persisted until, coming to the court, he encountered Queen Elizabeth, who by her splendour drove his humour out. Hers was the true transforming power. Though Jonson bowed to criticism and changed the ending, he thought well enough of his first version to defend it in the Quarto text, and to include in the Folio an alternative ending for presentation before the Queen, in which the essence of the original conclusion is preserved:

> Enuie is fled my soule, at sight of her,
> And shee hath chac'd all black thoughts from my bosome,
> Like as the sunne doth darkeness from the world.
> My streame of humour is runne out of me.   (ll. 4–7)

The transforming power attributed to the Queen was later to be attributed to King James in the court masques.

This unexpected linking of satire and masque is one of the
signs that Jonson's work is ultimately all of a piece. It may also
be a clue to the way we ought to respond to *Every Man out of his
Humour*. Criticism of the play makes it sound like hard work;
and Jonson himself, by the elaborate machinery of commentary
with which he surrounds the main action, helps confirm that
impression. But in his prefatory epistle to the Inns of Court he
offers the play as holiday reading. *'when the gowne and cap is off,
and the Lord of liberty raignes'* (ll. 20–1). Even without the special
ending involving the Queen, the play has affinities with the
court masque in its use of stylized characters and sudden transformations. The masque, in Jonson's hands, blended moral
instruction and festive entertainment, and perhaps we ought to
read this play in the same spirit, viewing its satire as raillery for
an Inns of Court revel. Admittedly, this would be easier to do if
the play were shorter and livelier than it is; but the intention is
there, and it comes close to being realized in the cleverly inter-
locking judgements of the last few scenes. Finally, in the way
Jonson juggles the characters of Macilente and Asper, there is a
fascination with sleight of hand for its own sake. It is no accident
that the scenes of judgement, here and elsewhere in Jonson's
work, are closely linked to scenes of transformation intended to
astonish the senses. Jonson the moralist and Jonson the artist
cannot finally be separated: when he judges his invented worlds,
he does so in ways that show his pleasure in puzzles, riddles and
games.

6
THE POET AS CHARACTER

I

In the game of shifting identities Jonson plays with Asper and
Macilente there is another puzzle still: to what extent is Jonson's
own identity involved? Is there an element of self-portrait in
Asper, of self-criticism in Macilente? Is the purging of Asper by
Macilente taken one step further as Jonson, through Asper,
purges himself? We cannot answer these questions exactly, any
more than we can determine exactly how much of Prospero is
Shakespeare or how much of Solness the Master Builder is
Ibsen. But it is reasonable to suspect that in each case the artist is
using an invented character as a way of embodying some of his
own experience of the artistic process. This is not the same thing
as saying Asper simply is Jonson, Prospero Shakespeare or
Solness Ibsen. But in Jonson's case in particular, there is no need
to shy away from seeing a strongly personal element in his
work, for he never made the pretence of being an impersonal
artist. While other Renaissance dramatists gracefully disappear
behind their characters, Jonson makes frequent appearances in
his own work. This is not just a private quirk of his: as Raphael
includes his own self-portrait in *The School of Athens*, so Chaucer
places among his Canterbury pilgrims the little man who tells
the tale of Sir Topas, and Milton makes the old blind poet one of
the important secondary characters of *Paradise Lost*. What is
unusual is not the device itself but its pervasiveness in Jonson's
work, and in particular his use of it in the traditionally impersonal medium of drama. Among English playwrights only
Bernard Shaw has been so obtrusive; and Shaw never matched
the rich variety of uses to which Jonson put the device of self-
portraiture.

But the analogy with Shaw implies an important warning.

The mask of 'G.B.S.' was a useful and entertaining device; but it was also a carefully constructed public performance, and could be a way not of embodying but of concealing the essential man. Similarly, when Jonson appears as a character in his own work an element of deliberate invention must be allowed for. We are seeing not the essential Jonson but a public front – one of many that he puts up, for varying artistic purposes, throughout his writing. These effects are worth studying in their own right, for the device is so pervasive that examining it may help us approach some conclusions about Jonson's art. Whatever it reveals about his private nature – and it may reveal a good deal, though not everything – it tells us much about Jonson's view of the artist's relations to his work, and to his audience.

Jonson's work is full of sly touches that remind us of the author, often at unexpected moments. They suggest he has become a public figure, knows it, and is willing to play on this as part of his art. He likes making an audience blink: it keeps them alert. And he likes to poke fun at himself. It was a fairly mature Jonson who wrote in *Epicoene*, 'shee may censure *poets*, and authors, and stiles, and compare 'hem, DANIEL with SPENSER, IONSON with the tother youth' (II. ii. 116–18). The most dangerous of his many scrapes with the law came when he did what every playwright has dreamed of doing: he killed an actor, and got away with it.[1] He was saved from execution by being able to read his 'neck-verse'. At the start of a play written not long afterwards the audience is told, 'First, the title of this play is CYNTHIAS *Reuels*, as any man (that hath hope to bee saued by his booke) can witnesse' (Induction, ll. 40–2); and in *Bartholomew Fair* Waspe proudly proclaims his illiteracy: 'I am no Clearke, I scorne to be sau'd by my booke, i'faith I'll hang first' (I. iv. 7–8). The later joke is more specific, as Jonson thinks the audience's memory may need more jogging. Both are mischievous throwaway effects, private jokes between the writer and those members of the audience who are quick enough to catch them. In *News from the New World Discovered in the Moon*, the poet who made the discovery is identified as the same one who walked to Edinburgh on foot (ll. 169–79); and some of his other propensities are glanced at:

FAC   I am sure, if he be a good Poet, hee has discover'd a good
     Taverne in his time.

I HER   That he has, I should thinke the worse of his Verse else.

(ll. 147–50)

For the most part, moments like these are incidental jokes shared with the audience. They are like the personal appearances of Alfred Hitchcock in his own films: one learns to watch for the familiar portly figure striding by. One may remark that the publicity does no harm either: it keeps the image of the artist before the public, and helps create a bond between them. The joking quality is carried over into more elaborate self-portraits, where the image of the fat drunken poet produces a friendly laughter, bred of familiarity:

> I am to dine, Friend, where I must be weigh'd
>   For a just wager, and that wager paid
> If I doe lose it: And, without a Tale,
>   A Merchants Wife is Regent of the Scale.
> (*The Underwood*, LIV: 'Epistle to Mr. Arthur Squib', ll. 1–4)

Like some of his own fools, he has become a physical thing: the gross body can be weighed like merchandise, for money. But the brain within it is still nimble: he fears he may be two pounds short, and takes the occasion to beg money from his friend. There may be a touch of sadness in the reminder of Jonson's poverty, but in making comic capital of it Falstaff could not have done better. When the court bureaucracy fails to pay his allowance of sack, he thinks it worth while to write a stinging epigram on the subject (*The Underwood*, LXVIII: 'An Epigram, to the Household'). If behind the bluster there is a serious point about the neglect of a poet, there is also a personal joke about the grounds on which Jonson has chosen to fight his battle. And there is a similar personal joke when he celebrates the virtues of Penshurst: 'Here no man tells my cups; nor, standing by, / A waiter, doth my gluttony enuy' (*The Forest*, II: 'To Penshurst', ll. 67–8). Amid the civilized grace and order of the estate, the hard-drinking poet may look like an intruder. But he has his function. Jonson, as we have seen, makes the pleasures of food and drink central to his view of the good life at Penshurst, and does so with playful wit. But there is a potential grossness in the idea, and Jonson's joking admission of his own gluttony both recognizes this view and exorcises it through comedy, thereby protecting Penshurst itself from the wrong kind of laughter.

Jonson's size and appetites are an important part of his comic self-image; in 'To Penshurst' he is the gargoyle who points out by contrast the grace of the rest of the structure. Our laughter at him is easy and relaxed. There is a more edgy laughter, however, when Jonson adds to the caricature a quarrelsome temper, for here we are closer to the man's real sensitivity about his work. Carlo Buffone, in the Induction to *Every Man out of his Humour*, gives us a portrait of Jonson veering uncertainly between the temperate life of the ideal poet and the self-indulgence of a particular man. On this occasion we are warned that drink does not improve Jonson's temper, and Buffone seems to glance anxiously over his shoulder as he speaks:

> This is that our *Poet* calls *Castalian* liquor, when hee comes abroad (now and then) once in a fortnight, and makes a good meale among Players, where he has *Caninum appetitum*: mary, at home he keepes a good philosophicall diet, beanes and butter milke: an honest pure Rogue, hee will take you off three, foure, fiue of these, one after another, and looke vilanously when he has done, like a one-headed CERBERVS (he do' not heare me I hope) and then (when his belly is well ballac't, and his braine rigg'd a little) he sailes away withall, as though he would work wonders when he comes home.
>
> (Induction, ll. 334–45)

At home, in the seclusion to which the good so often retreat in Jonson's work, the writer can be his best self; the players see him at his worst. Not only drink, but the theatre itself, seems to sour his temper, and Induction-figures in later plays have cause to fear that villainous look of which Buffone complains. The Stage-Keeper of *Bartholomew Fair* must, like Buffone, glance over his shoulder 'lest the *Poet* heare me, or his man, Master *Broome*, behind the Arras' (Induction, ll. 7–8). He has had trouble already: 'Hee has (*sirreuerence*) kick'd me three, or foure times about the Tyring-house, I thanke him, but for offering to putt in, with my experience' (ll. 28–30).

Gossip Mirth, at the opening of *The Staple of News*, reports a more painful scene:

> *Yonder he is within (I was i' the Tiring-house a while to see the*
> Actors *drest) rowling himself vp and downe like a tun, i' the midst of*
> *'hem, and spurges, neuer did vessel of wort, or wine worke so! His*
> *sweating put me in minde of a good Shrouing dish (and I beleeue*
> *would be taken vp for a seruice of state somewhere, an't were*
> *knowne) a stew'd* Poet! *He doth sit like an vnbrac'd Drum with one*
> *of his heads beaten out: For, that you must note, a* Poet *hath two*
> *heads, as a Drum has, one for making, the other repeating, and his*
> *repeating head is all to pieces: they may gather it vp i' the tiring-*
> *house; for hee hath torne the booke in a Poeticall fury, and put*
> *himselfe to silence in dead* Sacke, *which, were there no other*
> *vexation, were sufficient to make him the most miserable* Embleme
> *of patience.*   (Induction, ll. 61–74)

The comedy this time conveys a certain desperation. This picture combines several elements of the comic Jonson – the temper, the sensitivity to failure, the drinking – in a caricature that, for all the amusement it provides, seems to touch a raw nerve.

In an earlier play, *Cynthia's Revels*, Jonson seems at first to be a model of authorial restraint, everything he is not in *The Staple of News*. One of the boys reports:

> wee are not so officiously befriended by him, as to haue his
> presence in the tiring-house, to prompt vs aloud, stampe at the
> booke-holder, sweare for our properties, curse the poore tire-
> man, raile the musicke out of tune, and sweat for euerie veniall
> trespasse we commit, as some Authour would, if he had such
> fine engles as we.   (Induction, ll. 160–6)

This sounds like the ideal, against which Jonson measures himself, and mocks himself, in other self-portraits. But it is a constant theme in his work that ideals are hard to sustain in reality. Before long the Prologue is referring to 'Our doubtfull author' (Prologue, l. 4) who is hoping he has the right audience for his work; the facade of indifference is cracking a little. By the Epilogue, it has broken altogether:

> The Author (iealous, how your sense doth take
> His trauailes) hath enioyned me to make

Some short, and ceremonious *epilogue*;
But if I yet know what, I am a rogue:
He ties me to such lawes, as quite distract
My thoughts; and would a yeere of time exact.
I neither must be faint, remisse, nor sorry,
Sowre, serious, confident, nor peremptory:
But betwixt these. Let's see; to lay the blame
Vpon the Childrens action, that were lame.
To craue your fauour, with a begging knee,
Were to distrust the writers facultie.
To promise better at the next we bring,
Prorogues disgrace, commends not any thing.
Stifly to stand on this, and proudly approue
The play, might taxe the maker of *selfe-Loue*.
I'le onely speake, what I haue heard him say;
By (---) 'tis good, and if you lik't, you may.   (ll. 3–20)

That concluding line has contributed much to Jonson's reputation
for arrogance. In his very next play, he defends these words
against precisely that charge (*Poetaster*, Prologue, ll. 15–28). But
to get the full effect of the line we should study its context. The
actor draws a picture of an anxious author, fussing backstage
and issuing so many instructions that the actor finds his advice
useless and is thrown back on his own resources for inventing an
epilogue. He surveys and abandons several conventional ideas –
perhaps he is a bit rattled himself by now – and finally seizes on
one of the author's own remarks: not a formal statement, but
something overheard in an unguarded moment. Given the
image of a fussing author established in the speech, it can be seen
as a moment of excited bluster, springing from anxiety. The
brusque tone, reinforced by the oath, suggests as much. '*By (---)
'tis good*' may well be Jonson's considered estimate of his play;
but it is presented as the climax of a self-portrait whose main
effect is comic. Jonson knows, and virtually admits, that this is
an odd way for a play attacking self-love to end; but that in itself
is part of the joke.[2]

However, there is also an essential toughness in the Epilogue to
Cynthia's Revels that implies another Jonson beneath the comic
surface. This is a man who values square dealing and plain

speaking, and will not grovel before an audience. The belliger-
ent, hard-drinking poet is one public Jonson; for the most part
(though not exclusively) he is a creature of the theatre, with its
tensions and its rough-and-tumble battles with actors and
audiences. A more dignified Jonson appears in the private,
sophisticated world of the non-dramatic poetry. This is a man of
integrity, who may be dependent on patronage but will not buy
it by degrading himself:

> And though my fortune humble me, to take
> The smallest courtesies with thankes, I make
> Yet choyce from whom I take them; and would shame
> To have such doe me good, I durst not name.
> (*The Underwood*, XIII: 'An Epistle to Sir Edward Sackville,
> Now Earl of Dorset', ll. 15–18)

The virtue of Dorset remains generalized here; but the virtue of
Jonson is particular, and is the subject of the first part of the
poem. Once again we are aware of the tension and insecurity of
the writer's position; but this time he behaves not with comic
anxiety but with integrity and discrimination. Even when he is
praising one of the most powerful men in England, he insists
that what he writes is 'free / From seruile flatterie (common *Poets*
shame)' *Epigrams*, XLIII: 'To Robert Earl of Salisbury', ll. 10–11)
– for Salisbury is too good to need flattery. If Salisbury is
idealized here, so, by the same process, is Jonson. He is not only
(as we saw in Chapter 5) the ideal judge; he is a plain-speaking
man in a world of sycophants.

In his friendships, he presents himself as having a similar
integrity. To be one of the tribe of Ben is to be not the partisan
for a sect but the servant of Truth:

> I am neither *Author*, or *Fautor* of any sect. I will have no man
> addict himselfe to mee; but if I have any thing right, defend it as
> Truth's, not mine (save as it conduceth to a common good.) It
> profits not me to have any man fence, or fight for me, to
> flourish, or take a side. Stand for *Truth*, and 'tis enough.
> (*Timber*, ll. 154–9)

For all the importance of social conviviality in his life and work,
that too is dismissed as a basis of true friendship:

> Not like your Countrie-neighbours, that commit
>   Their vice of loving for a Christmasse fit;
> Which is indeed but friendship of the spit:
>
> But, as a friend, which name your selfe receave,
>   And which you (being the worthier) gave me leave
>   In letters, that mixe spirits, thus to weave.
>   (*The Underwood*, XXXVII: 'An Epistle to a Friend', ll. 7–12)

We seem a long way from the caricature of the hard-drinking
poet. Plain speaking and dedication to truth are the values this
sober Jonson espouses. Such a man can take honest criticism, as
well as administer it;³ and we will see later that Jonson was
capable of acknowledging rebukes and promising to do better.
But he prefers the stance of honest critic himself; even this sober
Jonson is more comfortable as an active figure than as a passive
one. When he praises Michael Drayton he takes care to
emphasize the value of that praise. Because the two men have
not corresponded much, 'It hath beene question'd, MICHAEL, if
I bee / A Friend at all; or if at all, to thee' (*Ungathered Verse*, XXX:
'The Vision of Ben Jonson, on the Muses of his Friend M.
Drayton', ll. 1–2). Now that he is ready to praise Drayton, it is
not through empty gregariousness, but because Drayton has
written something worth praising:

> And, though I now begin, 'tis not to rub
> Hanch against Hanch, or raise a riming *Club*
> About the towne: this reck'ning I will pay,
> Without conferring symboles. This's my day.   (ll. 7–10)

In passages like these, the discriminating Jonson seems to reject
the coarse animal vitality of the comic Jonson. He is as purely a
creature of judgement and intellect as the other is a creature of
the senses. It is one of the many attractions of 'Inviting a Friend
to Supper' that it manages to combine both Jonsons in a rich and
balanced whole.

Jonson claims a similar integrity and discrimination in dealing
with his public. He declares in the Prologue to *Every Man in his
Humour* that he does not need to do hack work to survive
(though we know that the historical Jonson, as a young man,
did). Just as he will not flatter a patron, he will not purchase the

audience's favour 'at such a rate, / As, for it, he himselfe must iustly hate' (ll. 5–6). Far from being anxious about the reception of his work, he is impervious to criticism if he has no respect for the critic: 'Thy praise, or dispraise, is to me alike, / One doth not stroke me, nor the other strike' (*Epigrams*, LXI: 'To Fool, or Knave', ll. 1–2). In his 'Epistle to Katherine, Lady Aubigny' (*The Forest*, XIII) he matches his view of her virtue – beleaguered but steadfast – with a similar view of his own. Presenting his credentials as Lady Katherine's praiser, he depicts himself as one who has preserved his integrity – in particular, his integrity as a writer – in a corrupt world (ll. 9–21). In that way he resembles other virtuous figures in his own work, including Lady Katherine herself. By his writing of the poem, the two characters, each an isolated figure of virtue, have made common cause.

Jonson claims here to be impervious to what the world says of him. That claim is made over and over in his work; it is generally accompanied by a savage attack on the fools and knaves to whom he professes indifference, and as Jonas A. Barish puts it, 'The oftener he protests his imperturbability, the less we are inclined to believe it.'[4] To make a public statement of one's indifference is to be less than purely indifferent: there are enemies to cow, friends (and oneself) to reassure. He maintains, as we have seen, that virtue cannot simply retreat from the world; sooner or later it must do battle. At the opening of *Poetaster* an armed Prologue – excusing his appearance by declaring ''tis a dangerous age' (l. 6) – beats down the spirit of Envy and goes on to defend the author's pride in his work. The final statement about the author's view of his enemies – 'Their moods he rather pitties, then enuies: / His mind it is aboue their iniuries' (ll. 27–8) cannot ring true under the circumstances, any more than does Horace's plaintive cry when asked to judge the poetasters, 'I am the worst accuser, vnder heauen' (v.iii.176). The tension we have seen in Crites we see here in Jonson himself: professing indifference to the world, he cannot help hitting back when injured. As George Parfitt has suggested, the story from his soldiering days of how he killed a man in single combat before both armies is 'psychologically true', whatever its basis in fact.[5] Several of his plays are surrounded by barbed-wire entanglements. Potential critics of *Every Man out of his Humour* are told:

> if we faile,
> We must impute it to this onely chance,
> "*Arte* hath an enemy cal'd *Ignorance*.   (Induction, ll. 217–9)

Similar warning shots are fired at the openings of *The Staple of News* – 'If that not like you, that he sends to night, / 'Tis you haue left to iudge, not hee to write' (Prologue for the Stage, ll. 29–30) – and *The New Inn*, where we are welcomed to a feast, promised that we will be royally entertained, and then scolded:

> *If any thing be set to a wrong taste,*
> *'Tis not the meat, there, but the mouth's displac'd,*
> *Remoue but that sick palat, all is well.*   (Prologue, ll. 7–9)

The tone is more ingratiating, but the message is the same. Jonson will defend his work, not by pointing out its merits (which ought to be obvious) but by attacking the judgement of those who presume to criticize. The possibility of real debate about the play is closed off; the stance is that of a fighter.

Even when Jonson professes to retreat from the battle in disgust, he is still really on the attack. The 'Ode to Himself' on the failure of *The New Inn* begins, 'Come leaue the lothed stage' and goes on to a detailed attack on the corruption of the theatre, ending with a suggestion that when he turns to a higher art Jonson will gain satisfaction not so much from the art itself as from the pain it gives his enemies (ll. 51–8). The tension between indifference and belligerence is also felt in the Apologetical Dialogue 'To the Reader' appended to *Poetaster*, where the figure of the Author answers in detail the charges to which he professes indifference,[6] and reveals an ambivalent attitude to the audience's bad taste: he is 'Pleas'd, and yet tortur'd, with their beastly feeding' (l. 48). That painful line suggests a problem like that of Crites: trying to maintain a sneering indifference to the folly of the world, he cannot help being pained by it and he cannot take his eyes off it.

Jonson, as we have seen, has also a double attitude to the idea of retreat from the world. It can be an escape from corruption, or an unhealthy seclusion from reality. Something of this tension is suggested by the Author's retirement in the *Poetaster* dialogue:

> I, that spend halfe my nights, and all my dayes,
>   Here in a cell, to get a darke, pale face,
> To come forth worth the iuy, or the bayes,
>   And in this age can hope no other grace –
> Leaue me. There's something come into my thought,
> That must, and shall be sung, high, and aloofe,
> Safe from the wolues black iaw, and the dull asses hoofe.
>
> (ll. 233–9)

The world being what it is, retreat from it is no disgrace; and it allows inspired vision. But the man pays a price, cut off from the normal conditions of life. Even in this somewhat undramatic 'dialogue' Jonson's dramatic sense is at work, allowing him to see the situation from more than one angle: the Author is both an inspired bard and a pale, unhealthy drudge.

In the actual circumstances of Jonson's later life, the seclusion was to become painful. Paralysed and confined to his room, he becomes a sad parody of the 'centred self':

> The *Muse* not peepes out, one of hundred dayes;
>
> But lyes block'd up, and straightned, narrow'd in,
> Fix'd to the bed, and boords, unlike to win
> Health, or scarce breath, as she had never bin.
>   (*The Underwood*, LXXI: 'To the Right Honourable,
> the Lord High Treasurer of England. An Epistle Mendicant',
>   ll. 9–12)

He is reduced to frank begging: from the Treasurer, from the King (*The Underwood*, LXXVI: 'The Humble Petition of Poor Ben. To the Best of Monarchs, Masters, Men, King Charles'); and most humiliating, from the theatre audience. In the Prologue to *The New Inn* he approaches the audience with something like his old truculence; but in the Epilogue he is reduced to playing on their heartstrings:

> *If you expect more then you had to night,*
>   *The maker is sick, and sad. But doe him right,*
> *He meant to please you: for he sent things fit,*
>   *In all the numbers, both of sense, and wit,*

> *If they ha' not miscarried! if they haue,*
> *All that his faint, and faltring tongue doth craue,*
> *Is, that you not impute it to his braine.*
> *That's yet vnhurt, although set round with paine,*
> *It cannot long hold out.*   (ll. 3–11)

Later in the Epilogue the old fires spring up again, as Jonson defends his decision to keep the below-stairs characters out of the last act; but by the end he is complaining of royal neglect (ll. 21–2) and the general impression is not of a fighter taking on all comers but of a sick, helpless old man asking the audience not to be too hard on him. His retreat formerly implied security – safe in his own integrity, aloof from the world. Now he is '*set round with paine*' and his retreat is an image of helplessness.

However, the arrogance of the public Jonson does not usually collapse in such a humiliating fashion. It is more characteristic to find it countered by a controlled, judicious self-effacement as Jonson defers, not to the public at large but to other men who have earned his respect. However he may have criticized John Donne in private, in the formal context of the *Epigrams* he submits gracefully to his judgement:

> Reade all I send: and, if I find but one
>   Mark'd by thy hand, and with the better stone,
> My title's seal'd.   (*Epigrams*, XCVI: 'To John Donne', ll. 7–9)

He still expects praise rather than adverse criticism; but he is prepared to entertain the possibility that the praise will not be wholesale. Writing to Francis Beaumont, he matches praise with praise and adds to it a surprising self-deprecation: 'When euen there, where most thou prayest mee, / For writing better, I must enuie thee' (*Epigrams*, LV: 'To Francis Beaumont', ll. 9–10). The fact that the praise is confined to specific passages of Beaumont's work makes it seem serious, not merely polite. This implies something like the ideal relationship of the poets in *Poetaster*, taking the measure of their own work and deferring gladly to those who can write better. Once again Jonson has placed himself in a situation similar to that in which he places his invented characters. And he is generous in praise of his old master William Camden

> to whom I owe
> All that I am in arts, all that I know,
> (How nothing's that?)
> (*Epigrams*, XIV: 'To William Camden', ll. 1–3)

Passages like these belong to the ideal world of the *Epigrams*, where Jonson has the role of the clear-eyed judge. He knows what is due to him, and rebuffs the attacks of the unworthy with his usual gusto. But having taken his own measure, he can also defer, in an open and manly spirit, to those he judges his betters.

He is also capable not just of courteous self-deprecation but of quite severe self-criticism. There are the grim admissions of 'To Heaven' (*The Forest*, XV): 'I know my state, both full of shame, and scorne' (l. 17).[7] The elegy, 'Tis true, I'm broke' (*The Underwood*, XXXVIII) begs a lady's forgiveness for some unspecified offence. Whatever it was, it seems to have involved the dark side of that conviviality Jonson so prized: something done (or more likely said) in company, when he was drunk:

> I will not stand to justifie my fault,
>   Or lay the excuse upon the Vintners vault;
> Or in confessing of the Crime be nice,
>   Or goe about to countenance the vice,
> By naming in what companie 'twas in,
>   As I would urge Authoritie for sinne.   (ll. 21–6)

These are explanations, not excuses; he lists them, but ultimately throws himself on the lady's mercy. That the offence is not named implies it is none of the reader's business; it is a matter between himself and the lady. But it is the reader's business to observe how an honest man can confess he has offended and ask forgiveness.

When he does accuse himself of particular offences, they are offences of central importance in his invented world, offences of which his fools and villains are also guilty. In retreat from criticism, he has lapsed into mere torpor:

> Where do'st thou carelesse lie,
>   Buried in ease and sloth?
> Knowledge, that sleepes, doth die;
> And this Securitie,
>   It is the common Moath,

That eats on wits, and Arts, and oft destroyes them both.
(*The Underwood*, XXIII: 'An Ode to Himself', ll. 1–6)

In the rest of the poem he makes a heroic recovery, scorning the base age and dedicating himself to his art, as at the end of the *Poetaster* dialogue: 'high and aloofe, / Safe from the wolves black jaw, and the dull Asses hoofe' (ll. 35–6). But this poem commands, I think, more respect than either the *Poetaster* dialogue or the *New Inn* ode, for it includes a greater measure of self-criticism. Jonson sees more fully around the situation, and sees in himself not just injured virtue but responsibilities neglected. His retreat from the stage has produced mere inaction, and he is spurred to work again not just by contempt for his enemies (as in the *New Inn* ode) but by an awareness that he has fallen beneath his own standards and must recover. Similarly, the unnamed figure in the Cary-Morison ode (*The Underwood*, LXX) who is told –

> Goe now, and tell out dayes summ'd up with feares,
> And make them yeares;
> Produce thy masse of miseries on the Stage,
> To swell thine age;
> Repeat of things a throng,
> To shew thou hast beene long,
> Not liv'd.   (ll. 53–9)

– may be, as Ian Donaldson has suggested, Jonson himself.[8] If so, his theatrical work, including his public complaints about the fate of his art, may be just one more instance of the meaningless activity, the life no better than death, that Jonson attacks in his satiric type-figures.

As we saw in Chapter 5, one of Jonson's favourite stances is that of the ideal judge, and some of his shrewdest irony is directed at incompetent pretenders to judgement. But, paradoxically, the ideal judge can judge himself, seeing and admitting his own failures of judgement:

> It is an Act of tyrannie, not love,
>   In practiz'd friendship wholly to reprove,
>   As flatt'ry with friends humours still to move.
>
> From each of which I labour to be free,

> Yet if with eithers vice I teynted be,
> Forgive it, as my frailtie, and not me.

> For no man lives so out of passions sway,
>   But shall sometimes be tempted to obey
>   Her furie, yet no friendship to betray.
>   (*The Underwood*, XXXVII: 'An Epistle to a Friend', ll. 25–33)

Jonson's integrity is still firm; but one of the terms of that integrity is an ability to see his own lapses of judgement, the moments when plain speaking becomes undue harshness or proper praise becomes flattery.

On the latter point in particular Jonson is sensitive. His praise of the good generally goes beyond anything a literally-minded appraisal of the people in question could sustain. The reader familiar with the poetry of the period may be willing to accept the conventions of encomium with no particular difficulty; but Jonson raises difficulties himself. His respect for the truth is such that he admits the gap between the poem and the reality, even while trying to excuse it:

> Though I confesse (as every Muse hath err'd,
> And mine not least) I have too oft preferr'd
> Men past their termes, and prais'd some names too much,
> But 'twas with purpose to have made them such.
>   (*The Underwood*, XIV: 'An Epistle to Master John Selden',
>   ll. 19–22)

The confession that he has praised particular 'names' too much is interesting, in view of the great importance we have seen him attach to names. His excuse is that he has tried to make the subjects of his poems live up to their names – to be, in other words, their own best selves. But as they have fallen short of their ideals, he has betrayed one of his own. He has not been completely frank with his friends; and before he suggests an excuse for this he allows the admission that the Muse has simply 'err'd'.

Similar admissions disturb the ideal world of the *Epigrams*. Jonson, creator and judge of that world, has made mistakes: he has written to order for 'Fine Grand' (*Epigrams*, LXXIII), prostituting his art to the unworthy (and worse still, not getting paid for it). Epigram LXV, 'To My Muse', contains a more damaging admission still:

> Away, and leaue me, thou thing most abhord,
>   That hast betray'd me to a worthlesse lord;
> Made me commit most fierce idolatrie
>   To a great image through thy luxurie.   (ll. 1–4)

His punishment, self-inflicted, is to admit his shame by writing this poem.[9] He vows that from now on he will write 'Things manly, and not smelling parasite' (l. 14). There is, however, a characteristic recovery at the end. The original poem still stands, and still represents what the lord ought to have been; it is valid not as praise but as rebuke: 'Who e're is rais'd, / For worth he has not, He is tax'd, not prais'd' (ll. 15–16). The poem still makes its own valid statement, however the poet may err. Jonson is also capable of the frank, disarming admission that he has undervalued a genuinely good man, Vincent Corbet:

> Much from him I professe I wonne,
> And more, and more, I should have done,
>   But that I understood him scant.
> (*The Underwood*, XII: 'An Epitaph on Master Vincent Corbet',
>   ll. 29–31)

If we are used to thinking of Jonson as the arrogant, opinionated figure of legend, poems like the Epitaph on Vincent Corbet come as a pleasant surprise. But a full reading of Jonson's work shows that that particular legend, though Jonson was undoubtedly responsible for its creation, was not the only face he presented to the world through his art. He plays many parts, and they shade into each other: the drunken, bad-tempered author is a comic version of a man who stands quite seriously on the value of his work, and will not brook criticism; the rebuttal of criticism mingles paradoxically with a stoic detachment from the world, an impulse to withdraw pulling against a more powerful impulse to go on fighting. The arrogance is justified in the name of plain speaking; but Jonson can turn the plain speaking upon himself, and when writing for an audience he trusts can rebuke himself as sharply as he rebukes his opponents. The public Jonson, then, is not a single character but a complex variety of roles, seemingly inconsistent at times but ultimately interconnected. Sometimes, especially in the Inductions to the plays, we are looking from outside at a comic figure; at other times, especially in the non-dramatic poems, we seem privileged to glance over the shoulder of a man writing in private to his friends. He is by turns laughable, embarrassing, impressive, and touching. It is tempting to call him the most fully human figure Jonson the writer ever created; and I think the assessment is just, provided we do not take it to mean that Jonson is baring his heart in an act of simple autobiography. The complex, multi-faceted figure he creates is engaged with the same problems as are the purely invented characters – the problem of true judgement; the attempt to live by ideals when the world is fallen, and one's own nature with it; the tension between retreat from the world and continued involvement with it; the dangers, responsibilities and delights of creation itself. Doubtless this figure reflects Jonson's life; but he is in the last analysis a creature of Jonson's art.[10]

II

Fundamental to that art is the disparity between the ideal and the reality: what men wish to be, or claim to be, and what they are. Jonson proclaims in *Timber* standards by which his own reported behaviour can be judged, and by which it sometimes appears lamentably wanting.[11] His own reaction to criticism is rebuked when he writes, 'A *Fame* that is wounded to the world, would bee better cured by anothers *Apologie*, then its owne: For few can apply medicines well themselues' (ll. 23–5). Jonson never waited for other men to write his 'Apologies' for him. Similarly, the hectoring tone of Jonson's lectures to his public, and even the bluff frankness of his poems to his friends, are hard to reconcile with the following:

> Next a good life, to beget love in the persons wee counsell, by dissembling our knowledge of ability in our selves, and avoyding all suspition of arrogance, ascribing all to their instruction, as an *Ambassadour* to his Master, or a *Subject* to his *Soveraigne;* seasoning all with humanity and sweetnesse, onely expressing care and sollicitude.   (ll. 93–8)

Even when he is generous with his praise and courteous with his advice, this is not the tone he uses: he takes care to point out the value of his opinions, and to insist on his own virtues.

The gap between the calm ideal and the arrogant man widens when we read the reports of Jonson's contemporaries. Drummond, at the end of the 'Conversations', summed up the main impression his guest made on him:

> He is a great lover and praiser of himself, a contemner and Scorner of others, given rather to losse a friend, than a Jest, jealous of every word and action of those about him (especiallie after drink) which is one of the Elements in which he liveth) a dissembler of ill parts which raigne in him, a bragger of some good that he wanteth, thinketh nothing well bot what either he himself, or some of his friends and Countrymen hath said or done. he is passionately kynde and angry, carelesse either to gaine or keep, Vindicative, but if he be well answered, at himself.[12]

It is worth recalling Marchette Chute's remark that if Drummond's 'earnest jottings do not give a complete picture of Jonson himself they give an excellent picture of Jonson's effect on Drummond'.[13] Towards the end of the paragraph Drummond seems to regain his composure, and a more balanced view of Jonson emerges. But the first impression is of shock. Jonson's massive self-confidence – whatever inner tensions it may have masked – looks like plain arrogance to Drummond. In particular, he cannot resist pointing out the gap between Jonson's view of himself and the reality: 'a dissembler of ill parts which raigne in him, a bragger of some good that he wanteth'.

A cooler and more damaging appraisal comes from one of the 'tribe of Ben', James Howell, who addressed Jonson in one letter as 'my honored friend and father'[14] but who wrote to Sir Thomas Hawkins:

> I was invited yesternight to a solemne supper by B.J. where you were deeply remembered, there was good company, excellent chear, choice wines, and joviall wellcome; one thing interven'd which almost spoyld the relish of the rest, that B. began to engrosse all the discourse, to vapour extreamely of himselfe, and by vilifying others to magnifie his owne *muse; T. Ca.* busd me in the eare, that though *Ben* had barreld up a

great deale of knowledge, yet it seemes he had not read the
Ethiques, which among other precepts of morality forbid self
commendation, declaring it to be an ill favour solecism in
good manners.[15]

This makes sad reading. Besides the easy criticism that the great
classicist has not profited from his study, there is a deeper
distress in watching Jonson spoil the sort of gathering he
describes so attractively in 'Inviting a Friend to Supper'. He is
not only falling below the ideals of the ancients but betraying his
own idea of the good social occasion. As an old friend, Howell is
inclined to be forgiving, partly because of Ben's age, and partly
because 'if one be allowed to love the naturall issue of his body,
why not that of the brain'.[16] But George Chapman, towards the
end of his life, was not inclined to forgive. 'An Invective of Mr.
George Chapman against Mr. Ben Jonson' is no playful literary
flyting, and leaves a nasty taste in the mouth:

> Thou must bee Muzzelde, Ringd, and led In Chaines
> Lest dames with childe abide vntymely paynes
> and Children perrish: didst thou not put out
> A boies right eye that Croste thy mankind poute?[17]

Jonson's hasty temper was not always funny.

Passages like these give us, if not the real Ben Jonson, the
unguarded Ben Jonson, who does not know he is being
observed and recorded for posterity. It is easy enough to point at
the ironies: the exponent of Stoic indifference who lays about
him when crossed; the boaster who wrote a satiric comedy
against self-love. But there are grounds for believing that Jonson
was well aware of these ironies, however he may have forgotten
himself in the heat of the moment. Behind the occasional self-
reproach we have already noted is an attempt at sustained self-
discipline, based on the gap he himself perceives between his
own behaviour and the virtues he preaches in his art. He writes
to the Earl of Dorset, 'I have the list of mine owne faults to
know, / Looke to and cure' (*The Underwood,* XIII: 'An Epistle to
Sir Edward Sackville, now Earl of Dorset', ll. 114–15); and in
'An Epistle to Master Arthur Squib' (*The Underwood,* XLV) he
takes the process one stage further:

What I am not, and what I faine would be,
  Whilst I informe my selfe, I would teach thee,
My gentle *Arthur;* that it might be said
  One lesson we have both learn'd, and well read.   (ll. 1–4)

To write is (in Ibsen's phrase) to sit in doomsday judgement on
oneself. If Jonson lectures his friends on proper conduct, it is not
from a position of superiority but from one of shared frailty. He
knows he has fallen short of his own ideals; and the advice he
sends for the betterment of his friends is also directed at himself.
It was not in Jonson's nature to admit this very often; but it was
not in his nature to conceal it either. The glimpses of the frail
man behind the confident, didactic art add to the latter an extra
dimension of drama.

The disparity between Jonson's proclaimed values and his actual
nature runs parallel to, and is involved with, a more general
disparity between the man and his art. This takes comic forms in
a number of the love poems. The effect is clearest in 'My Picture
Left in Scotland' (*The Underwood,* IX):

I now thinke, Love is rather deafe, then blind,
  For else it could not be,
        That she,
Whom I adore so much, should so slight me,
  And cast my love behind:
I'm sure my language to her, was as sweet,
        And every close did meet
    In sentence, of as subtile feet,
        As hath the youngest Hee,
  That sits in shadow of *Apollo's* tree.

Oh, but my conscious feares,
    That flie my thoughts betweene,
    Tell me that she hath seene
    My hundred of gray haires,
    Told seven and fortie years,
  Read so much wast, as she cannot imbrace
    My mountaine belly, and my rockie face,
And all these through her eyes, have stopt her eares.

                                        (ll. 1–18)

Normally a love-poet will not describe his own appearance, but he may describe the lady's in lavish (if conventional) detail. Jonson turns that device on its head: the lady disappears and the blazon becomes a point-by-point description of his own gross body. Yet his art is light, elegant and still youthful; his verse's feet are nimble even if he himself is not. In this case, the reality of the poet has interfered with the effect of his verse: no persuasion to love could survive the sight of the persuader, and the fact that the poem is not addressed to the lady suggests Jonson has given up. Yet the poem implies, I think, that the delicacy of Jonson's art is in some way dependent on the grossness of his body. He writes in conscious rivalry with younger men; and it may be that his awareness of his own unloveliness spurs him to make his verse as lovely as it can be.

The same incongruous figure appears as Charis's lover in 'A Celebration of Charis in ten Lyric Pieces' (*The Underwood*, II), contributing to the ironic context in which the graceful lyric passages are placed; and in one of the Elegies as the author of sophisticated love poetry whose apparent disqualifications have at least respectable classical precedents:

> Let me be what I am, as *Virgil* cold;
>   As *Horace* fat; or as *Anacreon* old;
> No Poets verses yet did ever move,
>   Whose Readers did not thinke he was in love.   ·
>   (*The Underwood*, XLII: 'An Elegy', ll. 1–4)

That passage suggests that the poetry is what matters; if it can persuade, it can override the infirmities of the poet, infirmities other great poets before him have borne.[18] 'An Epistle to my Lady Covell' (*The Underwood*, LVI) draws a contrast between the fat body and the nimble muse, and concludes, 'although you fancie not the man, / Accept his Muse' (ll. 25–6). But that separation of man and poet is too simple. Even the poems that claim the poet does not matter still call attention to him; and we may be closer to Jonson's real interest in the device in the poem he placed at the beginning of *The Forest*, 'Why I Write Not of Love'. (The irony is a favourite one at this period: a poem about frustrated composition also begins *Astrophel and Stella*, and *The*

Shepherd's Calendar opens with Colin Clout breaking his pipe.)
This poem apparently describes a failure. Jonson begins with a
sense of obligation to write love poetry: 'Some act of *Loue's*
bound to reherse, / I thought to binde him, in my verse' (ll.
1–2). Bound himself, he seeks to bind love, to control that
elusive experience in the shackles of art:

> Which when he felt, Away (quoth hee)
> Can Poets hope to fetter mee?
> It is enough, they once did get
> MARS, and my *Mother,* in their net:
> I weare not these my wings in vaine.
> With which he fled me: and againe,
> Into my ri'mes could ne're be got
> By any arte. Then wonder not,
> That since, my numbers are so cold,
> When *Loue* is fled, and I grow old.   (ll. 3–12)

Cupid's nimble freedom (felt in the rhythm of the lines) implies
his boyishness: and against it the stark simplicity of 'I grow old'
carries with it all the crippling disabilities Jonson confesses to so
jokingly in other poems. This time, he does not claim to
overcome them. Yet if he cannot write of love, he can write
impressively of that very failure. Confessing its own coldness,
his poetry – light though the tone is – becomes unexpectedly
moving. As Wordsworth (more solemnly, and at much greater
length) was to find inspiration in the failure of inspiration, so
Jonson was to find poetry in his disqualifications as a poet. The
gross reality of Ben Jonson the man does not just stimulate his
art as a kind of counter-irritant; by writing of it as he does he
brings it under the control of that art – or, as he writes elsewhere
of his own body:

> 'Tis true, as my wombe swells, so my backe stoupes,
> And the whole lumpe growes round, deform'd, and droupes,
> But yet the Tun at *Heidelberg* had houpes.
>   (*The Underwood*, LII: 'My Answer. The Poet to the Painter',
>   ll. 4–6)

The old fat poet who writes graceful lyrics is, like the irritable
dramatist, a comic figure; but Jonson makes richer and more
confident use of him, exploring through the comedy the

relations between the imperfect artist and the aspirations of his art. Two poems of private grief explore the same problem; and I think the failure of one and the success of the other are instructive. 'Eupheme' (*The Underwood*, LXXXIV) is a cycle of poems on Lady Venetia Digby. Jonson's praise of the lady and grief at her death, though they may be perfectly sincere, are uncomfortably hyperbolic in expression. In short poems Jonson's hyperbole can be masterful and persuasive; but it does not profit from being dragged out at length, and the cycle as a whole – parts of which are missing or unfinished – suggests strain and uncertainty. The ninth poem, 'Elegy on my Muse', regards Lady Venetia's death as the end of everything, and thus lays itself open to the charge of blasphemy that Jonson levelled at Donne's *Anniversaries*.[19] But there is an important difference. The lady's death is the end of everything *for Jonson*; the idea is presented not as objective truth but as a function of the poet's own grief. He addresses Nature:

> Looke on thy sloth, and give thy selfe undone,
> (For so thou art with me) now shee is gone.
> My wounded mind cannot sustaine this stroke,
> It rages, runs, flies, stands, and would provoke
> The world to ruine with it; in her *Fall*,
> I summe up mine owne breaking, and wish all.
>
> (ll. 21–6)

He adds later, in what may be a glancing reference to his own criticism of Donne, 'My Passion / Whoorles me about, and to blaspheme in fashion!' (ll. 31–2). The extravagance of the poem's opening ('Twere time that I dy'd too, now shee is dead') is thus excused; and having admitted the subjective nature of his grief Jonson goes on to celebrate the immortality of the soul in a series of excited exclamations that maintain the intensity of feeling but move it in another direction. But while Jonson shows an interesting self-awareness at this point, his admission that grief has made him frantic does not act as a counterbalance to the poem's extravagance, but rather as an excuse for it. The tension of his best work, in which we feel a critical self-awareness insisting on the most authentic thought and the clearest expression, is missing. Instead we have an

uncharacteristic soft-centred emotionalism, admitted but un-
controlled.

The epitaph 'On My First Son' (*Epigrams*, XLV) is another
matter:

> Farewell, thou child of my right hand, and ioy;
>   My sinne was too much hope of thee, lou'd boy,
> Seuen yeeres tho'wert lent to me, and I thee pay,
>   Exacted by thy fate, on the iust day.
> O, could I loose all father, now. For why
>   Will man lament the state he should enuie?
> To haue so soone scap'd worlds, and fleshes rage,
>   And, if no other miserie, yet age?
> Rest in soft peace, and, ask'd, say here doth lye
>   BEN. IONSON his best piece of *poetrie*.
> For whose sake, hence-forth, all his vowes be such,
>   As what he loues may neuer like too much.   (ll. 1–12)

This time there is a tension between the conventions of the
epitaph and the intractable reality of the poet's feelings.[20] The
poem sets forth the correct attitudes: grief balanced by resignation. The first line gives both an easy expression: the loss
seems to be both lamented and accepted. But the second line
gives a sudden twist of bitterness: Jonson's hope for his son was
not a natural, proper feeling but a sin for which he is punished.
We do not expect sarcasm in an epitaph; but this use of the word
'sin' is sarcasm that springs from authentic grief, and strikes very
deep, questioning the justice not only of the boy's death but of
the universe in which such things happen. In the third and fourth
lines Jonson brings the sceptical voice under control, and accepts
the justice of his son's fate. But the control is icy, the sarcasm
persists: what has happened is not natural justice but the cold
enforcement of a legal contract. 'O, could I loose all father, now'
suggests at first that Jonson wishes he had never had a son, if this
is the price he must pay for it. But the lines that follow give the
exclamation another meaning: Jonson rebukes his fatherly feelings, and sets against them another proper attitude: it is desirable
to be released from this miserable world, and a father should not
lament if his son has this privilege. Jonson does not include
bereavement as one of the world's miseries, though that may be

implied; but what he lists here we see elsewhere in his work – the world's rage, which he encountered in the theatre; the humiliations of the flesh, out of which he made self-mockery; and the miseries of age he was later to know all too well. Beneath the resignation to his son's death there is a continued protest at the conditions of his own life. The valediction 'Rest in soft peace' suggests that the passion is now spent, and the description of the boy as 'BEN. IONSON his best piece of *poetrie*' shows love and grief disciplined by wit. But the more we think about that line, the more we see that if the wit disciplines the feeling, it also deepens it. The words imply that Jonson valued his son more than he valued all his art; and we know how deeply, how painfully he valued his art. There is also, in the conceit of the boy speaking his own epitaph, the imagination's refusal to accept his death. In the bitter, difficult final couplet the sarcasm returns and 'O, could I loose all father, now' acquires again its first and natural meaning. Hurt by this bereavement, Jonson shrinks from any further emotional commitment to the world. If we have been tempted to see the conventional resignation as false, and the bitterness as authentic, the balance is redressed here. The poem as a whole makes us seriously question whether Jonson ever could narrow his feelings in this way; the man who refuses to feel is no more the true Ben Jonson than the man who accepts his son's death as mere justice.

Poetry can be a way of bringing grief under control. This poem strikes the notes proper to an epitaph: lament, resignation, valediction – though we might note that there is no hint of a life after death. Jonson tries very hard to express these feelings in the proper way. We know from the touching and decorous epitaph 'On My First Daughter' (*Epigrams*, XXII) that he could indeed master and accept his grief through art. But here the bitterness of loss keeps breaking the surface, twisting the ideas and the expression, threatening the control that the poem tries to impose on the writer's feelings and thus creating a darker, richer poem. The artist is struggling with his art, and out of that conflict grows one of Jonson's greatest poems.

As the artist himself is one of the subjects of his art, so the art is frequently its own subject. We have seen this already in some of the works just discussed. Art as its own subject is common enough in Renaissance literature; the sonnet cycles of Sidney, Spenser, Shakespeare and Drayton provide obvious examples, and in *The Faerie Queene* Spenser is constantly writing about the poem, as well as writing the poem. So is Milton in *Paradise Lost*. It is possible for the critic to extend this line of investigation too far, so that art becomes a series of mirrors reflecting mirrors, with no reference to life; and to do that with Jonson or any of his contemporaries is to do them a disservice for there must, after all, be something human for the mirrors to catch and reflect. But with that caution in mind, we may look briefly at the image of itself which Jonson's art creates, and at the ways in which this relates to Jonson's image – or rather his complex of images – of himself as an artist.

More than any other dramatist of his time, Jonson provided a running critical commentary on his own works. *Sejanus*, like *The Shepherd's Calendar* and *The Waste Land*, comes complete with its own scholarly footnotes. *Every Man out of his Humour* generates its own literary criticism as Cordatus and Mitis debate the writer's decisions: his preference for massed scenes with many characters over short scenes with fewer characters (II. iii. 288–301); his use of threatened violence in the dishumouring of Sordido (III. viii. 74–94). But Jonson calls our attention not just to the craftsmanship of particular works but to a sense of purpose and control that lies behind his entire output. Towards the end of his career he seems to be drawing his work together in a single *oeuvre*. There are increasing cross-references – sometimes joking, like the reminders of *The Devil is an Ass* and *Bartholomew Fair* in *The Staple of News* (First Intermean, ll. 34–46; Third Intermean, ll. 50–6), or the comparison of Inigo Jones to Adam Overdo (*Ungathered Verse*, XXXIV: 'An Expostulation with Inigo Jones', ll. 79–81). Beneath the jokes is the expectation that Jonson's public has been following his work as a whole, and is ready to make connections between one piece and another. Jonson himself makes a conscious effort to draw the threads together in *The Magnetic Lady*:

> The *Author*, beginning his studies of this kind, with *every man
> in his Humour;* and after, *every man out of his Humour:* and since,
> continuing in all his *Playes,* especially those of the *Comick*
> thred, whereof the *New-Inne* was the last, some recent humours
> still, or manners of men, that went along with the times,
> finding himselfe now neare the close, or shutting up of his
> Circle, hath phant'sied to himselfe, in *Idaea,* this *Magnetick
> Mistris.*   (Induction, ll. 99–106)

In the rest of the play there are references to the *Epigrams* (1.ii.
33–7), *The Staple of News* (Chorus to Act 1, 42–4), and the
second prologue to *Epicoene* (Chorus to Act 11, 27–30). These
cross-references suggest what the publication of the Folio had
already declared in a more solemn way: that Jonson intended to
leave to posterity not a collection of miscellaneous writings but a
single body of work to be read as a whole.

His art has a sense of purpose and his works – the plays
especially – frequently declare their own nature and function.
The Prologues to *Epicoene* and *The New Inn*, and the Epilogue to
The Alchemist, offer the play as a feast for our entertainment.
Even this genial view has its serious overtones, for we know the
value Jonson placed on social occasions; and the two Prologues
in particular stress the skill and judgement that go into making a
good banquet.[21] The play is also, more conventionally, a mirror
held up to the world, as Asper declares in the Induction to *Every
Man out of his Humour:*

> Well I will scourge those apes;
> And to these courteous eyes oppose a mirrour,
> As large as is the stage, whereon we act:
> Where they shall see the times deformitie
> Anatomiz'd in euery nerue, and sinnew,
> With constant courage, and contempt of feare.   (ll. 117–22)

The image has a curious double effect here. At first, there seems
to be a distinction between the 'apes' who are to be scourged and
the courteous audience who will watch the scourging. But in a
mirror 'opposed' to the audience, it is bound to see itself. The
audience is credited with enough critical intelligence to recognize its own follies, and accept the mirror image as a just
reflection. Jonson expects, in other words, the same capacity for

self-criticism that he shows – occasionally – himself. Conversely, the 'Epistle to Katherine, Lady Aubigny' (*The Forest*, XIII) presents itself as a glass in which the lady may see her own virtues (ll. 21–9) and in which the inner truth about her will be preserved through the vicissitudes of time (ll. 121–4). For Jonson the mirror of art, in whatever genre, reflects not the disorganized surface of life but the pure moral essence; folly, vice and virtue in their essential forms.

The Epistle to the two Universities that serves as preface to *Volpone* declares a stern moral purpose in the play's ending, '*it being the office of a* comick-Poet, *to imitate iustice, and instruct to life*' (ll. 121–2), just as it proclaims an ancient principle of the moral nature of the poet:

> For, if men will impartially, and not à-squint, looke toward the offices, and function of a Poet, they will easily conclude to themselues, the impossibility of any mans being the good Poet, without first being a good man. He that is said to be able to informe yong-men to all good disciplines, inflame growne-men to all great vertues, keepe old-men in their best and supreme state, or as they decline to child-hood, recouer them to their first strength; that comes forth the interpreter, and arbiter of nature, a teacher of things diuine, no lesse then humane, a master in manners; and can alone (or with a few) effect the businesse of man-kind: this, I take him, is no subiect for pride, and ignorance to exercise their rayling rhetorique vpon.
>
> (ll. 20–31)

This is perhaps Jonson's largest claim for the function of poetry.

Yet it is characteristic that this preface, with its stern declaration of the moral rectitude of true art, should introduce a play that appeals so engagingly to our lower natures, and concludes with a morally subversive epilogue. There was in Jonson a touch of mischief that led him to make such juxtapositions: delicate love-lyrics written by a fat old man, and a comical satire on self-love ending with the author's boast, '*By (---) 'tis good.*' And there may be more than just mischief at work here. As Jonson's image of himself is complex and varied, so his image of art is constantly shifting. The play is a feast, a lesson, a mirror. It asks us as judicious spectators to look at a collection of fools – who turn out to be ourselves. It promises to scourge and reform the world – and then demands our applause, to make the lean satirist 'as fat, as Sir IOHN FAL-STAFFE' (*Every Man out of his Humour*, v. xi. 86–7), as though the only purpose of art were pleasure. It proclaims a stern moral purpose and then gives the villain the last word. In short, the range of views Jonson presents about the purpose and function of his art corresponds to the range of images he presents of himself – a plain-speaking man of integrity and a self-indulgent glutton; a critic of the world, conscious of his own superiority; and sometimes a merciless critic of himself. Within such a range incongruities are bound to emerge, and Jonson does not shy away from them. Often he emphasizes them by juxtaposition, sometimes within a single work. As each Jonson we meet is to some extent a mask, rather than the true man, so each declaration about art is a statement of an ideal, a possibility, rather than a literal description of what a particular play or poem actually achieves. The disparity between *Volpone* and its preface is sufficient warning of that. It is not that Jonson is uncertain how to handle his material; rather, he is determined to see as many of its possibilities as he can. Idea and achievement are at odds; but instead of undercutting each other they combine to create a larger and more comprehensive vision.

This may help us understand one of Jonson's best known, most puzzling and most hotly debated poems – 'To the Memory of My Beloved, the Author Mr. William Shakespeare: And What he hath Left us' (*Ungathered Verse*, XXVI). The problem lies not so much in the poem itself as in the disparity between its unstinting praise of Shakespeare – his craftsmanship in particular – and Jonson's very different view of Shakespeare recorded elsewhere.[22] Jonson's blunt declaration to Drummond 'That Shaksperr wanted Arte'[23] is expanded in a more balanced and judicious assessment in *Timber*:

> *I remember,* the Players have often mentioned it as an honour to *Shakespeare,* that in his writing, (whatsoever he penn'd) hee never blotted out line. My answer hath beene, Would he had blotted a thousand. Which they thought a malevolent speech. I had not told posterity this, but for their ignorance, who choose that circumstance to commend their friend by, wherein he

> most faulted. And to justifie mine owne candor, (for I lov'd
> the man, and doe honour his memory (on this side Idolatry) as
> much as any.) Hee was (indeed) honest, and of an open, and
> free nature: had an excellent *Phantsie;* brave notions, and gentle
> expressions: wherein hee flow'd with that facility, that some-
> time it was necessary he should be stop'd. . . . His wit was in
> his owne power; would the rule of it had beene so too. . . .
> But hee redeemed his vices, with his vertues. There was ever
> more in him to be praysed, then to be pardoned.
>
> (ll. 647–68)

As so often, Jonson's comments on another man are also
comments on himself. He is a candid friend, genuinely admiring
Shakespeare but not allowing his admiration to become un-
critical flattery. He is out to rescue his friend not from calumny
but from false praise; more than once in commendatory verses
to other men's work, Jonson insisted that injudicious praise
could actually harm an author (*Ungathered Verse*, xx, xxi). Yet
his candour has been taken for malevolence; as usual he is under
attack, and as usual he is ready to defend himself.

The attack has persisted: Jonson's criticism has recoiled on
himself, in the conventional, much deplored but still persistent
contrast between Jonson's laboured art and Shakespeare's native
woodnotes wild. In its extreme form, it is the contrast between
the plodder and the genius. Dekker's caricature in *Satiromastix*
(I. ii.) of Jonson painfully hammering out a poem word by word
shows how early the legend took root. But if we are to get a
clear view of Jonson's account of Shakespeare, we need to look
more closely at his attitude to the right balance of labour and
inspiration in art. Once again, *Timber* is helpful. It is full of wise
advice about the craft of writing, much of it borrowed from
other writers, but embodying thoughts Jonson evidently considered worth borrowing; these include strictures against the
injudicious haste of which Jonson finds Shakespeare guilty:

> No matter how slow the style be at first, so it be labour'd, and
> accurate: seeke the best, and be not glad of the forward con-
> ceipts, or first words, that offer themselves to us, but judge of
> what wee invent; and order what wee approve. . . . For all that
> wee invent doth please us in the conception, or birth; else we
> would never set it downe. But the safest is to returne to our

Judgement, and handle over againe those things, the easinesse
of which might make them justly suspected.   (ll. 1705–23)

That presents one image of the poet – careful, judicious, self-
critical. But there is another image presented elsewhere in
Timber:

> For, whereas all other Arts consist of Doctrine, and Precepts:
> the *Poet* must bee able by nature, and instinct, to powre out the
> Treasure of his minde. . . . Then it riseth higher, as by a divine
> Instinct, when it contemnes common, and knowne con-
> ceptions. It utters somewhat above a mortall mouth. Then it
> gets a loft, and flies away with his Ryder, whether, before, it
> was doubtfull to ascend.   (ll. 2411–24)

Soaring inspiration, free of rules and traditions – this was for a
long time the conventional view of Shakespeare, and Jonson
espouses it here as a sign of the true poet. He returns shortly
after to his insistence on the necessity of slow, hard work
(ll. 2434–66) but he has said enough to show the importance of
natural inspiration and the free flow of invention. He writes
elsewhere that while the excesses of this facility can be cured,
nothing will cure the lack of it (ll. 1775–7). Turning back to
Jonson's account of Shakespeare, we notice that part of its
balance is an admiration for Shakespeare's natural inspiration; he
sees it not as a vice in itself but as an indispensable virtue that
occasionally leads to excess. When it suits him to do so, he also
claims this virtue for himself. In the Prologue to *Volpone* he
defends himself against the charge of plodding, and takes a
certain pride in the speed with which the play was composed
(ll. 11–16). When we look widely enough in Jonson's work we
see, on this issue of inspiration *versus* craftsmanship, a characteristic determination to see all around the subject.

When we come to the Shakespeare ode itself the first thing we
notice is – as in the passage from *Timber* – a feeling that
Shakespeare needs to be protected: 'To draw no enuy (*Shakespeare*) on thy name, / Am I thus ample to thy Booke, and Fame'
(ll. 1–2). Envy is Jonson's own enemy as an artist; as in his
'Epistle to Katherine, Lady Aubigny', he is making common
cause with one of the virtuous against a world full of detraction.

And he reiterates the warning against one insidious form of detraction, false praise: 'as some infamous Baud, or Whore, / Should praise a Matron. What could hurt her more?' (ll. 13–14). So 'blinde Affection' (l. 9) may do Shakespeare harm; what he needs is the frank, judicious praise of a good man – of Ben Jonson, in fact. As usual, the praiser is presenting his credentials; the first part of the poem – implicitly, at least – is about himself. But this does not introduce the sort of balanced critical assessment we find in *Timber*. This is a work for another kind of occasion, and there is something a little mischievous in the deliberate pose-striking with which the main part of the poem begins:

> I, therefore will begin. Soule of the Age!
>> The applause! delight! the wonder of our Stage!
> My *Shakespeare*, rise.   (ll. 17–19)

As Jonson varied his picture of himself throughout his work, so he varies his picture of Shakespeare. When writing seriously about art, he offered a balanced appraisal; when promoting his own brand of realistic comedy, he made impudent (but not, I think, unfriendly) jokes about plays where '*Chorus* wafts you ore the seas' (*Every Man in his Humour*, Prologue, l. 15) and actors

> with three rustie swords,
> And helpe of some few foot-and-halfe-foote words,
> Fight ouer *Yorke,* and *Lancasters* long iarres:
> And in the tyring-house bring wounds, to scarres.
>> (ll. 9–12)

(Part of the joke may be that the Chorus who wafts us o'er the seas in *Henry V* makes very similar complaints about battle scenes himself; Jonson was not saying anything he expected Shakespeare to resent deeply.) Now, on this occasion, he is celebrating Shakespeare's achievement in a public way, and he gives us Shakespeare triumphant. We have seen the importance Jonson attached to a sense of occasion in works as diverse as the court masques and *Bartholomew Fair;* we see it again in this poem.

His fondness for picturing artists in competition leads him to set Shakespeare against the other moderns and even, more surprisingly, against the ancients, and to show him beating them all: 'how farre thou didst our *Lily* out-shine, / Or sporting *Kid,* or *Marlowes* mighty line' (ll. 29–30). But the particular terms of his praise are more surprising still:

> Yet must I not giue Nature all: thy Art,
>   My gentle *Shakespeare,* must enioy a part.
> For though the *Poets* matter, Nature be,
>   His Art doth giue the fashion. And, that he,
> Who casts to write a liuing line, must sweat,
>   (Such as thine are) and strike the second heat
> Vpon the *Muses* anuile.   (ll. 55–61)

This is precisely the craftsmanship, the ability to think again, whose lack in Shakespeare Jonson deplores elsewhere. The inconsistency may be more apparent than real, for Jonson complains in *Timber* that '*sometime* it was necessary he should be stop'd' (my italics); Shakespeare would not have been the artist he was if he was never the craftsman at all. In the poem Jonson acknowledges that, and innumerable recent studies of Shakespeare's artistry have endorsed this judgement. But the balance and the emphasis have undoubtedly shifted from the criticism in *Timber*; and in the process Shakespeare, working hard at his anvil, sounds more like the conventional image of Jonson. The resemblance becomes more striking as Jonson goes on to credit Shakespeare with his own belligerence, battling against fools and poetasters: 'he seemes to shake a Lance, / As brandish't at the eyes of Ignorance' (ll. 69–70). Later, Shakespeare is commanded, 'Shine forth, thou Starre of *Poets,* and with rage, / Or influence, chide, or cheere the drooping Stage' (ll. 77–8). We can just about recognize Shakespeare the craftsman; but here the Shakespeare we know, who whatever his private views of the theatre may have been is always urbane and deferential with his audiences in public, disappears behind a Shakespeare who has become an imitation of Jonson.[24]

The craftsman, the fighter – these are two of Jonson's favourite masks. As masks, they are detachable, and I think what happens in this poem is that Shakespeare is allowed to borrow them. Describing an ideal Shakespeare, Jonson puts into the image the best of his own distinctive traits. He adds to it the

soaring inspiration he also insisted was necessary for the poet,
and with which he was always willing to credit Shakespeare:

> Sweet swan of *Auon!* what a sight it were
>   To see thee in our waters yet appeare,
> And make those flights vpon the bankes of *Thames,*
>   That so did take *Eliza,* and our *Iames!*   (ll. 71–4)

Against the clanging anvil, we may set the mounting swan. In
one passage in particular, natural facility and craftsmanship are
fused:

> Looke how the fathers face
> Liues in his issue, euen so, the race
> Of *Shakespeares* minde, and manners brightly shines
> In his well torned, and true-filed lines.   (ll. 65–8)

Shakespeare's art is as natural as the getting of children, and (if
there is a pun on 'race') it flows with ease; it also shows the fruits
of solid, careful work.

In this poem, Jonson combines the best of himself and the best
of Shakespeare to produce an image of the ideal poet. The
picture may transcend his own strictest view of Shakespeare's
achievement; but Jonson's awareness of the imperfections of
reality never stopped him from trying to picture the ideal. And
to transcend reality for a particular occasion is not to forget it.
Timber was not published until after Jonson's death, but he
presents his views there as widely known in Shakespeare's circle.
If we catch an echo of his more critical views in the very terms
he uses to praise Shakespeare, the effect may well be intentional.
The self-conscious 'I will begin' suggests a deliberate artifice, an
effort to exalt Shakespeare beyond his imperfections. The
juxtaposition of the ideal and the imperfect fascinated Jonson,
and when he writes of himself and his own art, we always have
to be alert for it. It allowed him to create, in the character of 'Ben
Jonson', a rich and complex figure; and it allowed him to present
in this poem an idealized Shakespeare who nonetheless calls to
mind the imperfect Shakespeare we meet in *Timber.* By his
appearances in his own work, Jonson reminds us at every turn
that poems are written by men – and that men are both
imperfect and capable of imagining perfection.

7
ART AND ITS CONTEXT

I

If Jonson was concerned with the sometimes complex relations between the writer and his work, he was even more preoccupied with the relations between a work and its audience – relations which for him were often painful and difficult. He warns Alphonso Ferrabosco of what happens when a work of art is turned out into the world:

> When we doe giue, ALPHONSO, to the light,
>   A worke of ours, we part with our owne right;
> For, then, all mouthes will iudge, and their owne way:
>   The learn'd haue no more priuiledge, then the lay.
>
> (*Epigrams*, CXXXI: 'To the Same', ll. 1–4)

He goes on to advise Ferrabosco not to care what the world thinks; but of course this was advice he found hard to take himself. The first of the Epigrams is addressed 'To the Reader' and asks, 'Pray thee, take care, that tak'st my booke in hand, / To read it well: that is, to vnderstand' (ll. 1–2). Beneath the admonition we detect anxiety and mistrust.

The mistrust deepens and finds detailed expression in the irritable address 'To the Reader in Ordinarie' prefixed to *Catiline*:

> *The Muses forbid, that I should restrayne your medling, whom I see alreadie busie with the Title, and tricking ouer the leaues: It is your owne. I departed with my right, when I let it first abroad. And, now, so secure an Interpreter I am of my chance, that neither praise, nor dispraise from you can affect mee. Though you commend the two first Actes, with the people, because they are the worst; and dislike the Oration of* Cicero, *in regard you read some pieces of it, at Schoole,*

and vnderstand them not yet; I shall finde the way to forgiue you. Be
anything you will be, at your owne charge.   (ll. 1–10)

As in the Epigram to Ferrabosco, Jonson declares he has parted
with his rights in the work by giving it to the world; but what
actually registers, of course, is the familiar tension between
professed indifference and actual concern. Jonson goes farther
than lecturing the reader: he makes him a dramatic character, his
vices imagined and particularized, so that we – the better readers
– can see him from outside, and judge him. Our responses are
thus directed: if we felt inclined to enjoy the blood and thunder
of the first two acts and to yawn at Cicero, we see now that we
ought to be ashamed of ourselves. (Such is Jonson's anxiety for
the proper reception of his work that he is willing to dispraise a
large part of it in order to protect what matters most.) Finally,
the 'Reader extraordinary', who is addressed immediately afterwards, is implicitly invited to make common cause with the
playwright against those who misunderstand the play.

Throughout his work Jonson shows an itch to defend, to
explain, to justify. The prologues and epilogues of play after
play testify to this. In the masques – the early ones in particular –
Jonson, while declaring that his allegorical devices should not
need explication, nonetheless provides it.[1] In the printing of some
of the later plays, the mistrust of the reader becomes almost
neurotic, as Jonson adds marginalia to make clear what was
perfectly clear already. The following dialogue from *The Devil is
an Ass* –

> FIT   S'light, that'll be iust *play*-time.
>   It cannot be, I must not lose the *play!*
> MER   Sir, but you must, if she appoint to sit.
>   And, shee is president.
> FIT   S'lid, it is the *Diuell!*   (III. v. 35–8)

– is accompanied by two marginal notes, '*He longs to see the* play'
and '*Because it is the* Diuell'. This seems to reflect not so much a
genuine desire to explain as sarcasm about the reader's intelligence. The problem with passages like these, with their
attack – direct or implied – on the stupid reader, is that they
make no attempt to create a bond with the intelligent reader.

The preface to *Catiline*, on the other hand, does; and the method
we see at work there was the method Jonson used most fully and
effectively in his campaign to control the audience.

The *Epigrams* include, among the foolish and vicious satirized
under their type-names, characters who betray themselves by
their reactions to these very poems: 'Censorious Courtling' who
damns with faint praise (*Epigrams*, LII); 'Groom Idiot' who
laughs at the wrong places (*Epigrams*, LVIII). By being made
characters within the poems, they are thus separated from the
ideal audience that is reading the poems; and that audience in
turn learns to keep a check on its own responses by seeing what
to avoid. There is an equivalent effect in the masques: the rabble
of vulgarians who press into the court in many of the antimasques help to define by contrast the genteel and understanding public the masque itself is written for. The courtly
audience (Jonson implies) has not just come to gape at a fine
show, like Notch the Brewer's Clerk in *The Masque of Augurs*: 'I
ha' seene the Lyons ere now, and he that hath seene them, may
see the King' (ll. 8–9). Unlike the 'Curious' of *Time Vindicated*
they know what they want, and why. In two notable instances
Jonson replied to criticism by giving it comic embodiment in an
antimasque. *Pleasure Reconciled to Virtue* had been attacked as a
dull way for the Prince of Wales to makes his debut;[2] Jonson
replied in a sequel, *For the Honour of Wales*, by inventing a gaggle
of comic Welshmen who reduce the masque in the same way that
the puppets of *Bartholomew Fair* reduce the story of Hero and
Leander: changing Mount Atlas to a Welsh mountain, and
offering to replace Hercules with one of their own local heroes:
'Or *Lluellin,* or *Reese ap Griphin,* or *Cradock,* or *Owen Glendower,*
with a Welse hooke, and a Goats skinne on his backe, had done
very better, and twice as well?' (ll. 190–2). If we laugh at them,
we are implicitly taking the author's side against critics of the
original masque. The fools of the plays, like those of the
masques and Epigrams, frequently embody the attitudes to
drama that Jonson wants his audience to avoid. In *Every Man in
his Humour* Matthew and Bobadill prefer *The Spanish Tragedy* to
contemporary drama (like Jonson's) (I. v. 46–64); Fitzdottrel in
The Devil is an Ass – who is so foolish in so many directions that

as a character he becomes somewhat blurred – displays the wrong reasons for going to the theatre:

> To day, I goe to the *Black-fryers Play-house*,
> Sit i' the view, salute all my acquaintance,
> Rise vp between the *Acts*, let fall my cloake,
> Publish a handsome man, and a rich suite.   (I. vi. 31–4)

Ironically, the play he wants to disrupt by his antics is *The Devil is an Ass*; even as he speaks the play is having the last laugh on him.

Jonson uses this technique of controlling the audience most fully in the Inductions. Even the early comedy *The Case is Altered*, which Jonson excluded from the Folio, has something like a rudimentary Induction in an early scene (I. ii. 39–83) in which Antonio Balladino speaks with pride of the appeal his plays and pageants have for a stupid, old-fashioned audience (as opposed to the sophisticated audience of the Blackfriars, where *The Case is Altered* was performed). A later scene contains a long satiric passage about playgoing in 'Utopia' where the audiences are capricious and hard to please (II. vii. 26–82). Both passages seem like digressions, added not for anything they contribute to the play proper but for the purpose of enlisting the audience's loyalty.[3] The taming of the audience is more elaborately contrived, however, in *Every Man out of his Humour*. There, Mitis obligingly raises objections so that Cordatus, on behalf of the author, can refute them, thus silencing whatever complaints the audience may have. When Mitis, satisfied on one point, declares he will still raise objections, Cordatus replies:

> O, what else? it's the speciall intent of the author, you should doe so: for thereby others (that are present) may as well be satisfied, who happily would obiect the same you doe.
>
> (II. iii. 305–8)

With engaging frankness, Mitis is shown to be the author's puppet; and his objections are carefully contrived to allow Jonson to defend his methods of working and his theory of comedy. Most satisfying of all, Mitis is eventually converted, and sits back to enjoy and admire the play.

But it is in the later plays that Jonson makes his most elaborate attempts to bring the audience under control.[4] The most engaging – and therefore the most successful – of these is the Induction to *Bartholomew Fair*, where the tone is light, the audience is more teased than bullied, and Jonson shows himself prepared to be accommodating. In the articles of agreement drawn up between the author and the public,

> It shall bee lawfull for any man to iudge his six pen'orth, his twelue pen'orth, so to his eighteene pence, 2. shillings, halfe a crowne, to the value of his place: Prouided alwaies his place get not aboue his wit. . . . mary, if he drop but sixe pence at the doore, and will censure a crownes worth, it is thought there is no conscience, or iustice in that.   (ll. 87–96)

Measuring the audience's wit in monetary terms is an ironic joke that recalls Morose's practical view of social relations. Behind the absurdity may be a certain exasperation: this is the only kind of discrimination between one level of intelligence and another the audience is capable of understanding. But we should note that all comers are accepted. As in the conciliatory prologue to *Epicoene*, all tastes will be appealed to – including, we might note, the taste of the Stage-keeper, who complains that the play falls short of his own ideas of the Fair, and offers to do some rewriting (ll. 13–35). The Book-holder orders him off the stage: yet he also promises that the tastes of the Stage-keeper and his like will be satisfied after all: 'For the *Author* hath writ it iust to his *Meridian,* and the *Scale* of the grounded Iudgements here, his Play-fellowes in wit' (ll. 55–7). There will be characters just as authentic, and incidents just as rowdy, as anything the Stage-keeper has suggested (ll. 117–23). Instead of scorning a taste for vulgar amusement, Jonson promises to satisfy it. What he claims is the right to satisfy it in his own way, with his own selection of material. (There is also a suggestion that he is writing of the contemporary Fair, while the Stage-keeper is recalling the Fair as it used to be – ll. 116–17.) Moreover, the Stage-keeper is not a direct representative of the audience, but rather a stagehand who is getting above himself. He can safely be laughed off the stage, while the taste he represents can in general be accepted as a fair expectation to bring to the play.

What Jonson wants most of all is that the audience will be

consistent. He is so himself – 'his *Ware* is still the same' (ll.
161–2) – and if the play is to work the audience must match the
writer's steadiness with its own. He has written a play to appeal
to the vulgar and the judicious; and perhaps the ultimate point of
the joke about entrance prices is that if each level of the audience
sticks to the kind of response most natural to it, there will be
something in the play to please everybody. The agreement also
includes the proviso

> that euery man heere, exercise his owne Iudgement, and not
> censure by *Contagion,* or vpon *trust,* from anothers voice, or
> face, that sits by him, be he neuer so first, in the *Commission of
> Wit:* As also, that hee bee fixt and settled in his censure, that
> what hee approues, or not approues to day, hee will doe the
> same to morrow.   (ll. 97–102)

There is even an ironic approval of the old-fashioned theatre-
goer who prefers *The Spanish Tragedy* and *Titus Andronicus*,
because 'such a one, the Author knowes where to finde him'
(ll. 111–12). Jonson sets his own integrity against the instability
of the audience, in a characteristic opposition of the virtuous
man and the uncontrollable world. But he does more than that:
he gives the audience a fixed image of itself – comically fixed, by
the different prices they have paid. He urges them to stay in their
places, and not just in the literal sense. By doing this, he
attempts to control the conditions of performance, to take the
risk out of theatre. As playwright, he can determine the material
of the play; and he tries to control the audience by making them
part of that material.

Jonson's stance in *Bartholomew Fair* is generally conciliatory.
In *The Staple of News* he is more aggressive, caricaturing the
foolish elements in the audience through the Gossips Mirth,
Tattle, Censure and Expectation. They raise stupid objections –
'*I cannot abide that nasty fellow, the* Begger; *if hee had beene a*
Court-Begger *in good clothes, a* Begger *in veluet, as they say, I
could haue endur'd him*' (First Interman, ll. 12–14); they betray
old-fashioned taste – '*I would faine see the* Foole, *gossip, the* Foole
is the finest man i' the company, they say, and has all the wit' (First
Interman, ll. 23–4); they look forward to the time when
Zeal-of-the-Land Busy and Rabbi Trouble-Truth will stop

schoolchildren from acting in plays (Third Intermean, ll. 50–6). In so far as they are the play's enemies, the Gossips are so flagrantly stupid that they seem hardly worth attacking; and to that extent the device misfires. But Jonson has a subtler use for them, one that recalls his use of the Stage-keeper in *Bartholomew Fair*. The actor who is to speak the Prologue asks for their indulgence:

> *The truth is, there are a set of gamesters within, in trauell of a thing call'd a Play, and would faine be deliuer'd of it: and they haue intreated me to be their Man-Midwife, the Prologue; for they are like to haue a hard labour on't.*   (Induction, ll. 54–7)

The elaborate obstetrical analogy reminds us that 'Gossip' means, among other things, godparent. The Gossips are there to assist this newborn play; their folly is part of its fun. Mirth, as her name implies, is more friendly to it than the others, and can appreciate some of Jonson's subtler effects. The play, with its story of a prodigal and its heavily explicit allegory, is in fact surprisingly old-fashioned, and Mirth points out that it has its vice-figures too: '*But now they are attir'd like men and women o' the time*' (Second Intermean, ll. 16–17). Without sacrificing his intention to write contemporary satire, Jonson has gone part way to meet the old-fashioned taste the Gossips represent; and Mirth appreciates this. For the most part, however, the Gossips are the enemies of the play, and the fact that they do not return at the end for a final comment suggests that the play has in some way swallowed them up. In the equivalent scenes of *The Magnetic Lady* battle-lines are drawn. Jonson's view of the theatre itself seems contracted here: it is no longer a feast or a mirror, but a shop where poetic wares are peddled (Induction, ll. 1–11). The Boy who is minding the shop as a representative of the theatre company is confronted by two representatives of the audience, Probee and Damplay, who correspond roughly to Cordatus and Mitis in *Every Man Out*. Damplay raises objections, Probee and the Boy defend the author. But Damplay, unlike Mitis, will not be won over (Chorus to Act III, 17–20). Jonson, still smarting from the failure of *The New Inn*, must have felt that some audiences were impossible to satisfy; and Damplay is his way of embodying that idea. Probee retorts with a description of the ideal audience as passive and deferential (Chorus to Act IV, 10–13). In *Every Man Out* a lively discussion of the play persisted right to the end; here, there is an effect of exhaustion as Jonson wishes the audience would just be quiet and let him get on with it. Damplay subsides with a grudging, 'Well, let us expect then: And wit be with us, o' the *Poets* part' (Chorus to Act IV, 35–6). Like the Gossips of *The Staple of News*, the Induction figures of *The Magnetic Lady* fail to return at the end. The play has absorbed the approval of Probee and the Boy and simply overridden the objections of Damplay.

The younger Jonson of *Every Man Out* was idealistic enough to imagine winning over a censorious member of the audience. The mature Jonson of *Bartholomew Fair* was prepared to meet his motley public half way, to appeal to their tastes without sacrificing his own integrity. He had taken their measure; all he asked was that they remained themselves, and he could deal with them. But the older, more cantankerous Jonson of *The Staple of News* and *The Magnetic Lady* tries to split the audience, cutting out the foolish and carping members for separate treatment, putting them into the play as objects of attack, and finally overwhelming them by inflicting on them the punishment he so often inflicts on his dramatic characters – a final reduction to silence.

It is a relief to note, however, that this was not Jonson's last word on his audience. The Prologue to *The Sad Shepherd* opens with one of his most conciliatory statements, and it is a pity no audience ever heard it:

> He that hath feasted you these forty yeares,
> And fitted Fables, for your finer eares,
> Although at first, he scarce could hit the bore;
> Yet you, with patience harkning more and more,
> At length have growne up to him, and made knowne,
> The Working of his Pen is now your owne.   (ll. 1–6)

There is some confusion here over whether the audience has educated Jonson or Jonson has educated the audience; but even that suggests a certain harmony of interest. The writer and his public have grown together. This is of course directly at odds with what Jonson has recorded elsewhere of his battles with the audience, and it is best read, I think, as one of those passages where Jonson oversteps the literal truth in order to depict an ideal.

There is no suggestion that the audience with which Jonson claims a rapport in this Prologue is a specially limited one. Normally, however, when Jonson depicted his ideal public in any detail he emphasized that it was a select, discriminating public. In two early Epigrams he opposes 'The Learned Critic' (XVII) to 'My Mere English Censurer' (XVIII). Significantly, the first Epigram is the shorter of the two, and simply declares that Jonson will submit to the judgement of such a critic. 'My Mere English Censurer', on the other hand, cannot properly judge Jonson's Epigrams, because he does not know the classical tradition in which Jonson is working. The notes on sources attached to the Quarto text of *Sejanus*[5] assume a scholarly reader; indeed, they would make no sense to anyone else. Jonson is openly condescending to the uninitiate in *Part of the King's Entertainment in Passing to his Coronation*, where he declares the allegorical devices were so presented

> as vpon the view, they might, without cloud, or obscuritie, declare themselues to the sharpe and learned: And for the multitude, no doubt but their grounded iudgements did gaze, said it was fine, and were satisfied.   (ll. 263–7)

The 'grounded iudgements' are also given something to satisfy them in *Bartholomew Fair*; but in this early entertainment, Jonson is more upon his dignity, the tone is colder, and the priority given to the learned is much firmer.

The appeal to learning, however, is just one special application of a general strategy of audience control. Those who approve of Jonson's work are presented not just as learned but as wise and good. Asper declares, 'Good men, and vertuous spirits, that lothe their vices, / Will cherish my free labours, loue my lines' (Induction, ll. 134–5). *Sejanus*, torn to pieces by the mob as its title character was, will be restored by *'the loue of good men'* (Epistle to Lord Aubigny, ll. 14–15). For Jonson, it is impossible

to be a good reader or audience without first being a good man.
One must also be alert and intelligent. Asper promises

> To please, but whom? attentiue auditors,
> Such as will ioyne their profit with their pleasure,
> And come to feed their vnderstanding parts.
>
> (Induction, ll. 201–3)

As the learning displayed in some of Jonson's work restricts the
number of readers who will appreciate it fully, so the frequent
complexity of his plots challenges the wits of the audience, and
means that only the acute will really understand the play. In the
Induction to *The Magnetic Lady* the Boy declares, on behalf of
the author:

> A good *Play,* is like a skeene of silke: which, if you take by the
> right end, you may wind off, at pleasure, on the bottome, or
> card of your discourse, in a tale, or so; how you will: But if
> you light on the wrong end, you will pull all into a knot, or
> elfe-lock; which nothing but the sheers, or a candle will undoe,
> or separate.   (ll. 136–41)

As Jonson's work includes satiric caricatures of hostile readers
and audiences, so it includes idealized images of good ones –
learned, keen-witted, ingenious at unravelling a complex work.
But the effect goes beyond simply flattering or intimidating the
audience. Jonson includes the reception of the work as part of
the work's vision, so that we are to reflect not just on our own
view of it but on how a work of art relates to its public in general
– what it can achieve, and how it is liable to be frustrated. The
reception of a play thus becomes part of its action. The debates
of Cordatus and Mitis, Probee and Damplay; the chattering of
the Gossips; the defeat of the monster Envy by the armed
Prologue – these are fuller ramifications of the conflict between
virtue and folly that the plays themselves show. The drama
within the play is thus extended to include what happens when
the play enters the world.

The creation of a select circle is another part of this drama: as the
doors are barred in the court scene of *Poetaster,* so the unworthy
are frequently warned off Jonson's plays. The Prologue to *The*

New Inn, having declared that we are '*welcome all*' (l. 1) goes on to suggest that some are more welcome than others (ll. 24–6). The Induction to *Bartholomew Fair* promises the play will give no offence to those that have 'the wit, or the honesty to thinke well of themselues' (l. 84). Passages like these suggest a separation of sheep and goats within a particular audience. The two Prologues to *The Staple of News*, on the other hand, imagine more than one kind of audience, and show that the function of the play changes as the audience does. 'The Prologue for the Stage' presents the author as a stern figure instructing and moulding his public:

> He must be one that can instruct your youth,
> And keepe your *Acme* in the state of truth,
> Must enterprize this worke.   (ll. 25–7)

Like the Epistle Dedicatory to *Volpone*, this presents a didactic view of art; and the Prologue itself is pedagogic in manner, loftily instructing the audience in the nature of art. 'The Prologue for the Court', on the other hand, assumes an audience that needs no instruction:

> *A Worke not smelling of the Lampe, to night,*
> *But fitted for your* Maiesties *disport,*
> *And writ to the* Meridian *of your* Court,
> *Wee bring; and hope it may produce delight:*
> *The rather, being offerd, as a* Rite,
> *To* Schollers, *that can iudge, and faire report*
> *The sense they heare, aboue the vulgar sort*
> *Of* Nut-crackers, *that only come for sight.*   (ll. 1–8)

The play is presented in rather a forbidding manner to the general public; but with the courtly and learned, Jonson's manner is more relaxed; to them the play offers delight. They will naturally appreciate it more than the vulgar do, and do not need to be lectured. For each audience, then, the play presents a different face. Only the reader – and this is a point I want to return to later – is privileged to have both Prologues, and to include in his experience of the play the added reflections on art and its public that come from putting the two together.

At times, even the most judicious and learned spectator is tacitly invited to stand aside while Jonson appeals to the one member of the audience who matters most of all. The deep perspective effect of *Oberon*, where after a series of discoveries the Prince is revealed at the very back of the set, would be fully appreciated from only one seat in the audience – the King's.[6] What the rest of us are aware of is a special relationship, a straight line of vision between the principal masquer, Prince Henry, and the principal spectator, King James. We are invited not to share it but to watch and admire it as an image of rapport between art and its audience at the highest level. We are also allowed to listen as Jonson makes a more jocular appeal to the King's special interests in *Bartholomew Fair*. Like the first Prologue to *The Staple of News*, the Induction is for the public stage, and for that stage only. At court it is not needed. The appeal to the King can be swifter and simpler; for one thing, he is already familiar with one of the play's subjects – Puritanism – and takes a special interest in it:

> *Your* Maiesty *is welcome to a* Fayre;
> *Such place, such men, such language & such ware,*
> *You must expect: with these, the zealous noyse*
> *Of your lands* Faction, *scandaliz'd at toyes,*
> *As* Babies, Hobby-horses, Puppet-playes,
> *And such like rage, whereof the petulant wayes*
> *Your selfe haue knowne, and haue bin vext with long.*
>
> ('The Prologue to the King's Majesty', ll. 1–7)

Unlike the public audience, the King does not have to be negotiated with; he can be simply welcomed. He does not need a full debate about Jonson's selection of material for the Fair scenes; he knows his kingdom well enough to know what to expect. And he can appreciate the satire on the Puritans better than any other man in England. He is also, the Epilogue declares, best able to judge the play as a work of art and to nullify by his approval whatever attacks the envious may make on it:

> *This is your power to iudge (great Sir) and not*
> *the enuy of a few. Which if wee haue got,*
> *Wee value lese what their dislike can bring,*
> *if it so happy be, t'haue pleas'd the* King. (ll. 9–12)

In the Epilogue to *The Magnetic Lady*, there is a similar appeal
from the author to King Charles, '*To which voice he stands, / And
prefers that, 'fore all the Peoples hands*' (ll. 7–8). The headnote
'Chorus changed into an Epilogue: to the King' suggests that
this appeal beyond the general public has at some stage replaced
a final appearance of Probee, Damplay and the Boy. In the end,
only the King matters.

   This implies a final despair about the public audience; but the
courtly audience Jonson addressed in the masques – an audience
of which the King was the centre – could be treated very
differently. This is partly because of the peculiarity of the
masque form itself. In the plays Jonson had to be constantly
reminding the audience of its responsibilities, as traditional
dramatic form does not automatically require the audience to be
conscious of itself. The masque is another matter. The audience
is a large part of the show: the King is celebrated, the disguised
masquers take out the ladies to dance; the audience's knowledge
of the true identity of the performers – who may be their friends
and kinsmen – is not an accident but an important part of the
total effect. Though its conventions present an idealized world,
the masque is in one sense about the audience sitting in the great
hall watching it and sometimes joining in. It does not present a
separate world they can relate to in one fashion or another, or
remain detached from, as the case requires; it presents an
idealized picture of their own world.[7] Accordingly, there are
times when Jonson's appeals to masque audience are more fully
worked into the fabric of the action than was possible in
conventional drama.

   Jonson seeks not just their approval but their involvement.
The Hags of *The Masque of Queens* threaten to 'Darken all this
roofe, / With present fogges' (ll. 241–2) – to darken, in other
words, the room where the masque is taking place, to put out
the candles. There is an implied threat to the audience here, and
when the Hags are driven out it is the audience itself that is
rescued. More often, they are appealed to as rescuers or judges.
The relationship of Love to the court ladies is particularly
important. In *The Haddington Masque* Venus, searching for the
missing Cupid, turns a pretty compliment by suggesting that

the audience itself may be the best place to search:

> Looke in all these ladies eyes,
> And see if there he not concealed lyes;
> Or in their bosomes, 'twixt their swelling brests:
> (The *wag* affects to make himselfe such nests).   (ll. 73–6)

The conceit is more elaborately developed in *Love Freed from Ignorance and Folly*, where Love, imprisoned by the Sphinx, asks the audience's aid:

> Hath this place
> None will pittie CVPIDS case?
> Some soft eye, (while I can see
> Who it is, that melts for mee)
> Weepe a fit.   (ll. 37–41)

The Sphinx, representing Ignorance, is a menace not only to Love but to the audience as well:

> And, in truth, ther's none haue reason,
> Like your selues, to hate the treason.
> For it practis'd was on beautie,
> Vnto whom LOVE owes all dutie.   (ll. 47–50)

As Love embarks on the ordeal of answering the Sphinx's riddle he takes heart 'From my Iudges heere, that sit / As they would not loose LOVE yet' (ll. 145–6).

But the beauty of the ladies, and their devotion to love, are not enough to effect a rescue. Love flounders in his attempt on the riddle, thinking the answer is 'a Lady'; he is, perhaps, too exclusively concerned with that part of his audience. About to be carried off and torn apart by the Sphinx, he appeals to them again, but sounds baffled and frustrated as he does so: 'Ladies, haue your lookes no power / To helpe LOVE, at such an hower?' (ll. 255–6). He has to be rescued by the priests of the Muses, who urge him to look again at his audience, but with a more discriminating eye:

> But they bid, that thou should'st looke
> In the brightest face here shining,
> And the same, as would a booke,
> Shall helpe thee in diuining.   (ll. 279–82)

The answer to the riddle is 'King James'. The appeals to the audience have given an urgency to the masque's message – we are all concerned in the freeing of love from ignorance and folly – but they do this without spoiling the light tone. Indeed, they enhance that tone by embodying the appeals to the ladies in witty compliments to their beauty. At the same time, the audience is made to reflect on the inadequacy of beauty by itself to save Love from its enemies. The rescue comes not from the ladies of the audience, but from the priests of the Muses and from the virtue embodied in the King. It is the contemplation of virtue, not of beauty alone, that saves Love from the forces that threaten to degrade it; and it is through poetry that we learn this truth. The ideas are deeply serious, but the device of the riddle keeps the tone light. And the involvement of the audience – first the ladies, and then the King – has the double effect of stressing the reality of the issues while keeping the entertainment itself witty and playful.

There is a similar appeal to the audience to come to Love's aid in *Love Restored* (ll. 210–17); the quarrelling Cupids of *A Challenge at Tilt* appeal to the ladies to settle their argument (ll. 6–14); and the conflict of *Lovers Made Men* is resolved by allowing the men to remain lovers 'For your faire sakes (you brighter starres, / Who have beheld these civill warres' (ll. 206–7). In each case the audience is involved in a central issue. Something like the power of the masque audience is attributed to the theatre audience at the end of *Every Man Out*, where their applause may make Macilente as fat as Falstaff, and at the beginning of *Poetaster*, where Envy is cowed not just by the Prologue but by 'this calme troupe' (Induction, l. 57) who have assembled to watch the play. But these are, by comparison, peripheral effects: the central conflicts of the plays have to be worked out by the characters Jonson has invented for the purpose. That is true to a great extent of the masques as well, of course; but the difference is that the characters of the masques can enlist the support of the audience, naturally and directly, while the central action is taking place. During the speeches, they are involved in imagination; and when they participate in the final dances – whose significance as an image of virtuous action is expounded in *Pleasure Reconciled to Virtue* – their involvement becomes direct and practical.

This sounds as though Jonson created in the masque the image of an ideal audience, not only sympathetic and understanding but able to take a direct role for good in the performance itself. But there were problems with the masque form, and indeed with the very device I have just been exploring. The constant awareness of the actual audience must have made the illusion precarious, for the reality of the Jacobean court was very far from the ideal the masques attempted to embody. There must have been times when the suspension of disbelief became impossible to sustain. Against the appeals to the beauty of the ladies in *The Haddington Masque* and *Love Freed from Ignorance and Folly* we may set Mercury's bawdy appeal for help in *Mercury Vindicated from the Alchemists at Court*:

> Ne're an olde Gentle-woman i' the house, that has a wrinckle
> about her, to hide mee in? I could run into a Seruing-womans
> pocket now; her gloue, any little hole. Some mercifull
> vardingale among so many, be bounteous, and vndertake me.
>
> (ll. 32–6)

Jonson seems to be parodying the appeals of Love in earlier masques; and in so doing he gets much closer to the reality of the court audience.

When *Bartholomew Fair* was performed in a second-rate theatre that doubled as a bear-baiting establishment the relation between art and reality must have seemed very close indeed. But when one of Jonson's more graceful masques was performed at the court of King James the disparity must have been painful. *The Masque of Blackness* makes charming reading; but a letter of Dudley Carleton gives us the gross reality of the original performance:

> The confusion in getting in was so great, that some Ladies lie
> by it and complaine of the fury of the white stafes. In the
> passages through the galleries they were shutt vp in seuerall
> heapes betwixt dores, and there stayed till all was ended. and in
> the cumming owt, a banquet which was prepared for the king
> in the great chamber was ouerturned table and all before it was

skarce touched. It were infinit to tell you what losses there
were of chaynes, Jewels, purces, and such like loose ware. and
one woeman amongst the rest lost her honesty, for which she
was caried to the porters lodge being surprised at her busines
on the top of the Taras.[8]

Bartholomew Fair sounds genteel by comparison.

While Jonson himself did not record such embarrassing
incidents he did comment, in the texts of several masques, on
the uncertainties of performance. This problem must have been
more acutely felt in a masque than in a play, for there was
usually one performance only, and therefore no chance to
correct mistakes on a later occasion. *The Entertainment at Althorp*
included a very tricky effect that could easily have gone wrong.
This is Jonson's account:

> At that, the whole wood and place resounded with the noyse of
> cornets, hornes, and other hunting musique, and a brace of choise
> Deere put out, and as fortunately kill'd, as they were meant to be;
> euen in the sight of her Maiestie.   (ll. 228–31)

In that '*fortunately*' one hears a small sigh of relief. Other parts of
the performance did not go so well: the speeches in the second
half of the entertainment were rendered inaudible by the crowd
(ll. 236–7; 295). The remarkable thing is that Jonson reports this
to the reader, instead of tactfully suppressing it. While he does
not say so explicitly, he seems to feel, even in this early entertainment, a sense of grievance at the ease with which the text of a
show like this could be spoiled, and a desire to share that
grievance with an understanding reader. Another complaint is
registered in the text of *The Haddington Masque*, and it is a
particularly revealing one. Jonson reports that the Epithalamion,
'*because it was sung in pieces, betweene the* daunces, *shew'd to be so
many seuerall* songs; *but was made to be read an intire* Poeme'
(ll. 340–2). Not just an accident of performance, but the basic
requirements of the form, spoiled the effect Jonson intended.
The music and dancing – both essential to a masque – meant that
the audience could not concentrate on the poem the way a reader
can.

The words '*made to be read an intire* Poeme' sum up Jonson's
discontent with the masque in performance, and suggest one

reason why the masque audience, idealized though it was in the
text, could not finally be the ideal audience Jonson was looking
for. The masque, by its very nature, was too full of accidents
and distractions to allow the audience to concentrate on the text
in the manner that Jonson intended. The reader is free of those
accidents, and to that extent is a better audience; but his
experience is so far from that of the masque in performance that
he is virtually dealing with a different genre.[9] Two examples
from *The Masque of Queens* illustrate the difference strikingly.
When the House of Fame is revealed and the Queens descend
Jonson not only describes the House but gives an account of each
Queen and her history. A few moments of performance become
well over two hundred lines of text (ll. 475–709); and the reader
is slowed down at a point when the audience must have felt the
pace quicken. The effect is reversed a few lines later, as Jonson
describes the dances of the masquers, 'entertayning the time,
almost to the space of an hower, with singular variety' (ll.
737–8). The main body of the performance is, for the reader,
despatched in a moment. The carefully prepared holograph of
this masque, presented to the Queen, shows that Jonson was
prepared to treat the masque as a work to be read; but it becomes
a very different work in the process. In the printing of some later
masques, Jonson took the opportunity to fight again battles he
had lost on the night itself. For example, a contemporary
account of *Time Vindicated to Himself and to his Honours* describes
three scene-changes of which only one is mentioned in Jonson's
text.[10] Jonson presents the masque as he wanted it to be, before
Inigo Jones meddled with it. In theory, a masque can realize
itself only in performance; but there were so many problems in
performance that Jonson in the end had to use the printed
version as the only safe way to convey his intentions. And a
masque in print is not really a masque. For all he attempted – and
achieved – in this form Jonson must have found it frustrating for
reasons that went deeper than a personality clash with Inigo
Jones. It may be worth noting that in Jonson's First Folio the
plays and poems are handsomely presented and given plenty of
space while the masques are, by comparison, cramped and
huddled at the end of the volume.

Jonson's final appeal to the reader shows where his touchy relations with his public ultimately led him. By caricaturing his stage audience and idealizing his masque audience, Jonson could get some measure of imaginative control over the uncertainties of performance. But of course the control was not literal. Even the best of texts could be spoiled by incompetent performers and insensitive audiences. Only in print could Jonson reach his public directly, without interference. The title page of *The New Inn* breaks all the rules of play publication by calling attention to the failure of the work in performance, declaring 'it was neuer acted, but most negligently play'd, by some, the Kings Seruants. And more squeamishly beheld, and censured by others, the Kings Subiects'. Jonson's usual honesty makes him qualify his attack on the players by admitting that the Host and Lovel were well acted (The Persons of the Play, ll. 1, 13–14) but nothing qualifies his rage at the audience. The Dedication to the Reader declares that any reader, however stupid, must be better than the theatregoing public:

> if thou canst but spell, and ioyne my sense; there is more hope
> of thee, then of a hundred fastidious *impertinents,* who were
> there present the first day, yet neuer made piece of their
> prospect the right way.   (ll. 3–7)

When Jonson tells the reader that he trusts to his 'rusticke candor' (l. 18) he seems to be turning away not only from the theatre but from the sophisticated city it draws on. There is no Elizabethan writer more bound to the city than Jonson; yet here he appears to be saying it is better to be read in a farmhouse than performed at the Globe.

Jonson's readers have special privileges. There are little typographical jokes – like the black letter used when Subtle addresses Face as 'Vlen Spiegel' (*The Alchemist,* II.iii.32), and used again throughout Vangoose's broken-English speeches in *The Masque of Augurs.* There are the scholarly notes to *Sejanus* and the elaborate glosses to *The Masque of Queens,* the latter provided at the command of Prince Henry (Dedication, ll. 32–41).[11] *Every Man out of his Humour* and *The New Inn* are introduced by short essays on the principal characters. As with the masques, battles lost in production could be won in print. *Every Man Out* was (not surprisingly) cut for performance; *Sejanus* in the theatre included work by another hand. In both cases Jonson suppressed the acting version and gave the reader the play as he intended it to be. No dramatist of his time took such elaborate care over the presentation of his work to the reader,[12] and no dramatist until Bernard Shaw would do so again. There must have been struggles here as well: Jonson once wrote to a friend, 'My Printer, and I, shall afford subiect enough for a Tragi-Comoedy.'[13] He must have been as uncomfortable a presence in the printing house as he was in the theatre. But, particularly in the magnificent First Folio, he succeeded in controlling the medium through which his work was presented as he never could in the theatre or at the court, and he used his power with flair and imagination. Simply as a piece of printing, his Folio is far more attractive than Shakespeare's.

The *Epigrams'* opening injunction 'to understand' is repeated in the address 'To the Reader' before *The Alchemist*: '*If thou beest more, thou art an Vnderstander, and then I trust thee*' (ll. 1–2). A similar trust is registered at the opening of *Catiline*, where the long satiric address 'To the Reader in Ordinarie' is followed by a brief note 'To the Reader extraordinary': 'You I would vnderstand to be the better Man, though Places in Court go otherwise: to you I submit my selfe, and worke. Farewell.' The brusqueness is in fact a compliment: between men who understand and trust each other, few words are needed. The same point is made in 'An Epistle to Master John Selden' (*The Underwood*, XIV) but here the trust is deeper: 'I know to whom I write. Here, I am sure, / Though I am short, I cannot be obscure' (ll. 1–2). Jonson also claimed to 'know' the audience of *Bartholomew Fair*, but that did not relieve his anxiety about them, as the elaborate negotiations of the Induction show. He knows Selden in another way: this is a particular man, whose response Jonson can trust because he knows him as an individual, not as a type. The addresses to the ideal reader in *The Alchemist* and *Catiline* have, perhaps, something wistful about them; this ideal reader is a creature more of hope than certainty. And there are – as we have seen – enough bad readers that Jonson's trust in 'the reader' as an abstraction cannot be absolute. As Jonson's images of virtue in the *Epigrams* are particular, named people, so his ideal audience, finally, is not an abstraction but a single person he can name, know and trust. This is the ultimate advantage of writing over performance: the theatre takes anyone who pays entrance money, the masque audience is made up of courtiers important enough or aggressive enough to find a place. Only in a poem written between friends can Jonson say, 'I know to whom I write'. The poem is not of course restricted to that one reader; it is offered to the public. But what the public sees is an image of the ideal bond between the writer and his audience; and it is typical of Jonson that the terms in which the ideal is expressed are not abstract but concrete and particular.

As the reader is privileged to overhear Donne's lectures to his mistress, or Herbert's dealings with his God, we are allowed to overhear Jonson's addresses to the most valued members of his circle. After contemplating the general, unsympathetic public he turns with relief to Elizabeth, Countess of Rutland:

> But let this drosse carry what price it will
> > With noble ignorants, and let them still,
> Turne, vpon scorned verse, their quarter-face:
> > With you, I know, my offring will find grace.
> > (*The Forest*, XII: 'Epistle to Elizabeth Countess of Rutland',
> > > ll. 27–30)

There is a certain exclusiveness to the working of good art, as there is to that of virtue in general. Presenting Donne's Satires to Lucy, Countess of Bedford, Jonson writes:

> > Rare poemes askes rare friends.
> Yet, *Satyres,* since the most of mankind bee
> > Their vn-auoided subiect, fewest see:
> For none ere tooke that pleasure in sinnes sense,
> > But, when they heard it tax'd, took more offence.
> They, then, that liuing where the matter is bred,
> > Dare for these poemes, yet, both aske, and read,
> And like them too; must needfully, though few,
> > Be of the best: and 'mongst those, best are you.
> > (*Epigrams*, XCIV: 'To Lucy, Countess of Bedford, with
> > > Mr. Donne's Satires', ll. 6–14)

There is a general principle about the good reader here, who
must know the world and yet be free of its vices in order to
appreciate satire fully; but that principle is identified with a
particular woman.

As we see in *Poetaster*, a good poet can also trust another good
poet; in his commendatory verses, and in the Shakespeare ode,
Jonson presents himself in this light, as the understanding friend
who can appreciate the work of his colleagues. Jonson sees
Donne as having the same function for him:

> Who shall doubt, DONNE, where I a *Poet* bee,
>   When I dare send my *Epigrammes* to thee?
> That so alone canst iudge, so'alone dost make:
>   And, in thy censures, euenly, dost take
> As free simplicitie, to dis-auow,
>   As thou hast best authoritie, to'allow.
> Reade all I send: and, if I find but one
>   Mark'd by thy hand, and with the better stone,
> My title's seal'd. Those that for claps doe write,
>   Let pui'nees, porters, players praise delight,
> And, till they burst, their backs, like asses load:
>   A man should seeke great glorie, and not broad.
>   (*Epigrams*, XCVI: 'To John Donne', ll. 1–12)

Donne is not just named but particularized. He is, like Jonson
himself, a plain speaker; and he too writes epigrams. On both
counts his opinion is worth having. 'Reade all I send' suggests
that Jonson is in the habit of showing him not the odd poem here
and there, but a substantial part of his work. In return, he gets a
mixture of praise and censure. 'Great glorie, and not broad' has
two implications: as Donne is discriminating in his choice of
poems to praise, so Jonson is discriminating in his choice of
readers. This is the ultimate source of the rapport between them:
they share, recognize and value in each other a critical intelligence that is content with nothing but the best.

While the theatre audience, all too often, is simply bludgeoned
into submission, Jonson treats his particular readers with respect.
He also allows touches of good humour, and in one poem in
particular acknowledges that however his poetry matters to
him, he cannot expect it to have quite the same importance for

his readers. In 'An Epigram to my Muse, the Lady Digby, on her Husband, Sir Kenelme Digby' (*The Underwood*, LXXVIII) he adds to the epigram in praise of Digby a little dramatic scene in which he imagines Lady Digby showing the poem to her husband:

> Goe, *Muse,* in, and salute him. Say he be
>   Busie, or frowne at first; when he sees thee,
> He will cleare up his forehead, thinke thou bring'st
>   Good *Omen* to him, in the note thou sing'st,
> For he doth love my Verses, and will looke
>   Upon them, (next to *Spenser*'s noble booke,)
> And praise them too.   (ll. 19–25)

He has just praised Digby as a man of public affairs, and in this passage there is a jocular acknowledgement that to present him with a poem may look like an intrusion on the time of a busy man. But Jonson's relations with Digby are such that he knows the intrusion will be forgiven, and he goes on to imagine Digby's approval of his verse leading to the approval of the Treasurer, Lord Weston, and to widespread interest – 'what copies shall be had, / What transcripts begg'd?' (ll. 29–30) – as one good judge sets the example for his whole circle. There may also be a standing joke between Jonson and the Digbys implied in the reservation about Spenser, whom Sir Kenelm still prefers. Spenser was not one of Jonson's favourite authors,[14] but he suggests that he knows enough not to lecture Sir Kenelm on the subject. Jonson expects his poem to be praised, of course; but he shows its reception as one point in a busy day, and he places Digby's interest in his work in the context of his general taste. He shows, in short, the poem making its way in the traffic of the world. This was another reason why Jonson took as his ideal public particular, named individuals, instead of creating fictional readers whose one function was to study and admire Ben Jonson: he wanted readers who knew the real world, and lived in it, for he wanted his art to be part of that world.

II

To study Jonson's view of his audience, then, is ultimately to be led to the deeper issue of the relations between a work of art and

the reality that surrounds it, feeds it, and responds to it. In the
'Epistle to Katherine, Lady Aubigny' (*The Forest*, XIII) the lady is
both the reader and the subject of the poem, and as we read it we
seem to see two ladies – one within the poem, the other without:

> Where,
>   If it may stand with your soft blush to heare
> Your selfe but told vnto your selfe, and see
>   In my character, what your features bee,
> You will not from the paper slightly passe:
>   No lady, but, at some time, loues her glasse.
> And this shall be no false one, but as much
>   Remou'd, as you from need to haue it such.
> Looke then, and see your selfe. I will not say
>   Your beautie; for you see that euery day:
> And so doe many more.   (ll. 21–31)

The poem is a mirror reflecting the lady's true nature; but in
declaring this it gives us, as readers, a broader view: we are
aware of Lady Katherine studying this mirror, aware of her
natural face as well as of the perfect image. This awareness
comes through the friendly joke about female vanity, 'No lady,
but, at some time, loues her glasse' that adds a light touch of
mockery to the controlling image, suggesting a joke shared
between Jonson and the real Lady Katherine. And the lady
whose concentrated attention the poem now claims (and whose
retirement from the world Jonson will praise) is shown as
having in fact a full social life: her beauty is seen by many, every
day. But that is merely her physical beauty: 'My mirror is more
subtile, cleere, refin'd, / And takes, and giues the beauties of the
mind' (ll. 43–4). The face she presents to the world, even to
herself, is one thing; but the poem promises to show her true
nature, something the ordinary world does not always give her
time to study.

This true nature is not subject to time: this mirror, unlike the
mirrors that reflect physical beauty, holds its image forever. The
poem ends:

> and as long yeeres doe passe,
> *Madame*, be bold to vse this truest glasse:
> Wherein, your forme, you still the same shall finde;
>   Because nor it can change, nor such a minde.   (ll. 121–4)

This may mean that while the lady's appearance will change through time, her mind cannot, and the poem reflects her mind's constancy. But it can also mean that while the lady's nature may change the poem will hold her virtues – her true self, whatever time does to her – fixed forever. In the last line, the mind that cannot change may be not the lady's mind, but her mind as the poem depicts it. If she ever feels her nature weakened, she can return to the poem for an image of what she ought to be. In the opening section of this poem Jonson complains of the dangers to virtue and depicts the lady and himself as two good people making common cause against a world where good is under siege. But when it comes to the lady's own nature, Jonson plays a subtler game, contrasting the lady who reads the poem – admirable but potentially imperfect – with the perfect lady shown within the poem.

There is a similar effect, more simply presented, in *Hymenaei*, where performers take the parts of the bride and groom so that the actual bride and groom in the audience are seen to be looking at idealized images of themselves. The view of the audience in general includes both couples. Elsewhere, the mirror effect is more satirical. There is a teasing parallel between the real court and the play court when the Epistle Dedicatory to *Cynthia's Revels* is addressed 'To THE SPECIALL FOVNTAINE OF MANNERS: The Court' (ll. 1–4), and we remember that the play's subtitle – its main title in the Quarto – is *The Fountain of Self-Love*. The Hope Theatre is as stinking as Smithfield; there is a parallel between our attending it and our attending Bartholomew Fair. There may be a similar parallel in the fact that Lovewit's house, like the theatre we attend to watch *The Alchemist*, is in the Blackfriars.[15] In general, when Jonson sets a comedy in London he lays on the local colour heavily, to emphasize that the play is a reflection of the city its audience lives in and will return to at the end of the performance. In *The Devil is an Ass* the effect is more complicated. The first scene takes place in Hell; at the end of it, with nothing to indicate a change of setting, Satan shows Pug 'Fitz-dottrel . . . *coming forth*' (I. i. 152). Hell becomes London; and London becomes the stage. Throughout the play Fitzdottrel fusses about wanting to see a new play, *The Devil is an Ass*. Later, there are references to a real player, Dick Robinson, who may well have been in the original cast (II. viii. 64–78). This self-conscious theatricality takes us back to the starting point, for Jonson's Hell is created largely in terms of old-fashioned theatrical devices – the laughing devil, the vice with his jingling verse. Are we in Hell, London, or the theatre? The answer is that we are in all three, and each is a mocking reflection of the other two.

In passages like these the relation of art to the world around it is that of a mirror, mocking or idealizing as the case may be, but claiming to give a direct reflection. At other times, there is an effect of critical dislocation. *Bartholomew Fair* at court must have been – in intention at least – very different from *Bartholomew Fair* at the Hope Theatre, with the beauty, wit and sophistication of the court audience putting the low-life characters firmly in their place.[16] A similar effect must have resulted – more decisively, for hers was a more severe court – when the fools of *Every Man out of his Humour* were paraded before Queen Elizabeth. A courtly audience seems required for the rustic comedy of *A Tale of a Tub*, and not just because Jonson used it as part of his campaign against Inigo Jones. The Prologue promises '*to shew what different things / The* Cotes *of* Clownes, *are from the* Courts *of* Kings' (ll. 11–12). Throughout the play the characters' rustic stupidity is conveyed by their garbled references to English history, and to classical history and mythology; the jokes are geared for a learned audience, and their effect is to cast the mocking shadows of the great behind the tiny figures of the clowns. If there is something academic in Jonson's picture of rural life, it may be because he does not finally see the rustics as having a valid life of their own. They are incomplete beings, defined not by what they have but by what they lack – the intelligence and sophistication of their audience.

This attention to the world that lies around the work of art is connected with the realism Jonson sometimes proclaimed as the key to his work. The promise of verisimilitude in the Prologue to *Every Man in his Humour* – 'deedes, and language, such as men doe vse' (l. 21) – is, like the didacticism of the preface to *Volpone*, at best a half-truth about the play. But if surface realism is not essential to Jonson's style, a reverence for hard facts is.[17] We have seen how he made a point of using actual people in his poems. Though he was never in Venice, he is careful to give us all the right place-names in *Volpone*. The characters of *Every Man Out* may be cartoons, but we find them at the opening of Act III in the middle aisle of St Paul's Cathedral. A constant attention to the facts recorded in his sources gives Jonson's Roman tragedies at certain points the quality of documentary[18] – sometimes at the expense of theatrical convenience, as when eavesdroppers in *Sejanus* are required to hide between the roof and ceiling[19] or *Catiline* grinds to a halt so that Cicero can deliver a version of one of his actual speeches. Jonson's 'realism' is not so much a consistent reproduction of the surface of life as an attempt to keep his invented worlds in constant touch with the real one.

We have seen that when Jonson depicted the ideal masque audience he allowed them to share in the perfection of the masque's inner vision. But Jonson knew – better than we do – that the real court was not like that. And at times he worked this knowledge into the masques themselves, to create an interplay between the ideal court and the real one. It was safest to do this in a jocular way. When the comic Irishmen of *The Irish Masque at Court* have some difficulty in recognizing the King (ll. 13–17) this can be passed off as a joke about their own ignorance; but it also suggests that the King is not the far-beaming blaze of majesty the masques would usually have us believe. The abstract perfection of monarchy is also broken down in Pan's impudent address to the King and Queen in *The Entertainment at Highgate*, where the King is seen as fond of hunting and the Queen (as becomes a Dane) of drinking (ll. 219–28). But the most elaborate exercise of this kind is *The Gypsies Metamorphosed*, whose constant playful impudence makes it one of the most engaging – and least typical – of Jonson's masques. The fortune-telling sequence plays on the actual natures of the people involved – the King is told by the Captain of the Gypsies:

> You are no great wencher, I see by your table,
> Although your *Mons Veneris* sayes you are able,

You liue chaste and single, and haue buried your wife,
And meane not to marrie by the line of your life.

(ll. 287–90)

If James himself had not been so unabashed about his preference
for young men this would have been a dangerous speech; as it is,
Jonson can add to its piquancy by giving it to Buckingham. And
the later, more serious part of the King's fortune glances at the
particular relations of the two men: discussing fortunes, the
Captain declares, 'Yet are you Maker, Sir, of mine' (l. 341).
Other passages in the masque also refer to James not as ideal
sovereign but as particular man, glancing for example at his
detestation of tobacco (ll. 1359–63). The picture of James is still
flattering – he is generous, peaceable, learned – but it includes
enough of his quirks and eccentricities to bring us closer than
any other masque does to the man himself.[20]

The other 'fortunes' are variable in effect. Some are solemn,
some are genial; but others take the impudence of the address to
the King even farther, notably when Buckingham's rapacious
mother is called 'The greatest felon in the land' (l. 498) –
because, the speaker quickly adds, she steals hearts.[21] More
seriously, the Lord Treasurer is reminded of his responsibilities,
and that all is not well at court:

> Your fortune is good, and will be to sett
> The office vpright, and the *Kinge* out of debt;
> To putt all that haue pensions soone out of theire paine,
> By bringing th'Exchequer in Creditt againe.   (ll. 594–7)

The jovial tone of the masque is maintained; but a real political
problem is glanced at. The holiday mood of the masque is also
touched with reminders of the workaday world in *The Irish
Masque at Court*, when James is hailed as the King who 'Should
end our countreyes most vnnaturall broyles' (l. 157). There is a
more detailed political commentary in *Neptune's Triumph*, where
the joy at Charles and Buckingham's return from Spain includes
sharp reminders of the dangers of that ill-conceived and un-
popular venture – which included the attempts of the Spanish to
win Charles to Catholicism:

And how the *Syrens* woo'd him, by the way,
What Monsters he encountred on the coast,
How neare our generall Ioy was to be lost,
Is not our subiect now: though all these make
The present gladnesse greater, for their sake.   (ll. 145–9)

The reminder of the Prince's danger (besides the threats to his Protestantism, he was at one point nearly lost at sea)[22] is intended to strengthen the mood of rejoicing; but it also adds a touch of political reality to the fantasy of the masque.

The effect, once again, is not to devalue the fantasy but to show it as an invention that has its roots in the real world. The same is ultimately true, I think, of Jonson's many references to the evanescence of the masque itself. In *Timber*, attacking the shows put on for the visiting King of Denmark, he made the obvious moralizing point about their transience: 'The bravery was shewne, it was not possess'd; while it boasted it selfe, it perish'd. It is vile, and a poor thing to place our happinesse on these desires' (ll. 1411–13). But when he was working within the form, he could be subtler. The masques that – like *Oberon* and *The Vision of Delight* – admit their own transience can, paradoxically, claim a more solid basis in reality, since this final honesty places the vision of beauty in the context of a normal world. And sometimes the endings achieve more than that. In the final songs of *Love Freed from Ignorance and Folly* Time, the enemy of the masque, is first attacked and then absorbed into the masque vision:

For he so greedie to deuoure
   His owne, and all that hee brings forth,
Is eating euery piece of houre
   Some obiect of the rarest worth.
Yet this is rescued from his rage,
As not to die by time, or age.
   For beautie hath a liuing name,
   And will to heauen, from whence it came.

The going out.
Now, now. Gentle *Loue* is free, and *Beautie* blest
   With the sight it so much long'd to see.
Let vs the *Muses* PRIESTS, and GRACES goe to rest,

> For in them our labours happie bee.
> Then, then ayry *Musique* sound, and teach our feet,
>   How to moue in time, and measure meet:
> Thus should the *Muses* PRIESTS, and GRACES goe to rest,
> Bowing to the Sunne, throned in the West.   (ll. 362–78)

The first song makes a simple opposition between devouring
time and the ideal permanence of beauty, whose essence is
beyond time. But the second song shows that the masque is not
just destroyed by time, but has used time in its own vision.
Music and dance depend on time, and in the freeing of love from
its enemies the expectation the audience brought to the masque
has been satisfied. Through time things are ended; but through
time they are also ordered, measured and fulfilled. The awareness of reality appears first to destroy the masque, but ends by
confirming it.

There is a similar effect at the end of *Love Restored*:

> Giue end vnto thy pastimes, LOVE,
>   Before they labors proue:
> A little rest betweene,
> Will make thy next showes better seene.
>   Now let them close their eyes, and see
>   If they can dreame of thee,
> Since morning hasts to come in view,
> And all the morning dreames are true.   (ll. 293–300)

The ending of the masque is in fact a blessing, for endless revelry
would spoil the balance of life and become wearisome in itself.
There will be more masques, more celebrations of love; as in
Love Freed the rhythms of time made the masque itself possible,
so here they allow the alternation of pleasure and business that
means the vision can return again in another form. And meanwhile, it can be held in the memory – a dream, but a true one.

As we have seen, Jonson's other major attempt to create an
ideal world was in the *Epigrams*. There too there are reminders
of the greater world that lies around the ordered vision. The
Epistle to the Earl of Pembroke admits that there are real people
behind the idealized figures of vice and virtue,

> *Amongst whom, if I have praysed, vnfortunately, any one, that doth
> not deserue; or, if all answere not, in all numbers, the pictures I haue*

made of them: I hope it will be forgiuen me, that they are no ill
pieces, though they be not like the persons. (ll. 21–5)

The praise of actual people is an important part of Jonson's
concept of virtue; and here he admits that behind the perfect
figures of the poems may be some imperfect individuals. In such
cases the poems must stand on their own merits, like portraits
that may be good paintings without being good likenesses. The
same admission is made in the Epigrams themselves, when two
poems praising Salisbury are followed by 'To My Muse' (LXV),
in which Jonson accuses himself of praising a worthless lord, but
goes on to insist that the poem has its own validity as a statement
about virtue, even if the poet and his subject have both fallen
short of perfection. The vicious are concealed behind type-
names; but there are teasing suggestions that Jonson has particular people in mind here as well, from the comment in the
Epistle to Pembroke – '*I would rather know them by their visards,*
still, then they should publish their faces, at their perill, in my Theater'
(ll. 38–41) – to the poems in which he hints that 'Person Guiltie'
is better known by another name (XXX, XXXVIII). Such reminders of outside reality disturb what looks at first like a
self-contained world. There are also reminders of mortality: a
number of epitaphs, including the moving poems on Jonson's
own children, 'On my First Daughter' (XXII) and 'On My First
Son' (XLV). The latter in particular (discussed in the last chapter)
shows a struggle between the ordered consolations of poetry and
philosophy and the reality of grief. Another, 'Epitaph on
Elizabeth, L. H.' (CXXIV), mysteriously suggests that the small,
perfect epitaph leaves out something of the nature – even the
name – of its subject:

> If, at all, shee had a fault,
> Leaue it buryed in this vault.
> One name was ELIZABETH,
> Th'other let it sleepe with death. (ll. 7–10)

But the most massive disturbance of the order of the *Epigrams*
comes at the end of the collection, in 'The Famous Voyage'
(CXXXIII), where we are taken on a mock-heroic tour of the
London sewers. We are made, in effect, to inspect the plumbing

that lies beneath the ideal world. If the grave is one reminder of
our imperfect natures, then for Jonson, as for Swift – as, indeed,
for a long tradition of satirists – the privy is another. The dignity
of the state vanishes in references to 'the graue fart, late let in
parliament' (l. 108) and 'the Lord *Maiors* foist' (l. 120); so does
the dignity of poetry itself:

> In memorie of which most liquid deed,
> The citie since hath rais'd a Pyramide.
> And I could wish for their eterniz'd sakes,
> My *Muse* had plough'd with his, that sung A-IAX.
>
> (ll. 193–6)

(On the composition of the pyramid, we will not speculate.)
Throughout the journey we feel overwhelmed with stench and
noise, as all that seems left of humanity is its grossness. The
adventurers are warned:

> How dare
> Your daintie nostrills (in so hot a season,
> When euery clerke eates artichokes, and peason,
> Laxatiue lettuce, and such windie meate)
> Tempt such a passage? when each priuies seate
> Is fill'd with buttock? And the walls doe sweate
> Vrine, and plaisters? when the noise doth beate
> Vpon your eares, of discords so vn-sweet?   (ll. 164–71)

The speaker of that warning is Bankes the juggler, his soul trans-
migrated into the body of a cat; and the descent to the sewers
puts us in touch with the animal world at its foulest: 'The sinkes
ran grease, and haire of meazled hogs, / The heads, houghs,
entrailes, and the hides of dogs' (ll. 145–6). More important, this
is a descent into Hell, drawing implicitly on medieval traditions
of the stench of Hell but more obviously on classical descents to
the Underworld: 'Arses were heard to Croake, in stead of frogs;
/ And for one CERBERVS, the whole coast was dogs' (ll. 13–14).
The poem is full of classical references, juxtaposed with London
ones: 'A *Docke* there is, that called is AVERNVS, / Of some *Bride-
well*' (ll. 41–2).

The main effect of the poem is an interplay of the scatological
and the classical; and this is a clue to its place in the *Epigrams*.

Our first impression is of startling incongruity: in place of the careful balancing of praise and satire, we have a vision of overwhelming corruption, presented with an air of perverse enjoyment. It is as though Jonson, having built a carefully ordered moral vision in the collection as a whole, decided – in a fit of childish glee – to smash it in the last poem. But the mock-classical references preserve a certain literary artifice: 'The Famous Voyage' is the recreation of a learned artist, not the diary of a sewerman. The poise of the *Epigrams* is indeed challenged by the vigorous scatology of this last poem; but the poem has its own internal poise, its own self-correcting reminders that there is more to life than sewage. Despite the initial shock, Jonson preserves enough sophistication in 'The Famous Voyage' to let it fit – if only just – into the *Epigrams* as a whole. As in the endings of certain masques, he has created an ideal, ordered world; then reminded us of a world elsewhere; and finally brought the two worlds together in a fuller, more complex vision.

Jonson's most interesting use of this technique – the evocation of a surrounding reality, and its absorption into the work of art itself – was in his love lyrics. That the author of *Bartholomew Fair* and 'The Famous Voyage' was one of the masters of this form may seem at first surprising; but it is less so when we examine what he did with the form. According to Wesley Trimpi, Jonson 'places the experience of love in the context of his experience as a whole'; for him 'Real lovers exist in a real world.'[23] What this means can be seen in three songs, each addressed (conventionally enough) to 'Celia'. The first (*The Forest*, v) appears also in *Volpone*, and sets the persuasion to love against the certainty of death, making that certainty, in fact, the main grounds of the persuasion: 'Time will not be ours, for euer: / He, at length, our good will seuer' (ll. 3–4). As the love affair is hedged about with mortality, so it is rendered precarious by circumstance:

> Cannot we delude the eyes
> Of a few poore houshold spyes?
> Or his easier eares beguile,
> Thus remoued by our wile?   (ll. 11–14)

The suggestion of a furtive, adulterous affair has, like the reminder of mortality, a long ancestry in the literature – not to mention the experience – of love. Jonson combines two traditional motifs to suggest a love made vulnerable both by its own nature and by the universal nature of man. It is also a secret love, and like so many secret activities in Jonson it requires a special language:

> 'Tis no sinne, loues fruit to steale,
> But the sweet theft to reueale:
> To be taken, to be seene,
> These haue crimes accounted beene.   (ll. 15–18)

The twisting of familiar words reminds us, as so often, of the normal ethical scheme in which those words have their proper values. All this makes the poem sound highly critical, and of course that is not its effect: the light, graceful rhythm prevents too solemn a response. Moreover, everything that threatens the love affair is admitted with wit, and turned to account as part of the persuasion; there is an edge of daring that makes the speaker's attitude attractive. That, at least, is the effect when the poem appears in *The Forest*. Its nature alters in the different context of *Volpone*, where Celia's horror and the suggestion of play-acting in the rest of Volpone's wooing add fresh layers of irony. The words are the same, but by putting them in a different context Jonson produces a more sharply ironic response. The effect of the poem in *The Forest* is subtler and I think more satisfying: it implies a surrounding reality, without depicting it too obviously; and it uses that reality to create a fine balance between self-criticism and persuasion.

'To the Same' (*The Forest*, VI) carries on the persuasion, and its concluding lines also find their way into *Volpone*. But here the surrounding reality is more factual, its effect simpler. The speaker demands more and more kisses from the lady:

> First giue a hundred,
> Then a thousand, then another
> Hundred, then vnto the tother
> Adde a thousand, and so more:
> Till you equall with the store,

All the grasse that *Rumney* yeelds,
Or the sands in *Chelsey* fields,
Or the drops in siluer *Thames*,
Or the starres, that guild his streames,
In the silent sommer-nights,
When youths ply their stolne delights. (ll. 8–18)

The expansion from a hundred to a thousand kisses suggests a playing with impossibilities: the next demand will surely be for a million. When it turns out to be another hundred (Jonson teases us by putting the second 'hundred' after the line break), the fantasy seems to circle back toward reality, as though the lovers have to pause to get their energy back. Then, with the intrusion of local place names 'the ideal classical world has suddenly become seventeenth-century England';[24] the effect would be sharpened for the learned reader by the poem's obvious debt to Catullus. The fantasy of infinite love-making is thus placed, with ironic effect, in a factual world. But the irony is not brutal: the Thames is silver, not full of dead dogs, and the reference to young couples making love by the river bank at night, though it belongs to a world we know, is delicately stylized. So is the final appeal to the lover, in the last reference to the infinite number of kisses the speaker wants:

That the curious may not know
How to tell' hem as they flow,
And the enuious, when they find
What their number is, be pin'd. (ll. 19–22)

The 'curious' and 'enuious' have just enough reality to make the love affair seem both furtive and defiant; and no more. This time the relation between the love affair and its context is one of simple opposition (apart from the lovers by the river, who may be part of the persuasion) but the balance between them is still delicate.

The best known 'Song to Celia' (*The Forest*, IX) also makes subtle use of a surrounding reality:

Drinke to me, onely, with thine eyes,
    And I will pledge with mine;
Or leaue a kisse but in the cup,
    And Ile not looke for wine.

The thirst, that from the soule doth rise,
  Doth aske a drinke diuine:
But might I of IOVE's *Nectar* sup,
  I would not change for thine.
I sent thee, late, a rosie wreath,
  Not so much honoring thee,
As giuing it a hope, that there
  It could not withered bee.
But thou thereon did'st onely breath,
  And sent'st it backe to mee:
Since when it growes, and smells, I sweare,
  Not of it selfe, but thee.   (ll. 1–16)

This implies a very different love affair from the persuasions and demands of the other Celia poems. Here, there is a certain distance: the closest the lovers get to kissing is to drink from the same cup. And the distance increases in the second part of the poem, as the implied scene of two lovers in the same room, exchanging glances, is replaced by a scene of the lovers in separate houses, sending tokens back and forth. This is not to say that they are drifting apart: that scene is placed in the past, and they are now together. But in the past, when they were apart, an exchange of tokens took place. Now, in the present, the exchange is simply asked for. In short, the lyric is surrounded by an implied action in which the relations between the lovers undergo delicate shifts, but a fine balance between sympathy and distance is always maintained. This surrounding reality sharpens the beauty of the lyric, making it poignant by suggesting not a menace to the lovers but a certain reserve in the affair itself. A wider context is also suggested in 'The thirst, that from the soule doth rise, / Doth aske a drinke diuine' (ll. 5–6). This flirts with a serious Christian image, the water of life.[25] But if that image really came into this poem of secular love, it would wreck it. The ensuing reference to 'IOVE's *Nectar*' is therefore both a relief and the culmination of a joke played on the reader: we feared for a moment that the poem was going to be inappropriately serious. But the flirtation with a higher love leaves, perhaps, a faint shadow behind, just enough to suggest that for all its charm and courtesy this love affair is a small thing, and the poet knows it.

But the most elaborate exercise in putting love lyrics in context is the cycle 'A Celebration of Charis in Ten Lyric Pieces' (*The Underwood*, II). This also includes, as the Celia poems do not, the poet and his audience as part of that context. In fact, the first character we meet is not Charis but the poet:

> Let it not your wonder move,
> Lesse your laughter; that I love.
> Though I now write fiftie yeares,
> I have had, and have my Peeres;
> Poëts, though divine, are men:
> Some have lov'd as old agen.
>
> ('His Excuse for Loving', ll. 1–7)

This is the familiar figure of the fat man, getting on in years, who writes love poetry. It provides an ironic, distancing context for everything that follows.

At the end of this opening poem, Charis is seen as a stylized figure whose beauty has power to 'make the old man young' (l. 20); there is the hope, perhaps, that her ideal beauty will transform Jonson's gross reality. But in the second poem, 'How He Saw Her', Jonson, Charis, and Cupid engage in an allegorical action that veers between masque-like stylization and farce. Jonson, trying to strike the lady with Cupid's arrow, is struck instead himself:

> she threw
> Such a Lightning (as I drew)
> At my face, that tooke my sight,
> And my motion from me quite;
> So that, there, I stood a stone,
> Mock'd of all: and call'd of one
> (Which with griefe and wrath I heard)
> *Cupids* statue with a Beard,
> Or else one that plaid his Ape,
> In a *Hercules*-his shape.   (ll. 23–32)

Far from restoring his youth, Charis fixes him in a caricatured shape, incongruously decking his own stout body with the attributes of Cupid. If there is an allegorical point to the episode, it is that her beauty has not restored him but made him more humiliatingly aware of his defects. The idea of the transformation of love is parodied. So too is the familiar convention of the killing glance of the lady: the face that turns the viewer to stone is the face of the Gorgon. We are being prepared, I think, for the more critical view of Charis that emerges later in the cycle. And the unnamed figure who mocks Jonson suggests another point that will be developed later – a larger society, viewing and commenting on the affair. In the first poem, the relations between the fat poet and the inspiring lady were fairly simple and self-contained; in the second poem, they open out and become more complicated, as beneath the masque-like action we detect suggestions of a real affair, with Jonson teasing Charis even as he celebrates her beauty and her power over him.

In the third poem, 'What He Suffered', the scope of the action contracts again. We are no longer aware of Jonson's stout body, simply of his relations with Charis, who releases him from bondage on condition that he gives Cupid's bow and arrow to her so that she may restore them to their owner. He does so; Cupid strikes him; Charis repents, and Jonson declares that her repentance comes too late; he will now have his revenge on her. Though the action of this poem is more varied than that of the previous one, it depicts an allegorical love-game in a purer form, with fewer mischievous suggestions of a realistic world. It is as though Jonson is now more absorbed in the game, more committed to it. And his 'revenge' in the fourth poem is extraordinary. It is the high point of his celebration of Charis, 'Her Triumph', in which the lady becomes a figure from the masque world, with no obvious comic overtones. The dangers opposed to her – 'Thorough Swords, thorough Seas, whether she would ride' (l. 10) – are too stylized to suggest any threatening outside reality. In the second stanza, she appears to be the centre of a new creation, a special private world of love:

> Doe but looke on her eyes, they doe light
>   All that Loves world compriseth!
> Doe but looke on her Haire, it is bright
>   As Loves starre when it riseth!
> Doe but marke, her foreheads's smoother
>   Then words that sooth her!
> And from her arched browes, such a grace

> Sheds it selfe through the face,
>   As alone there triumphs to the life
> All the Gaine, all the Good, of the Elements strife.
>
> (ll. 11–20)

Even the discord of the world has been brought into harmony
by the power of her beauty. The world she lights is like one of
those secondary worlds we examined in Chapter 1, an invented
creation with its own sun. She seems absolute in that world; but
it is Jonson's habit, as we have seen, to put such worlds, sooner
or later, against the real one. In the word 'soothe' there may be a
suggestion that Charis is susceptible to flattery,[26] and in the final
stanza the beauty, though more breathtaking than ever, is now
transient and about to be stained:[27]

> Have you seene but a bright Lillie grow,
>   Before rude hands have touch'd it?
> Have you mark'd but the fall o' the Snow
>   Before the soyle hath smutch'd it?   (ll. 21–4)

In the context of *The Devil is an Ass*, the same poem is subjected
to a sharper irony, as Wittipol paws Mistress Fitzdottrel, and
Fitzdottrel himself interrupts the courtship.[28] As with Volpone's
song to Celia, the irony is more delicate in the non-dramatic
context; but it is still there. And it prepares for a descent to the
mundane in the rest of the cycle.

The fifth poem, 'His Discourse with Cupid', reports a conversation in which Cupid compares Charis to his mother Venus,
giving her conventional attributes of beauty. But this time
Cupid is praising not the lady herself but the description of her
in one of Jonson's poems (ll. 20–2); a gap is opening between the
stylized beauty and the real woman; and in the following poem,
'Claiming a Second Kiss by Desert', there is a startling change of
context:[29]

> You were more the eye, and talke
> Of the Court, to day, then all
> Else that glister'd in *White-hall*.   (ll. 14–16)

We have moved from the world of the masque to the world
where masques are performed. And it is suddenly a crowded
world, no longer a neutral background against which the figures

of Charis, Cupid and Jonson stand out in high relief. Cupid disappears – as he has to, now that we are in a mundane England – and Charis becomes the subject of ordinary flattering gossip. She is no longer engaged in an allegorical action; she is dancing at court, during the celebration of a marriage (ll. 17–28). She has also, the title of the poem tells us, given her old, fat lover a kiss; and in the seventh poem, 'Begging Another, on Colour of Mending the Former', the kissing becomes intimate and sensuous (ll. 15–18). This is as close as the lovers get. For the rest of the cycle, the concentration on Jonson's love for Charis is broken, and there is a much broader view of the activities of the two characters and their circle. It is as though Jonson, having finally got what he wants, can relax and allow a more detached view of his relations to Charis.

The eighth poem, 'Urging her of a Promise', refers not (as we might expect) to another kiss, or indeed to any sign of her love for him, but to a promise made to their circle at large, that

> she would tell
> What a man she could love well:
> And that promise set on fire
> All that heard her, with desire. (ll. 3–6)

The love of Jonson and Charis is now seen as just one more game of courtship in a circle where such games are common; it is cheerfully abandoned as Jonson asks her to prescribe the sort of man she really wants. And, with his new detachment, he no longer has to pay stylized tributes to her beauty. Instead, he threatens to reveal the secrets of her cabinet:

> You shall neither eat, nor sleepe,
> No, nor forth your window peepe,
> With your emissarie eye,
> To fetch in the Formes goe by:
> And pronounce, which band, or lace,
> Better fits him, then his face;
> Nay, I will not let you sit
> 'Fore your Idoll Glasse a whit,
> To say over every purle
> There; or to reforme a curle;

Or with Secretarie *Sis*
To consult, if *Fucus* this
Be as good, as was the last:
All your sweet of life is past,
Make accompt, unlesse you can,
(And that quickly) speake your Man.   (ll. 15–30)

We are now in the world of *Epicoene*, or the 'cosmetics' scenes of *Sejanus* and *Catiline*. Charis is more particularized than ever, and the results are anything but flattering. Like Jonson, she is not so young as she was; the beauty so eloquently praised earlier in the cycle now has to be worked for. And there is something wistful in the picture of her sitting at her window admiring the men who go by; this provides the context for the next poem, 'Her Man Described by her own Dictamen'.

   In this poem Charis herself speaks. The focus of the cycle thus becomes wider still, as Jonson's is no longer the only controlling voice. And, as Jonson can be sardonic with her, she can retort in kind. The perfect man she describes is young, smooth, delicate and titled – everything Jonson is not. Most of Charis's prescription is concerned with the young man's physical appearance, though towards the end she asks for valour, bounty and honesty as well (ll. 41–4). With the previous poem in mind, this prescription seems to be the erotic daydream of an older woman with a taste for pretty young men, and this gives it a delicate balance of satire and pathos. There is also, in the care with which the ideal young man is constructed, the implication that the perfect man can only be dreamed of. In Charis's world there are no perfect men – only old, fat lovers like Ben Jonson. The final poem, 'Another Lady's Objection Present at the Hearing', widens the focus still further, bringing in another new speaker, one whose presence is unprepared and surprising. Her addition to Charis's catalogue of the attributes of the perfect man seems to bring the whole house of cards tumbling down: 'What you please, you parts may call, / 'Tis one good part I'ld lie withall' (ll. 7–8). For this lady, as for satirically reduced characters elsewhere in Jonson, only one organ matters (and presumably this applies to her view of herself, no less than of her man). This devastatingly frank, practical and reductive ending makes the whole elaborate structure of courtship seem like a way of dressing up one basic physical act.

But we should recall that this is neither Jonson nor Charis speaking, but an anonymous 'other lady'. She has the last word, but in the cycle as a whole her perspective is just one of many. Jonson plays the courtship game with wit and skill, and we are meant to enjoy it for its own sake. But we are meant to see it in its context. That context is first suggested for us by the comic figure of the old fat poet, but he is as stylized in his own way as the ideal Charis of the early poems. What finally emerges is a suggestion of a whole circle of courtiers, among whom Jonson and Charis take their places. They are a bit jaded and cynical, they are not as young as they were, and they have a lot of time on their hands. But they are capable of wit and eloquence, and of disarming frankness with each other, as well as mere gossip. They are playing their courtship games against time, and they know it; it is their way of keeping off mortality, and of dealing with their own physical desires. The suggestion of this court circle around the lyrics adds both irony and pathos, underlining the deliberate silliness of the Cupid poems, and making 'Her Triumph' more poignant by the contrast with what surrounds it.

In this cycle Jonson gives us a series of poems whose vision includes the subjects of those poems, independent of the stylization of art; it also includes the poet who writes them, and the audience who listens to them. Jonson's attempt throughout his work to control his audience by depicting it in his own art is part of a deeper strategy to deal with the imperfections of reality. It is his responsibility as an artist to create visions of perfect order; but it is also his responsibility not to lie about the world. The result is a paradoxical double vision, in which the image of perfect order is placed against an acknowledgement of the real world, a world that both gives the lie to the vision and makes it doubly necessary. To tell the full truth about the world, one cannot be content with saying that it is imperfect: it contains – indeed, it generates – the works of art that show man a pure reality. And the interplay between the pure vision and its impure context gives Jonson's art surprising subtlety and depth.

CONCLUSION

Ben Jonson seems at first glance to be the master of the plain statement, the single-minded vision. His manner is robust and dogmatic. He does not leave us to judge his invented worlds for ourselves; he is always there, taking us by the elbow and telling us what to think. But the more we read of him the more we realize this first appearance is deceptive. *Volpone* is a case in point: it presents a closed, intensely realized world of greed and double-dealing. Yet that world is not as self-sufficient as it first appears to be: the preface reminds us of a larger moral vision, by which the predators can be judged: there is – or should be – more to life than eating and being eaten. Yet when the final judgement closes in on Volpone and his victims, morality itself suddenly looks like an intolerably closed system, and Volpone's subversive epilogue allows a larger view, setting against the judicial condemnation of the Fox a delight in his energy. Moreover, the concentrated satiric vision of the main plot is countered by the lighter, more inconsequential subplot of Sir Politic Would-be, whose seeming irrelevance may be the most important thing about him. He gives us a chance to relax, a breath of air from another world. In short, we can look past the concentrated central images of *Volpone* and see in the work as a whole an unexpected largeness of vision. Yet 'Negative Capability' would not be quite the right term to express this largeness of vision. Jonson does not abstain from judgement: instead, he shows an impulse to judge that will not rest until it has seen all sides of the question, and that goes on judging to the end. Volpone's last words ask us not just to applaud the play but to make a decision about it – a decision different from the one we were invited to make a few lines earlier.

What we see in *Volpone* is characteristic of Jonson's work as a whole. The single-minded vision – whether of vice, folly, beauty or order – is dramatized in such a way as to suggest a larger context. So the follies of *Epicoene* are touched with reminders of serious social life, and even – in Truewit's opening speeches – of man's spiritual destiny. The delicate love lyrics are set against the real problems of lovers – mortality, and the humiliations of the body. The visions of perfect order in the court masques admit implicitly that they are available for one night only. The sense of occasion is, as we have seen, of vital importance for Jonson: the language and values of a masque, a memorial ode, or a fair are valid for that occasion, and deserve to be taken seriously; but they are never the whole truth. Jonson's fools and villains create intensely limited worlds, and try to shut out reality; they even create special languages for those worlds. The final difference between their enterprise and Jonson's is that while he too will create special worlds (as any artist does) he will never cut them off completely from the rest of life. Always, we are aware of the surrounding reality. As characters in Jonson's plays are continually watching and commenting on each other, so the plays themselves, always aware of artist, public and theatre, are watched and commented on; the masques actually build the audience into the spectacle; and the non-dramatic poems make their own readers an important part of the subject matter.

But if all this tempts us to attribute to Jonson a Shakespearian richness and variety, we should note that the works in which he actually tries to show a great variety of life – *Poetaster*, *The New Inn*, *The Speeches at Prince Henry's Barriers* – while they may tell us much about his values, are not his most successful artistic achievements. His true genius lies in giving us a concentrated vision, and implying the rest. In *The Alchemist*, we can just sense the larger England that lies outside Lovewit's house. In 'To Penshurst', we need a bit of scholarly research to learn that the owner of the house was in financial trouble; but once we know – as Jonson's first readers knew – the poem's vision of the good life becomes more moving, the praise of the family more tactful and delicate. The companion poem, 'To Sir Robert Wroth', which admits the darkness of the world more openly, is less concentrated and subtle, and does not work so deeply on the imagination. This capacity to work by implication results at times in a remarkable lightness of touch: Jonson's most serious values are often conveyed through jokes, riddles and games, and through poems that look like light occasional pieces. In *Love Freed from Ignorance and Folly*, a serious allegory of the nature of love is conveyed through a riddle and a few clever compliments to the ladies in the audience; yet its seriousness is never compromised. The most effective judgements in the comedies are presented in a spirit of game and revelry; and if we want to see Jonson's social ideals most effectively embodied in his art we need to turn not to the panorama of England in *Prince Henry's Barriers*, or the working model of the good society in *Poetaster*, but to a cheerful epigram in which the poet invites a friend to supper.

The tension between ideals and the imperfection of reality is not always explicit at the centre of a Jonson work – though one can think of exceptions, like 'On My First Son' and the 'Epode'. But it is never far from his mind. The figure of Cicero dramatizes fully an ideal of the good magistrate, while implying the failures and compromises that result when virtue operates in the world. He is never openly humiliated; but as we listen to the chorus of praise for him that ends the play, we record certain mental reservations. By the same token, Overdo seems the perfect figure of the foolish judge; but behind his folly we catch echoes of what the good judge should be. Sometimes the tension between ideal and reality that other writers will build into the centre of a work – *Measure for Measure* is an obvious example – Jonson will express instead as a tension between the work itself and the world that surrounds it. His praise of Shakespeare in the famous memorial ode is unruffled – except by our memory of what he said of Shakespeare elsewhere, a memory the poem manages to stir without once being openly critical. The *Epigrams* present a perfect world, in which virtue and vice have their ideal forms; but in the man who writes them and in the men and women who are their subjects, there is a flawed reality around the perfect vision. In some of the plays that surrounding reality, embodied in a hostile audience, becomes a direct menace to the work of art itself. And Jonson will occasionally take the more difficult route of allowing the audience, not the art, to embody perfection – as when Queen Elizabeth watches *Every Man out of his Humour* or the court audience rebukes by its very presence the folly and disorder of an antimasque.

If Jonson was a realist, it was not in the narrow sense of reproducing the observable details of life. Many such details do occur, of course – cosmetics, tobacco pipes, privies – but the essential vision of Jonson's works, whether ideal or satiric, is too stylized to be called realistic in that sense. When the Stage-Keeper demands that *Bartholomew Fair* simply reproduce the Fair as he remembers it, he is kicked off the stage. Jonson's realism is of a more fundamental kind. It lies in his awareness that the vision of any work of art is limited and provisional, that there is always a larger life outside it. Yet this does not lead to despair or cynicism about art, for we need its special insights to show us our highest aspirations and our greatest dangers. Merely to surrender to the flux of life is to become a dead thing. Indeed, Jonson seems at times to exploit the limited nature of art, to make the outlines of a work as sharp as possible: the masques seem to aim at the ultimate in beauty and order, *Bartholomew Fair* in squalor, *Sejanus* in terror. There is no pretence at being fair or balanced, at giving the other side a hearing. Nor, in the *Epigrams*, do individual poems allow the virtuous flaws or the vicious any touch of redeeming worth. This stylization is, paradoxically, another aspect of Jonson's honesty: if the function of art is to distill the essence of life, then Jonson aims to do this boldly and without compromise. By doing so, he calls our attention to the limits of each work, and that other aspect of his honesty – his admission of the larger world that lies around the limited vision – comes into play.

The apparent solidity of each individual work may be one reason why Jonson's art has, all too often, elicited respect rather than excitement. He seems, simply, a bit too organized. Even today his most laudatory critics can sound as though they are asking us to take our medicine – this is good for you, and you ought to enjoy it. That Jonson is good for us is, I think, beyond question. His warnings on how men and societies are degraded, and his corresponding view of the good life – free, cultured, and founded on mutual respect – are as needed now as they ever were. But we do not have to stop there. One of the surprises of reading the Journals of Dorothy Wordsworth is to discover how often the Wordsworths – who seem, in the nature of their interests and achievements, to be as far from Jonson as they could be – read and discussed his work. The entry for 11 February 1802 is particularly revealing:

> William still poorly. We made up a good fire after dinner, and William brought his Mattrass out, and lay down on the floor. I read to him the life of Ben Johnson and some short Poems of his which were too *interesting* for him, and would not let him go to sleep.[1]

If Jonson lived up to his reputation as the cold, solid writer who had everything in order he would surely have been a better soporific for a Romantic poet than this. But there is in his work a profound tension and excitement. The organizing mind admits the disorder around it, and seizes what victories it can. The struggle to live by high ideals is matched by a ruthless honesty about the world as it is; yet sometimes, in a small poem or a casual gesture, we see an ideal become reality. And there is a profound urgency about what is at stake – as music, dance and poetry will create a vision of the highest order, so satire will call up a nightmare in which life dissolves into terrifying absurdity. Small wonder that Jonson, like Wordsworth, was a bad sleeper. And it is somehow appropriate that the man who pushed fantasy to its limits but never lost sight of the real world should have spent his sleepless nights watching armies of the imagination do battle around his great toe.

NOTES

PREFACE

1 *Elizabethan Dramatists* (London: Faber & Faber, 1963), p. 68.

CHAPTER 1   FALSE CREATIONS

1 According to Robert Ornstein, 'Jonson leaves the impression . . . that he has mistakenly cast a minor character in the lead while the genuine hero lurks in the wings.' *The Moral Vision of Jacobean Tragedy* (Madison and Milwaukee: University of Wisconsin Press, 1960), p. 90.
2 For another discussion of Jonson characters who set up private worlds, see Gabriele Bernhard Jackson, *Vision and Judgment in Ben Jonson's Drama* (New Haven and London: Yale University Press, 1968), pp. 77–94. She works from a different perspective (emphasizing the private world as a shelter for the characters' obsessions) and uses a rather different set of characters. She also takes a much darker view of *The Alchemist* than I have.
3 Conversations with William Drummond of Hawthornden (Herford and Simpson, I, 141).
4 See Jonas A. Barish, 'Jonson and the Loathed Stage', *A Celebration of Ben Jonson*, ed. William Blissett, Julian Patrick and R. W. van Fossen (Toronto: University of Toronto Press, 1973), pp. 51–2.
5 Robert Ornstein comments, 'Catiline and his fellow cutthroats inhabit a bizarre Senecan demimonde in a larger, more realistically conceived Roman society' (*Moral Vision*, p. 98). He sees this as a weakness in the writing; I suspect it may be a deliberate effect.
6 See Jackson, *Vision and Judgment*, pp. 82–3; and John J. Enck, *Jonson and the Comic Truth* (Madison: University of Wisconsin Press, 1957), p. 241.
7 See Barish, 'Loathèd Stage', pp. 27–53; and Thomas M. Greene,

'Ben Jonson and the Centered Self', *Studies in English Literature*, 10 (1970), 331.

8   See Stephen Orgel, *The Jonsonian Masque* (Cambridge, Mass.: Harvard University Press, 1965), p. 191.

9   See Jonas A. Barish, 'Bartholomew Fair and its Puppets', *Modern Language Quarterly*, 20 (1959), 3–15.

10 In Richard Eyre's Nottingham Playhouse production in 1976, Damon and Pythias were costumed as Quarlous and Winwife. The same identification was made in Michael Bogdanov's Young Vic production in 1978. In that production the identifications were carried further, with Grace as Hero, Cokes as Leander, Knock'em as Cupid and Leatherhead as Dionysus.

11 'Order and Judgement in *Bartholomew Fair*', *University of Toronto Quarterly*, 43 (1973), 61–2.

12 On Ursula's booth as Hellmouth, see R. B. Parker, 'Themes and Staging of *Bartholomew Fair*', *University of Toronto Quarterly*, 39 (1970), 294. It may also be worth recalling the ending of Middleton's *A Game at Chess*, in which the pieces are gathered into a bag.

13 T. S. Eliot, *Elizabethan Dramatists* (London: Faber and Faber, 1963), p. 72.

14 See, for example, *The Underwood*, xxxvi: 'A Song': 'Where Love doth shine, there needs no Sunne' (l. 5).

15 In Leon Rubin's production at Hart House Theatre in Toronto (1978) a golden light shone from the casket Volpone opened as he addressed his gold.

16 See E. B. Partridge, *The Broken Compass* (London: Chatto and Windus, 1958), p. 74.

17 There is a similar double suggestion – ecstasy and damnation – when Marlowe's Doctor Faustus kisses the spirit impersonating Helen of Troy: 'Her lips sucke forth my soule, see where it flies.'

18 See Alexander W. Lyle, 'Volpone's Two Worlds', *Yearbook of English Studies*, 4 (1974), 70–6.

19 See J. A. Bryant, Jr, *The Compassionate Satirist: Ben Jonson and his Imperfect World* (Athens, Georgia: University of Georgia Press, 1972), p. 79.

20 William Empson has reminded us that Jonson's audience would be less squeamish about the freaks than we are. See 'Volpone', *The Hudson Review*, 21 (1968–9), 654–5. That is worth remembering; all the same, Jonson's interest in false creation means that the freaks, as distortions of nature, would be more serious for him than for many of his contemporaries.

21 'Centered Self', p. 337. Greene develops this interpretation on pp. 337–43.

22 See Alvin B. Kernan, Introduction to the Yale edition of *Volpone* (New Haven and London: Yale University Press, 1962), pp. 7–13.

23 The argument that follows I have developed at greater length in 'The Suicide of Volpone', *University of Toronto Quarterly*, 39 (1969), 19–32.

24 At the end of Leon Rubin's production, all the characters froze except Volpone. He passed among them, regarding each with wry amusement before stepping forward to deliver the Epilogue. They were still fixed in the play; he was free.

25 *Broken Compass*, pp. 127–34.

26 ibid., p. 117.

27 See Alan C. Dessen, *Jonson's Moral Comedy* (Evanston: Northwestern University Press, 1971), p. 109.

28 In Tyrone Guthrie's modern-dress production at the Old Vic in 1962, Surly was dressed in a dinner-jacket and kept his hands busy by toying expertly with a deck of cards.

29 *Comic Truth*, p. 160.

30 This was suggested at the end of Trevor Nunn's production for the Royal Shakespeare Company in 1977, when, according to one reviewer, Face 'clinks his ill-gotten coins slowly through his fingers and sizes up the audience in front of him.' Rosemary Say, 'Food for Thought', *Sunday Telegraph*, 29 May 1977.

31 See Richard Levin, 'The New *New Inn* and the Proliferation of Good Bad Drama', *Essays in Criticism*, 22 (1972), 41–7.

32 See Harriet Hawkins, 'The Idea of a Theater in Jonson's *The New Inn*', *Renaissance Drama*, 9 (1966), 205–26.

33 See Partridge, *Broken Compass*, p. 195.

34 ibid., p. 194.

CHAPTER 2 THAT DEAD SEA OF LIFE

1 See, for example, Epigrams CII, CIII and CIV. This has been variously explained by critics. Judith Kegan Gardiner, in *Craftsmanship in Context: The Development of Ben Jonson's Poetry* (The Hague and Paris: Mouton, 1975), refers to 'the generality of vice in contrast to the specific rarity of virtue' (p. 32). According to Anthony Mortimer, 'vice destroys the personality whereas virtue fulfills it'; see 'The Feigned Commonwealth in the Poetry of Ben Jonson', *Studies in English Literature*, 13 (Winter, 1973), 72. I return to this issue in Chapter 5.

2 Herford and Simpson, I, 151.

3 The image of the sinking towers reads like a deliberate inversion of

the address to London in *Part of the King's Entertainment in Passing to his Coronation*:

> Now London reare
> Thy forehead high, and on it striue to weare
> Thy choisest gems; teach thy steepe Towres to rise
> Higher with people.   (ll. 276–9)

4   Gabriele Bernhard Jackson, *Vision and Judgment in Ben Jonson's Drama* (New Haven and London: Yale University Press, 1968), p. 146. The image recurs, in a spirit of simple playfulness, in *Hymenaei*: 'Then, coyne them, 'twixt your lips so sweet, / And let not *cockles* closer meet' (ll. 525–6).

5   On the handling of this theme in Jonson's last plays, see Edward B. Partridge, 'The Symbolism of Clothes in Jonson's Last Plays', *Journal of English and Germanic Philology*, 56 (1957), 396–409.

6   The last exclamation is repeated, almost word for word, in *The Devil is an Ass*, IV. iv. 191–2.

7   Introduction to the Yale edition of *Sejanus* (New Haven and London: Yale University Press, 1965), p. 24.

8   John J. Enck notes Jonson's use of the flood image, relating it to Bergson's sense of the mechanical as the basic principle of comedy. See *Jonson and the Comic Truth* (Madison: University of Wisconsin Press, 1957), p. 56.

9   See Enck, *Comic Truth*, p. 179.

10 On the constant presence of death in the play, see Ian Donaldson, 'Volpone: Quick and Dead', *Essays in Criticism*, 21 (1971), 121–34.

11 'The Incredibility of Jonsonian Comedy', *A Celebration of Ben Jonson*, ed. William Blissett, Julian Patrick, and R. W. van Fossen (Toronto: University of Toronto Press, 1973), p. 10.

12 Stephen Orgel, *The Jonsonian Masque* (Cambridge, Mass.: Harvard University Press, 1965), pp. 160–1. In the original performance the inanimate was also endowed with life, as Mount Atlas rolled its eyes and moved (Herford and Simpson, x, 586). It is not clear that this comic effect had Jonson's approval, since he does not report it in his text of the masque; he specifies merely that the mountain is topped by the figure of an old man.

13 E. A. Horsman, Introduction to the Revels edition of *Bartholomew Fair* (London: Methuen, 1960), p. xxvi.

14 See R. B. Parker, 'Themes and Staging of *Bartholomew Fair*', *University of Toronto Quarterly*, 39 (1970), 297.

15 In Richard Eyre's production at the Nottingham Playhouse in 1976, the play ended with Overdo shaking his head in exasperation at Cokes, as if to say, 'You're incorrigible!'

16 William Blissett describes the Fair as 'a place of licence within a

world of law; it combines maximum impurity with minimum danger.' See 'Your Majesty is Welcome to a Fair', *The Elizabethan Theatre*, 4, ed. George Hibbard (Toronto: Macmillan, 1974), p. 91.

CHAPTER 3   IMAGES OF SOCIETY

1   According to 'An Execration upon Vulcan' Jonson's life of Henry V was destroyed in the burning of his study (*The Underwood*, XLIII, 97–100).

2   *Jacobean Pageant* (Cambridge, Mass.: Harvard University Press, 1962), p. 228.

3   See John C. Meagher, *Method and Meaning in Jonson's Masques* (Notre Dame: University of Notre Dame Press, 1966), p. 183.

4   'Jonson's Large and Unique View of Life', *The Elizabethan Theatre*, IV, ed. George Hibbard (Toronto: Macmillan, 1974), pp. 165–6.

5   See Herford and Simpson, V, 144.

6   'Goodness and Greatness: An Essay on the Tragedies of Ben Jonson and George Chapman, *Renaissance and Modern Studies*, 11 (1967), 16.

7   For a full discussion of Jonson's dramatic use of jargon, see Alexander H. Sackton, *Rhetoric as a Dramatic Language in Ben Jonson* (New York: Columbia University Press, 1948), pp. 46–112.

8   *Jonson and the Comic Truth* (Madison: University of Wisconsin Press, 1957), p. 155.

9   As Brian Gibbons puts it, 'Disrespect for the rules of art, like disrespect for the law, must be censured with the authority and weight of a whole society.' *Jacobean City Comedy* (London: Rupert Hart-Davis, 1968), p. 73.

10 See Jonas A. Barish, 'Feasting and Judging in Jonsonian Comedy', *Renaissance Drama*, n.s.5 (1972), 17.

11 See Gabriele Bernhard Jackson, *Vision and Judgment in Ben Jonson's Drama* (New Haven and London: Yale University Press, 1968), p. 26.

12 See Robert C. Jones, 'The Satirist's Retirement in Jonson's "Apologeticall Dialogue"', *English Literary History*, 34 (1967), 462.

13 The following discussion is based in part on arguments developed in my article, 'Morose and his Tormentors', *University of Toronto Quarterly*, 45 (1976), 221–35.

14 See J. A. Bryant, Jr, *The Compassionate Satirist: Ben Jonson and his Imperfect World* (Athens, Georgia: University of Georgia Press, 1972), p. 97.

15 'Farce and Fashion in *The Silent Woman*', *Essays and Studies*, n.s.20 (1967), 40–3.

16 *The World Upside-Down* (Oxford: Oxford University Press, 1970), p. 31.

17 See Michael Shapiro, *Children of the Revels* (New York: Columbia University Press, 1977), p. 83.

18 Donaldson, *World Upside-Down*, p. 39.

19 See G. R. Hibbard, 'The Country House Poem of the Seventeenth Century', *Journal of the Warburg and Courtauld Institutes*, 19 (1956), 165.

20 'Pastoral and Counter-Pastoral', *Critical Quarterly*, 10 (1968), 286.

21 See Herford and Simpson, XI, 33–4.

22 Jonson complained in these terms of his treatment at Lord Salisbury's table; see his Conversations with Drummond of Hawthornden (Herford and Simpson, I, 141).

23 See Earl Miner, *The Cavalier Mode from Jonson to Cotton* (Princeton: Princeton University Press, 1971), p. 7.

24 'Jonson, Lord Lisle, and Penshurst', *English Literary Renaissance*, I (1971), 250–60.

25 For a discussion of this method in Jonson's poetry as a whole, see Richard C. Newton, '"Ben. / Jonson": The Poet in the Poems', *Two Renaissance Mythmakers: Christopher Marlowe and Ben Jonson*, ed. Alvin Kernan (Baltimore and London: The Johns Hopkins University Press, 1977), pp. 166–70.

26 See Hugh Maclean, 'Ben Jonson's Poems: Notes on the Ordered Society', *Essays in English Literature from the Renaissance to the Victorian Age Presented to A. S. P. Woodhouse*, ed. Millar MacLure and F. W. Watt (Toronto: University of Toronto Press, 1964), p. 51; and Miner, *Cavalier Mode*, p. 298. In 'An Epistle Answering to One that Asked to be Sealed of the Tribe of Ben' (*The Underwood*, XLVII) Jonson takes the occasion of an appeal for his friendship to deliver a wide-ranging lecture on manners, morals and the role of a good man in public life.

27 See Herford and Simpson, XI, 21.

CHAPTER 4 VIRTUE'S LABYRINTH

1 This is suggested by Ian Donaldson, 'Jonson's Ode to Sir Lucius Cary and Sir H. Morison', *Studies in the Literary Imagination*, 6 (1973), 147.

2 The effect of this, and of the similar split of the name 'Ben Jonson' at ll. 84–5, is discussed by John Hollander, Introduction to *Ben Jonson* (The Laurel Poetry Series: New York: Dell, 1961), pp. 19–20; and by Donaldson, 'Jonson's Ode', p. 150.

3 See Donaldson, 'Jonson's Ode', p. 151.

4 'Ben Jonson's "Chast Booke" – the *Epigrammes*', *Renaissance and Modern Studies*, 13 (1969), 84.

5 Cob's comic pedigree has its precedents in earlier drama: see C. R. Baskervill, *English Elements in Jonson's Early Comedy* (Austin, Texas: University of Texas Bulletin, 1911), pp. 131–2. But if the device is traditional it has also – like the traditional satiric motifs examined in Chapter 2 – a special significance for Jonson.

6 The implications of this idea are explored by Thomas M. Greene, 'Ben Jonson and the Centered Self', *Studies in English Literature*, 10 (1970), 325–48.

7 The tortoise was a traditional emblem of politic caution: see Ian Donaldson, 'Jonson's Tortoise', *Review of English Studies*, n.s.19 (1968), 163.

8 The *Poetry of Conservatism* (Cambridge: Rivers Press, 1973), 30–1.

9 This positive view of Celia is developed by Charles A. Hallett, 'Jonson's Celia: A Reinterpretation of *Volpone*', *Studies in Philology*, 68, (1971), 50–69.

10 In Leon Rubin's 1978 production at Hart House Theatre in Toronto, Celia was played straight, with full emotional power. But as she pleaded with Volpone, the freaks stood behind her in mocking attitudes of piety; and as her plea reached its climax Volpone began to take his clothes off.

11 This objection is voiced by Alan C. Dessen, *Jonson's Moral Comedy* (Evanston: Northwestern University Press, 1971), p. 88.

12 Many critics have commented on the helplessness of the virtuous in *Sejanus*. The fullest discussion is Marvin L. Vawter, 'The Seeds of Virtue: Political Imperatives in Jonson's *Sejanus*', *Studies in the Literary Imagination*, 6 (1973), 41–60. His final attitude to these figures is rather more hostile than mine.

13 See Vawter, 'Seeds of Virtue', p. 45; and William D. Wolf, *The Reform of the Fallen World: The 'Virtuous Prince' in Jonsonian Tragedy and Comedy* (Salzburg: Institut für Englische Sprache und Literatur, 1973), p. 35.

14 Vawter sees the disagreements among the Germanicans as representing 'a sad state of ambiguity and confusion' ('Seeds of Virtue', p. 48). I think it represents a healthy spirit of free discussion.

15 See George Parfitt, *Ben Jonson: Public Poet and Private Man* (London: J. M. Dent & Sons, 1976), pp. 40–2.

16 The last song of *Pan's Anniversary* advises the shepherds not to trust hirelings (ll. 271–8); this is obvious political advice to the court, and it corresponds to Overdo's concern.

17 See my discussion of this character and other stock usurers in

Citizen Comedy in the Age of Shakespeare (Toronto: University of Toronto Press, 1973), pp. 24–8.

18 See G. R. Hibbard, 'Goodness and Greatness: An Essay on the Tragedies of Ben Jonson and George Chapman', *Renaissance and Modern Studies*, 11 (1967), 28; and Gabriele Bernhard Jackson, *Vision and Judgment in Ben Jonson's Drama* (New Haven and London: Yale University Press, 1968), pp. 37–8.

19 His refusal to act against Caesar has been defended by Jackson, *Vision and Judgment*, p. 36; and by Wolf, *Reform of the Fallen World*, p. 26. Wolf in particular makes the point that condemnation of Cicero's policy must depend on our knowledge of 'outside sources', i.e. the subsequent history of Rome. But by implicating Caesar in the conspiracy beyond what his sources warranted, and by building his part up more than would be necessary if he were simply interested in Cicero's victory over Catiline, Jonson has encouraged us to think of Caesar's later role in destroying the republic. See Joseph Allen Bryant, Jr, 'Catiline and the Nature of Jonson's Tragic Fable', *Publications of the Modern Language Association of America*, 69 (1954), 265–77.

20 T. S. Eliot, *Elizabethan Dramatists* (London: Faber and Faber, 1963), p. 70.

21 There are full discussions of Cicero's weakness in Michael J. C. Echeruo, 'The Conscience of Politics and Jonson's *Catiline*', *Studies in English Literature*, 6 (1966), 341–56; and Michael J. Warren, 'Ben Jonson's *Catiline*: The Problem of Cicero', *Yearbook of English Studies*, 3 (1973), 55–73. Warren in particular takes a far more hostile line than I have, practically reading the play from Caesar's point of view; Echeruo's view of Cicero is more balanced.

22 *The Jonsonian Masque* (Cambridge, Mass.: Harvard University Press, 1965), p. 184.

CHAPTER 5 JUDGEMENT AND TRANSFORMATION

1 See Stephen Orgel, 'To Make Boards Speak: Inigo Jones's Stage and the Jonsonian Masque', *Renaissance Drama*, n.s. 1 (1968), 124.

2 See Harriet Hawkins, 'Jonson's Use of Traditional Dream Theory in *The Vision of Delight*', *Modern Philology*, 64 (1967), 285–92.

3 See Orgel, 'To Make Boards Speak', p. 124.

4 See Edward Partridge, 'Jonson's *Epigrammes*: The Named and the Nameless', *Studies in the Literary Imagination*, 6 (1973), 194–7; and David Wykes, 'Ben Jonson's 'Chast Booke' – the *Epigrammes*', *Renaissance and Modern Studies*, 13 (1969), 85.

5   See Anthony Mortimer, 'The Feigned Commonwealth in the
    Poetry of Ben Jonson', *Studies in English Literature*, 13 (1973),
    72.

6   See Wesley Trimpi, *Ben Jonson's Poems: A Study of the Plain Style*
    (Stanford: Stanford University Press, 1962), p. 140.

7   See Ian Donaldson, 'Jonson's Tortoise', *Review of English Studies*,
    n.s.19 (1968), 165.

8   'Ben Jonson's *Epigrammes*: Portrait-Gallery, Theater, Common-
    wealth', *Studies in English Literature*, 14 (1974), 108.

9   See Jonas A. Barish, 'Feasting and Judging in Jonsonian Comedy',
    Renaissance Drama, n.s.5 (1972), 11.

10 'Feasting and Judging', p. 15.

11 Judd Arnold has suggested that Cynthia's indignation at the un-
    veiling of the fools may itself be tongue-in-cheek, since there is
    evidence earlier in the play that Cynthia was in on the plot from
    the beginning. See *A Grace Peculiar: Ben Jonson's Cavalier Heroes*
    (University Park, Pennsylvania: Pennsylvania State University,
    1972), p. 32. If true, this would strengthen my case about the light
    tone of the ending. However, I would have preferred a clearer
    reference to Cynthia's complicity in the last scene itself, and it may
    be that Arnold is reading an artificial play too literally.

12 Herford and Simpson, I, 141, 142.

13 'Ben Jonson Full of Shame and Scorn', *Studies in the Literary
    Imagination*, 6 (1973), 199–217.

14 Kerrigan, 'Ben Jonson', p. 208.

15 Introduction to the Yale edition of *Bartholomew Fair* (New Haven
    and London: Yale University Press, 1963), p. 10. cf. Epigram
    LXXV, 'On Lippe, the Teacher': 'Though LIPPE, at PAVLS, ranne
    from his text away, / To'inueigh 'gainst playes: what did he then
    but play?' (ll. 3–4).

16 Eugene M. Waith points out that the suddenness of the trans-
    formations, rather than the use of allegory, gives the play its
    masque-like quality. See 'Things as They Are and the World of
    Abolutes in Jonson's Plays and Masques', *The Elizabethan Theater*,
    4, ed. George Hibbard (Toronto: Macmillan, 1974), p. 117.

17 E. B. Partridge, *The Broken Compass* (London: Chatto and
    Windus, 1958), p. 114.

18 *The Cankered Muse* (New Haven: Yale University Press, 1959),
    pp. 158, 161.

19 See Jackson I. Cope, *The Theater and the Dream: From Metaphor to
    Form in Renaissance Drama* (Baltimore and London: Johns Hopkins
    University Press, 1973), p. 235.

20 See Cope, *Theater and the Dream*, p. 229.

21   See R. B. Parker, 'The Problem of Tone in Jonson's "Comicall Satyres"', *Humanities Association Review*, 28 (1977), 59; and Arnold, *A Grace Peculiar*, p. 20.

CHAPTER 6   THE POET AS CHARACTER

1   See Herford and Simpson, I, 18–19.

2   On the joking quality of the last line, see R. B. Parker, 'The Problem of tone in Jonson's "Comicall Satyres"', *Humanities Association Review*, 28 (1977), 57.

3   See Earl Miner, *The Cavalier Mode from Jonson to Cotton* (Princeton: Princeton University Press, 1971), p. 46.

4   *Ben Jonson and the Language of Prose Comedy* (Cambridge, Mass.: Harvard University Press, 1960), p. 87.

5   *Ben Jonson: Public Poet and Private Man* (London: J. M. Dent and Sons, 1976), p. 9.

6   See Robert C. Jones, 'The Satirist's Retirement in Jonson's "Apologetical Dialogue"', *English Literary History*, 34 (1967), 447–67. Jones discusses the general problem of Jonson's feigned indifference, referring also to the *New Inn* ode.

7   William Kerrigan regards this line as a central moment of self-revelation. See 'Ben Jonson Full of Shame and Scorn', *Studies in the Literary Imagination*, 6 (1973), 212.

8   See Chapter 4, n.1.

9   See Edward Partridge, 'Jonson's *Epigrammes*: the Named and the Nameless', *Studies in the Literary Imagination*, 6 (1973), 163.

10   As E. B. Partridge suggests, Jonson's '"best piece of poetry" may not have been his son, but his self.' See 'Jonson's Large and Unique View of Life', *The Elizabethan Theatre*, 4, ed. George Hibbard (Toronto: Macmillan, 1974), p. 147.

11   See Parfitt, *Ben Jonson*, p. 33.

12   Herford and Simpson, I, 151.

13   *Ben Jonson of Westminster* (London: Robert Hale, 1954), p. 248.

14   Herford and Simpson, XI, 417.

15   ibid., pp. 419–20.

16   ibid., p. 420.

17   ibid., p. 407.

18   See Judith Kegan Gardiner, *Craftsmanship in Context: The Development of Ben Jonson's Poetry* (The Hague and Paris: Mouton, 1975), p. 113.

19   Conversations with Drummond of Hawthornden, Herford and Simpson, I, 133.

20   According to Judith Kegan Gardiner, 'In this single poem the

objective public voice of the poet . . . is overwhelmed by the private voice of the author, Ben Jonson, even as it tries to come to terms with this moving and dissenting second voice' (*Craftmanship in Context*, p. 45). I agree that there are two voices at work, but I do not see the struggle between them as quite so one-sided.

21 On the implications of art as food, see Don K. Hedrick, 'Cooking for the Anthropophagi: Jonson and his Audience', *Studies in English Literature*, 17 (1977), 233–45.

22 For a survey of the problem, see T. J. B. Spencer, 'Ben Jonson on his beloved, the Author Mr. William Shakespeare', *The Elizabethan Theatre*, 4, ed. George Hibbard (Toronto: Macmillan, 1974), pp. 22–40.

23 Herford and Simpson, I, 133.

24 It may also be that Jonson is allowing himself a jocular imitation of Shakespeare, in the poem's heavy – and for Jonson uncharacteristic – reliance on puns. (I owe this suggestion to Hugh MacCallum.)

CHAPTER 7   ART AND ITS CONTEXT

1 See Stephen Orgel, *The Illusion of Power* (Berkeley, Los Angeles and London: University of California Press, 1975), p. 25.

2 Herford and Simpson, x, 575–6.

3 Michael Shapiro sees this technique as characteristic of plays written for the children's companies in particular: see *Children of the Revels* (New York: Columbia University Press, 1977), p. 74. But Jonson at least used it throughout his career, in plays written for a variety of companies.

4 See D. F. McKenzie, '"The Staple of News" and the Late Plays', *A Celebration of Ben Jonson*, ed. William Blissett, Julian Patrick and R. W. van Fossen (Toronto: University of Toronto Press, 1973), pp. 86–7.

5 See Herford and Simpson, IV, 472–85, where these notes are reprinted.

6 See M. C. Bradbrook, 'Social Change and the Evolution of Ben Jonson's Court Masques', *Studies in the Literary Imagination*, 6 (1973), 126.

7 See Stephen Orgel, *The Jonsonian Masque* (Cambridge, Massachusetts: Harvard University Press, 1965), pp. 6–7.

8 Herford and Simpson, x, 449.

9 For a detailed discussion of *Pleasure Reconciled to Virtue* from this point of view, see Stanley Wells, *Literature and Drama with Special Reference to Shakespeare and his Contemporaries* (London: Routledge and Keegan Paul, 1970), pp. 69–83.

10 Herford and Simpson, x, 649.

11 For a full discussion of these, see W. Todd Furniss, 'The Annotation of Ben Jonson's *Masqve of Qveenes*', *Review of English Studies*, n.s.5 (1954), 344–60.

12 See Jonas A. Barish, 'Ben Jonson and the Loathèd Stage', *A Celebration of Ben Jonson*, ed. William Blissett, Julian Patrick and R. W. van Fossen (Toronto: University of Toronto Press, 1973), pp. 32–4.

13 Herford and Simpson, I, 211.

14 See Conversations with Drummond of Hawthornden (Herford and Simpson, I, 132); and *Timber*, ll. 1806–8. On Digby's writings on Spenser, see Herford and Simpson, XI, 99.

15 See C. G. Thayer, *Ben Jonson: Studies in the Plays* (Norman, Oklahoma: University of Oklahoma Press, 1963), p. 108.

16 See William Blissett, 'Your Majesty is Welcome to a Fair', *The Elizabethan Theatre*, 4, ed. George Hibbard (Toronto: Macmillan, 1974), p. 105.

17 See E. B. Partridge, 'Jonson's Large and Unique View of Life', *The Elizabethan Theatre*, 4, ed. George Hibbard (Toronto: Macmillan, 1974), pp. 154–6.

18 On Jonson's respect for historical truth in these plays, see Joseph Allen Bryant, Jr, 'The Significance of Ben Jonson's First Requirement for Tragedy: "Truth of Argument"', *Studies in Philology*, 49 (1952), 195–213.

19 See William A. Armstrong, 'Ben Jonson and Jacobean Stagecraft', *Jacobean Theatre*, ed. John Russell Brown and Bernard Harris (London: Arnold, 1960), pp. 52–3.

20 William Blissett has argued for similar jocular references to King James in the character of Overdo. See 'Your Majesty is Welcome to a Fair', pp. 91–5.

21 See Dale B. J. Randall, *Jonson's Gypsies Unmasked* (Durham, North Carolina: Duke University Press, 1975), pp. 105–6. Randall's study gives a full account of the masque's background in the relations between James and the Villiers family.

22 Herford and Simpson, x, 665.

23 *Ben Jonson's Poems: A Study of the Plain Style* (Stanford: Stanford University Press, 1962), p. 209.

24 William V. Spanos, 'The Real Toad in the Jonsonian Garden: Resonance in the Nondramatic Poetry', *Journal of English and Germanic Philology*, 68 (1969), 8.

25 *John*, iv. 5–14.

26 See S. P. Zitner, 'The Revenge on Charis', *The Elizabethan*

Theatre, 4, ed. George Hibbard (Toronto: Macmillan, 1974), p. 133.

27 See Judith Kegan Gardiner, *Craftsmanship in Context: The Development of Ben Jonson's Poetry* (The Hague and Paris: Mouton, 1975), p. 104; and Zitner, 'Revenge on Charis', p. 134.

28 See Zitner, 'Revenge on Charis', pp. 129–30.

29 See Paul Cubeta, '"A Celebration of Charis": An Evaluation of Jonsonian Poetic Strategy', *English Literary History*, 25 (1958), 172.

CONCLUSION

1 *The Journals of Dorothy Wordsworth*, ed. Mary Moorman (Oxford: Oxford University Press, 1971), p. 88.

INDEX

Note: Only references to specific works have been entered under Jonson; for other references see under subject entries, in particular, art, audience, epigrams, judge-figure, masques, poet, self-portraiture, virtue.